POSTCOLONIAL RESISTANCE:
CULTURE, LIBERATION, AND TRANSFORMATION

DAVID JEFFERESS

Postcolonial Resistance:

Culture, Liberation, and Transformation

UNIVERSITY OF TORONTO PRESS
Toronto Buffalo London

© University of Toronto Press Incorporated 2008
Toronto Buffalo London
Printed in Canada

ISBN 978-0-8020-9190-1

Printed on acid-free paper

Library and Archives Canada Cataloguing in Publication

Jefferess, David, 1971–
  Postcolonial resistance : culture, liberation and transformation / David Jefferess.

  (Cultural spaces)
  Includes bibliographical references and index.
  ISBN 978-0-8020-9190-1 (bound)

  1. Postcolonialism.   2. Social change.   I. Title.   II. Series

  JV51.J44 2008   325'.3   C2007-905682-2

University of Toronto Press acknowledges the financial assistance to its publishing program of the Canada Council for the Arts and the Ontario Arts Council.

University of Toronto Press acknowledges the financial support for its publishing activities of the Government of Canada through the Book Publishing Industry Development Program (BPIDP).

Stories are the secret reservoir of values: change the stories individuals and nations live by and tell themselves, and you change the individuals and nations.
> – Ben Okri, *A Way of Being Free*

We need not identify revolution with violence or with a sudden capture of power. Even where such events occur, the essential transformation is indeed a long revolution. But the absolute test, by which revolution can be distinguished, is the change in the *form* of activity of a society, in its deepest structure of relationships and feelings.
> – Raymond Williams, 'Tragedy and Revolution'

There is no discussion taking place in the world today that is more crucial than the debate about strategies of resistance.
> – Arundhati Roy, *Public Power in the Age of Empire*

Contents

Acknowledgments ix

Introduction: Postcolonialism and Resistance 3

1 Colonial Discourse/Power and 'Spectacular Resistance' 23

2 Opposition and the (Im)Possibility of Liberation 57

3 Gandhism and Resistance: Transforming India 95

4 Reconciliation as Resistance: Transforming South Africa 136

Conclusion: Postcolonialism and Transformation 179

Notes 187
Bibliography 213
Index 225

Acknowledgments

This project began in Nkhota-Kota, Malawi, and was influenced by the poetry of Jack Mapanje and the reggae lyrics of Lucius Banda, and particularly his album *Ceasefire*, which was played nearly continuously at bottle-stores throughout 1997 and 1998. Their meditations on political power and history and their invocations of a politics of transformation inspired many wonderful conversations, in particular with my friends Lino Kamphonda and Gift Jeremaya-Phiri.

My doctoral supervisor, Susie O'Brien, and Imre Szeman, as well, have been wonderful mentors, and I cherish their constructive criticism, guidance, support, and encouragement over the past number of years. I would also like to thank Diana Brydon and Simon Gikandi, as well as the anonymous readers at UTP, for their critical assessments of the work at various points, which helped immeasurably my thinking on this topic. I am grateful to my editor, Siobhan McMenemy, for her guidance and support throughout this long process. I very much appreciate the careful copy-editing of the manuscript by Wayne Herrington, the work of Naomi Pauls, who provided the index for the book, and Frances Mundy for managing all of this and getting the book produced.

Marlo Edwards, Jake Kennedy, Andrew Loucks, and Daniel Coleman have provided inspiration, wonderful debate, and, most importantly, a grounding of the intellectual in the politics of the everyday. I would also like to thank Jodey Castricano for her support during the later stages of this project. My parents and brothers have been ever-supportive in whatever I have chosen to do. And, I thank Anita Kanwar for her support, her patience, and so much else.

This book was written with the assistance of a graduate scholarship from McMaster University, a Dalley Fellowship at McMaster, doctoral and postdoctoral fellowships from the Social Sciences and Humanities Research Council of Canada, and a grant from the Faculty of Creative and Critical Studies, UBC Okanagan.

POSTCOLONIAL RESISTANCE:
CULTURE, LIBERATION, AND TRANSFORMATION

Introduction:
Postcolonialism and Resistance

The idea of 'resistance' provides a primary framework for the critical project of postcolonialism. Resistance is a continual referent and at least implicit locus of much postcolonial criticism and theory, particularly in terms of the analysis of the failure, or deferral, of liberation in Africa, South Asia, and the Caribbean. On the one hand, this emphasis upon resistance limits the purview of (post)colonial experience, in that it 'denies any other kind of life to the people doing the resisting.'[1] Yet, the concept of resistance functions as an amorphous concept in postcolonial studies, identifying a diverse range of modes, practices, and experiences of struggle, subversion, or power. Despite the centrality of the concept for the development of the field, resistance is a concept that has received only limited theoretical examination.[2] For some, resistance signifies little more than the failure of colonial power to be total; indebted to psychoanalytic and poststructural literary theories, resistance, as mimicry, hybridity, or the ambivalence of colonial power, subverts the binary thought and essentialist identities produced by colonial knowledge. For others, drawing upon the theories of anticolonial intellectuals, resistance constitutes organized political and military struggle against colonial rule and the structures of the colonial economy.

Frantz Fanon's conception of liberation, however, constitutes not just the eviction of foreign rule or national self-affirmation but a transformation of structures of inequality and, significantly, the narratives and values that legitimize colonial power. The African novelist Ben Okri contends: 'Stories are the secret reservoir of values: change the stories individuals and nations live by and tell themselves, and you change the individuals and nations.'[3] While this sentiment appears utopian, and problematically suggests that the transformation of 'stories' or culture precedes, and is a condition for, the transformation of social, political, and economic relationships, I believe it captures the libratory potential of resistance to which anti-colonial thinkers such as Fanon allude; as well, it imbues the critical expectations of the postcolonial project. In this book, I interrogate the dominant ways in which resistance has been conceptualized within postcolonial studies; namely, (1) resistance as the subversion of colonial authority, or the failure of colonial power to be performed as it is imagined, and (2) resistance as opposition against the colonizer, framed in terms of a Manichean conflict, and largely confined to the rules of recognition of colonial knowledge. I posit as an alternative way of conceiving resistance, transformation. Through the examples of Mohandas Gandhi's critique of modernity and his philosophy of struggle as well as the role of the notion of reconciliation in the South African liberation struggle, I take up Fanon's conception of decolonization as requiring a radical restructuring of global relationships articulated within a 'new humanism' as an ethic and a politics of transformation.

Postcolonial studies began as a critique of the English literature canon and European colonial historiography, and it focused on the politics of representation; as a result, the academic project of postcolonialism has been conceptualized as resistance itself. For instance, African, South Asian, and Caribbean literatures that had been excluded by the discipline of English literature were read in the context of colonialism, and the struggle against it, as cultural projects of representation and identification. This engagement with 'Commonwealth' or 'Third World' literatures challenged the canon of English literature as well as the assumptions surrounding culture and cultural critique of which this body of literature and its criticism were an example. Similarly, the collective of historians involved in the Subaltern Studies project initially endeavoured to acknowledge and record peasant insurgents as subjects of their own history within but not reduced to colonial power, and outside the determination of the homogenized Indian nation of an elite imagination. Based on this work, and indebted to the anti-colonial critique of intellectuals such as Frantz Fanon and C.L.R. James, postcolonialism developed as a field that, to borrow from Sanjay Seth, provides 'a set of questions and a style of thought which are made possible by colonialism and its aftermath, and which seek to rethink, and redescribe, its own enabling conditions.'[4] Hence, the field is primarily concerned with analysing and problematizing the culture of colonialism; for instance, the way in which slavery, the appropriation of land and resources, and various attempts at the assimilation of indigenous peoples into European systems and practices were rationalized through discourses of civilization, modernity, and humanism.

Leela Gandhi defines current formulations of postcolonialism as an 'ethics of hybridity' and contends that its 'proposal for a non-violent reading of the colonial past through an emphasis on mutual transformation of coloniser and colonised, and its blueprint for a utopian inter-civilisational alliance against institutionalised suffering is, indeed, salutary'; further, she contends that this turn to 'the rhetoric of postnationalism seriously humanises the world we have inherited,' though she cautions against the 'euphoric utopianism' that such a position produces.[5] The hope of liberation as an 'alliance against institutionalised suffering' is certainly evident in the work of anti-colonial intellectuals such as Fanon and has been taken up by postcolonial theorists such as Edward Said and Gayatri Chakravorty Spivak, among many others. However, Leela Gandhi's emphasis upon the concepts of 'hybridity' and 'postnationalism,' as the defining terms of postcolonial thought, imagines a utopian alternative to the totalizing and Manichean binaries of colonial difference that fails to contend with the material inequalities produced by the colonial economy, an economy conceived of and rationalized within the civilizing project of European imperialism and its attendant discourse of Manichean difference. The identification of hybridity both in the colonial era and in more recent formulations of cosmopolitan postnational identities posits an alteration in our understanding of colonial identities in a way that, as a number of critics of the field have argued, privileges the postcolonial rereading of colonial experience as, itself, a politics of change, rather than examining how the structures of colonialism were changed through, for instance, daily practices or struggles for national or social liberation.

Simon Gikandi contends that the 'moment of theory, which enabled many of us to develop important critiques of Eurocentrism and its veneer of humanity, also excluded a serious engagement with the human values' that informed the struggle for liberation.[6] Hence, the critical and theoretical framework of the field, and particularly its poststructuralist and Marxian influences, disregarded certain kinds of knowing and acting. Gikandi argues that the influence of poststructural thought on postcolonial studies has meant the occlusion of much African literature, in which 'a concern with political commitment is often mitigated by a desire to map out moral economies.'[7] Arif Dirlik articulates a similar critique, but one that is based in a materialist analysis. Dirlik argues that postcolonialism's preoccupation with the discursive (i.e., the cultural production of race) not simply ignores but repudiates the foundational role of capitalism in colonial history.[8] While Gikandi sees the poststructural preoccupations of the field as eliding the ethical demands of struggle, Dirlik – as well as other critics of the field, such as Aijaz Ahmad, Benita Parry, and E. San Juan, Jr – contends that the field's emphasis upon colonial discourse is ahistorical and apolitical; it elides more properly materialist concerns of exploitation, and it fails to speak to contemporary relationships of inequality globally. Although their perspectives and concerns are different, I think Gikandi and Dirlik both lament the way in which postcolonialism seems to have lost sight of its 'object,' a politics of decolonization and liberation.

This sort of criticism reflects the conflict that has emerged within and around the field in which discursive approaches are emphasized over the material, or vice versa. For instance, in *Beyond Postcolonial Theory* (1997), E. San Juan, Jr, critiques postcolonialism's utopianism, specifically challenging notions such as 'hybridity' and 'postnationalism.' Like Leela Gandhi, however, he invokes a revised humanism in the service of material transformation. He argues that the recurring rhetoric of human dignity in anti-colonial movements reflected 'not the revival of Renaissance humanism or biblical eschatology but the concept of a world society in which problems of poverty, ecology, genocide, and human rights implicate every human across nation-state boundaries.'[9] Here, San Juan alludes to what he calls a 'planetary' ethics; he identifies this ethics as the foundation for the transformation of political and economic structures and relationships. Despite their significant differences in perspective, both Leela Gandhi and E. San Juan, Jr, acknowledge the way in which an alternative to colonialism requires a discourse and a politics of interdependence across regions and differences that must transcend both the post-Enlightenment rhetoric of humanism and the model of exploitative and oppressive economic and political governance that that rhetoric rationalized in the service of the colonial project.

Significantly, recognition of the ongoing project to challenge and transcend colonial modes of production (both cultural and material) implicitly problematizes the 'post' in postcolonial by emphasizing analysis not just of colonial knowledge/power but of how current relationships of inequality are linked to the failure of the post-colonial state to fulfil the ideals of anti-colonial liberation movements, ideals that transcended the idea of the violent overcoming of the colonizer, described by Fanon in *The Wretched of the Earth* (1961). Dirlik contends that the discipline of postcolonialism, specifically as it has emerged in the United States academy, celebrates the end of colonialism, 'as if the only tasks left for the present were to abolish its ideological and cultural legacy.'[10] While a basic assumption of my analysis, that postcolonial theories of resistance must engage with both material and discursive relations simultaneously, seems trite, this sort of criticism of the field reveals the discord between 'discursive' and 'materialist' modes of analysis. Ben Okri's musings on 'story' position discursive change as a precondition for structural change; here, Dirlik contends that postcolonial studies assumes that the post-colonial state signifies the structural end of colonialism and hence turns its attention to the cultural or discursive change (or deconstruction) that must follow. For Ngugi wa Thiong'o, in contrast, decolonization requires the simultaneous transformation of the political apparatuses of colonialism and its legitimizing narratives: 'Our propensity to action or inaction or to a certain kind of action or inaction, can be profoundly affected by the way we look at the world.'[11] By interrogating the use and function of the concept of resistance within postcolonial studies, I necessarily foreground analysis of how discourse, narrative, and language inform material relations of exploitation and inequality.

Leela Gandhi's contention that postcolonialism provides a reading practice that emphasizes the 'mutual transformation of coloniser and colonised' seems incongruous with the dominant notions of resistance within the field. Critics who focus on 'deconstructing' colonial knowledge 'transform the colonizer and colonized' in that practice of reading that is postcolonial analysis – 'the rethinking and redescribing of colonialism's enabling conditions' – rather than identify resistance as acts, processes, or values that perform a politics of transformation, both in terms of material relationships between those who are privileged and those who suffered within the colonial economy, as well as how these subjects were represented. For instance, while the forms of social and cultural resistance identified by the Subaltern Studies group include acts of will or agency, Homi Bhabha's formulations of 'ambivalence,' 'mimicry,' or 'hybridity' limit resistance to the failure of colonial authority to be performed as it is represented. Such a theory seems to negate the possibility of structural change, simply illuminating the impossibility of colonial authority. The analyses of critics such as Bhabha, however, cannot be simply dismissed, as some critics seek to do. As I will argue in chapter 1, aspects of Bhabha's colonial discourse theory are redeemable for theorizing an ethic and politics of transformation; specifically, Bhabha's 'spectacular resistance' provides an important critical perspective on how colonial power is dependent upon the inculcation of particular ways of understanding the world.

Reacting against colonial discourse theory, E. San Juan, Jr, seeks to recover the historical materialist sensibility of anti-colonial thinkers such as C.L.R. James by redirecting the critical gaze (back) at what he characterizes as 'actual movement[s] of resistance or opposition to imperial domination.'[12] While San Juan appeals to a more authentic material form of resistance, the term 'resistance,' specifically, is largely absent in the writings of the anti-colonial intellectuals who are most prominent in postcolonial studies. Apart from Amilcar Cabral's notion of 'cultural resistance,' Cabral, Aimé Césaire, Léopold Senghor, C.L.R. James, and Frantz Fanon invoke notions of 'struggle,' 'revolt,' 'revolution,' 'national liberation,' and/or 'decolonization' rather than 'resistance.' In the wake of poststructural critiques of modern Western knowledge and, specifically, universal(izing) notions of equality, justice, power, and narratives of emancipation, the ideal of liberation that underwrote the struggle against colonialism becomes untenable. Indeed, the concept of resistance may be seen as the replacement for liberation after humanism has been discredited. Poststructural critiques of Western knowledge and, more importantly, reconfigurations of power, such as Michel Foucault's critique of the notion of sovereign power, dismiss 'liberation' as an ideal or possibility and construct resistance as, paradoxically, an impediment to and enabler of power. Resistance becomes a function of power.

In *Post-Colonial Transformation* (2001), Bill Ashcroft argues that resistance should be conceptualized as 'any form of defence in which an invader is "kept out,"' as these 'sometimes even unspoken forms of social and cultural resistance ... [these] forms of saying "no" ... are most interesting because they are most difficult for imperial powers to combat.'[13] Such a formulation of resistance – like that of Bhabha, or Hardt and Negri in *Empire* (2003) as well – seems to be a replacement for, rather than a condition of, 'revolution' or 'liberation,' and hence forecloses the possibility of social and cultural change. The post-independence disappointment inflected in so much African literature – such as Ayi Kwei Armah's *The Beautyful Ones Are Not Yet Born* (1969) – reveals the way in which liberation signifies something other than the creation of the post-colonial nation-state. Revolution, as simply overcoming the oppressor or turning the tables, does not constitute liberation. Raymond Williams argues that revolution is not constituted by the seizure of power from an oppressor but by the transformation of a society's 'deepest structure of relationships and feeling.'[14] Indeed, Williams characterizes revolution in terms of the 'total redemption of humanity,' or the recognition of the humanity of the other.[15] Resistance, then, constitutes both the expression of an alternative and the means of affecting a revolution, as an altered state of affairs.

As Linda Tuhiwai Smith reminds us, the claim to humanity has been a consistent and significant aspect of anti-colonial discourses, articulated in terms of the demand for human rights, the capability to create history and knowledge, or the claim to subjectivity and agency.[16] In *Conscripts of Modernity* (2005), David Scott argues, through an analysis of C.L.R. James's representation of Toussaint L'Ouverture and the 1791 Haitian Revolution, that the formulation of anti-colonial discontent as a response to the degradation and dehumanization of the colonized traps the colonized in a romantic vision of vindicationalist revolution in which 'rehumanization' is the aim of resistance and can only be achieved by 'overcoming' the colonist.[17] On the one hand, Scott contends that the native is trapped in the discursive framework of the colonizer, and so seeks to 'achieve' humanity in the terms of European notions of civilization; yet, Scott focuses on the idea that such status can only be achieved by destroying the settler. In chapter 1, I draw upon Scott's analysis to critique the struggle of Indian migrants in South Africa for political rights. Yet, the ideal of a revised humanism was also articulated in anti-colonial discourses in a way that does not depend upon the vindication of the colonized's humanity in terms of European rules of recognition. As I will argue in chapter 2, for instance, while Fanon's and Said's appeal to a 'new humanism' is certainly indebted to a European tradition, liberation constitutes not the achievement of human status for the colonized – in the European's terms – but an altered set of relationships among people that relies on a discourse of human dignity and interdependence.

The notion of revolution as a humanistic project, whether in terms of the vindication of human subjectivity or the ideal of an egalitarian society, appeared intellectually untenable as a result of the challenge of poststructuralism. However, in many ways, the deconstruction of humanism performed by Jacques Derrida or Michel Foucault echoed the critique of humanism levelled by the anti-colonial critics I have named above. The humanistic rhetoric of the colonial project revealed the hypocrisy of the ideal. While post-Enlightenment discourses of the human posited universal rights and liberties, the violence of colonial conquest and occupation was rationalized by the very same discourse; the humanity of the European was defined in relation to the infrahumanity of the native who had to be either 'raised' into the human family or managed, disciplined, or destroyed. Indeed, in the practice of colonialism, the universal human was revealed to be the white man, and, hence, vindication was never possible. Yet, a reconceptualized humanistic imperative appears in various guises in the recent work of critics such as Leela Gandhi and E. San Juan, Jr, as well as Gikandi, Spivak, Hardt and Negri, Arundhati Roy, and Paul Gilroy.

In *Against Race* (2000) and *Postcolonial Melancholia* (2005), for instance, Gilroy argues for a planetary humanism, as a replacement for the racialized demarcation of human differences and in contrast to planetary identity being fashioned through the spread of consumer capitalism. Gilroy proposes an alternative vision of humanism, which he contends 'simply cannot be reached via any retreat into the lofty habits and unamended assumptions of liberal thinking.'[18] He acknowledges, however, that while 'the ability to imagine political, economic, and social systems in which "race" makes no sense is ... essential,' such work has fallen into 'disrepute,' for the guiding framework for such work appears to resonate so strongly with liberal political thought.[19] Nonetheless, he unashamedly claims that such an ethic of humanism is necessary: 'The challenge of being in the same present, of synchronizing difference and articulating cosmopolitan hope upward from below rather than imposing it downward from on high provides some help in seeing how we might invent conceptions of humanity that allow for the presumption of equal value and go beyond the issue of tolerance into a more active engagement with the irreducible value of diversity within sameness.'[20] Like Fanon and other anti-colonial thinkers, Gilroy's formulation of humanism cannot escape the dualisms that underpin colonial or neo-imperial thought. He concludes *Against Race* by arguing that 'our challenge should now be to bring even more powerful visions of planetary humanity from the future into the present and to reconnect them with democratic and cosmopolitan traditions that have been all but expunged from today's black political imaginary.'[21] The future Gilroy appeals to is the futurism of sci-fi imaginings of invasions by 'aliens' from outer-space. How do we imagine a collective identity or transnational solidarity, however, that is not dependent upon the threat of a 'foreign' and menacing Other? How can the human be imagined otherwise than against the 'savage'? And how do discourses of post-Enlightenment humanism or renewed appeals for human connection relate to the material relationships of the (neo)colonial political economy?

The seeming impasse between materialist and discursive approaches to the postcolonial critical project hinges upon the possibilities for social change assumed within these approaches. In her critique of Michael Hardt and Antonio Negri's *Empire*, Crystal Bartolovich argues that having 'shifted their discourse to "Empire," Hardt and Negri find themselves hard-pressed to say what the multitude should do, what or whom it should struggle against, since the enemy has now become (suddenly and perversely, I would add) "rather abstract."'[22] Does resistance require a 'concrete' enemy or Other to oppose? Must resistance be conceived of as a struggle *against* something (whether the settler or capitalism) rather than *for* something? How can resistance be conceived in a way that accounts for the influence of Foucault, among others, in reconstituting the meaning of power without reducing it to simply a function of power? Gilroy, Leela Gandhi, Dirlik, Gikandi, and San Juan are all very much concerned with contemporary configurations of global politics, economics, and culture. While these structures and attitudes may be different from the era of European colonialism, they are imbedded in that history, and so the 'past' of colonial authority and anti-colonial struggle cannot be dismissed as failing to speak to the contemporary moment. Hence, when Arundhati Roy claims in her writings on 'Empire' and her advocacy for global justice that discussions of resistance are some of the most crucial discussions of the contemporary moment,[23] I believe that in order to respond to this demand it is important to interrogate the concept of resistance, and the way in which it shapes the field of postcolonial studies; resistance is an ambiguous concept, signifying the failure of colonial power to be total, yet, at the same time, it is seemingly synonymous with anti-colonial notions of struggle and opposition.

Frantz Fanon begins the introductory essay to *The Wretched of the Earth*, 'Concerning Violence,' with the seemingly categorical statement that decolonization is 'always a violent phenomenon.'[24] This first invocation of the term 'decolonization' appears to signify only the end of colonial rule: the colonized overcoming the colonizer. However, while Fanon's arguments about violence and national liberation in *The*

Wretched of the Earth are often conflated within postcolonial studies with the notion of resistance, I want to foreground his use of the term 'decolonization' as a process. Fanon's description of decolonization in *The Wretched of the Earth* as necessarily violent and oppositional, I will argue in chapter 2, is presented in a way that illuminates its own ambiguity; to borrow from Ato Sekyi-Otu's analysis of Fanon, the sentiments expressed in 'Concerning Violence' are shaped by the 'horizon of immediacy' of the anti-colonial movement and *describe* a structure of attitude and reference rather than propose a theory of resistance.[25] According to Fanon, the 'minimum demand' of the colonized – though it appears as the extent of the demand in the remainder of the chapter – is the replacement of the colonist; the native peasant seeks the land of the settler farmer, for instance.

Yet, decolonization, as Fanon goes on to describe it, is both a historical moment and a process defined by the relationship between the colonizer and the colonized: 'The need for this change exists in its crude state, impetuous and compelling, in the consciousness and in the lives of the men and women who are colonized,' and the 'possibility of this change is equally experienced in the form of a terrifying future in the consciousness of another "species" of men and women: the colonizers.'[26] Decolonization, therefore, is seemingly marked by opposition and experienced as antagonism, wherein the image of liberation for the colonized is the colonizer's terror. On one level, decolonization is the historical fulfilment of the expulsion of European direct rule; yet, the 'change' Fanon describes in the conclusion to *The Wretched of the Earth* is not synonymous with national independence and the post-colonial African state. He writes: 'It is a question of the Third World starting a new history of Man, a history which will have regard to the sometimes prodigious theses which Europe has put forward, but which will also not forget Europe's crimes, of which the most horrible was committed in the heart of man.'[27] Fanon envisions, here, a revolution that is more akin to that articulated by Raymond Williams; revolution constitutes a 'change in the *form* of the activity of a society'[28] rather than simply the 'overcoming' of the 'oppressor.'

Fanon prophetically argues that the replacement of the colonizer by the colonized as the establishment of the African nation is doomed to disappointment for the peoples of the continent. The entrance of African nations into modernity is not the liberation Fanon envisions, for the emergence of European modernity is interdependent with the colonial project; 'Europe' and 'reason' are produced in relation to their Others.

Fanon notes that colonialism was initiated and maintained with the bayonet and cannon, yet he also constructs the very relationship within which decolonization is conceived as a product of colonialism: 'The settler is right when he speaks of knowing "them" well. For it is the settler who has brought the native into existence and who perpetuates his existence. The settler owes the fact of his very existence, that is to say, his property, to the colonial system.'[29] This formulation of the relationship between colonizer and colonized, and these subjectivities themselves, identifies, at once, both a discursive and material relationship; indeed, the material and the cultural are inseparable. Colonial identity is a function of, rather than prior to, the dominance/privilege of the colonizer and the suffering/subjugation of the colonized in the colonial political economy. Fanon's seeming recognition, here, of the interdependence of discursive constructions of identity and material relations of power undermines the idea that the 'answer' to the degradation and dehumanization of the colonial experience can only be the immediate 'overthrow' of the colonizer; colonization is not constituted simply by the presence of the settler, and it is not only the exploitative system of labour and landownership; it is also the conceptual framework that constructs such structural inequities as legitimate and makes alternatives to such relationships appear impossible.

In both *Black Skin, White Masks* and *The Wretched of the Earth*, Fanon alludes to a notion of liberation conceived of as the result of a narrative of progression; for instance, he suggests that liberation can only emerge after a violent political revolution constructed in oppositional terms. Yet, Fanon also describes liberation as transcending such an opposition. The 'new humanism' Fanon postulates requires not simply the destruction of economic and political structures marked by dominance and subjugation but the transformation of discursive structures of power establishing and maintaining colonial identities. The producer of culture – the writer or artist – consequently holds a privileged place within Fanon's theory of decolonization. Indeed, Fanon theorizes a series of stages in which the native artist moves from desiring to assimilate the dominating culture, to assuming the role of the 'awakener' of the people by fashioning a revolutionary 'literature of combat.'[30] Only in addressing the 'people' can the writer take his (and the writer and nationalist imaginary are very much masculine) place with the people as a producer of a new culture. While Fanon frames cultural resistance within a militaristic discourse, and critics such as Barbara Harlow have taken up this idea of literature as a weapon of oppositional politics,

Fanon is describing what postcolonial critics have come to identify as counter-discursive writing.

In *Culture and Imperialism* (1993), Edward Said argues that 'stories are at the heart of what explorers and novelists say about strange regions of the world; they also become the method colonized people use to assert their own identity and the existence of their own history.'[31] Like many postcolonial critics, Said concentrates upon the literary text as a site that illuminates colonialism's discursive constructions of power and identity. He argues that European literature, from travelogues to novels, served both to assert European identity and history and, as part of the project of colonial education, to produce and manage the identity of the colonized. Literature is privileged as the primary mode through which the colonial order is produced culturally. While a number of critics of postcolonial studies argue that such a perspective elides the material relations of (neo)colonial power and ignores the way in which colonial authority was maintained through violent repression and/or opposed by militant insurgency, the economic and political structures of colonialism cannot be so easily separated from the 'stories' the beneficiaries of colonialism constructed to understand and legitimize them. Reiterating Césaire's and Memmi's critiques of colonialism, Ngugi wa Thiong'o argues that the liberation of the colonized from material exploitation and political repression requires the 'decolonization of the mind.'

In this book, I am not specifically concerned with 'cultural resistance' as it is defined by critics such as Said or as it has shaped postcolonial literary studies. Literature, as a particular form of cultural production, is not the primary object of my study. However, specific works of literature have a prominent place in my analysis. For instance, I analyse Tsitsi Dangarembga's *Nervous Conditions* (1988), and, more importantly, critical interpretations of the novel, to argue for the way in which, despite the so-called 'discursive turn' in postcolonial studies, the postcolonial critical perspective, even in its deconstructive manifestations, often reinforces the binary and oppositional narrative of conflict. For the most part, however, I turn to works of literature such as J.M. Coetzee's *Waiting for the Barbarians* (1980) or Sindiwe Magona's *Mother to Mother* (1998) to examine the way in which works of literature take part in, and comment upon, the cultural frameworks of storytelling or narrative that inform colonial authority and the ideal of liberation. Before turning to this analysis, however, I would like to briefly trace how the construction of 'cultural resistance' in postcolonial literary studies reveals the limitations of postcolonial conceptions of resistance.

In *The Empire Writes Back* (1989) – the text that signals the transition from Commonwealth literary studies to postcolonial studies, a project of canon (re)formation based on the geographical boundaries of the former British Empire to the dominant practice within the Euro-American university of organizing and reading these literatures – Ashcroft, Griffiths, and Tiffin prescribe postcolonial literature as being concerned with the appropriation of English and reconstitution of various englishes, the adaptation of metropolitan genres and epistemologies, as well as the native subject's displacement due to dislocation or denigration. By their own admission, they compare widely divergent works on the basis that they depict a struggle for community within a binary that pits the colonial periphery against the European centre.[32] Postcolonial literature is defined, then, as a response to European colonial representation of the colonial project and the colonized. Such critical practices assume, and are limited to, an oppositional paradigm between apparently fixed communities of the colonizer and the colonized, the European and the native. By focusing upon the contest of competing versions of history and identity, such formulations privilege this narrative of contest over the act of articulating the story, or the idea that the story – as narrative of identity and experience – is a fundamental part of the contested field on which the struggle is taking place.

Within this postcolonial critical practice, literature is read as 'resistance' in so far as (1) colonial narratives are 'rewritten' or (2) postcolonial literature is constructed as the Other to the colonial narrative. Ashcroft et al. recognize post-colonial works as constituent of various national or regional literatures, and thereby link the act of writing to that of nation-building, a 'vital stage of the process of rejecting the claims of the centre to exclusivity.'[33] For the authors of *The Empire Writes Back*, '"Post-colonial" seems to be the choice that both embraces the historical reality and focuses on that relationship which has provided the most important creative and psychological impetus in the writing.'[34] Derived from this political experience, all post-colonial or 'dominated' literature subverts European power 'through nationalist assertion, proclaiming itself centre and self-determining,' yet at the same time radically 'questioning the bases of European and British metaphysics, challenging the world-view that can polarize centre and periphery in the first place.'[35] To support this claim, they point to such writers as Wilson Harris, Chinua Achebe, J.M. Coetzee, Margaret Atwood, and Jean Rhys, who they argue have rewritten texts of the English canon in a way that posits alternative 'realities' by reversing hierarchical order and by 'interrogating the philosophical assumptions on which that order was based.'[36] To what extent, however, does privileging texts that literally *write back* to prior European texts allow for such autonomy to be gained or recognized?

To read literatures of the colonized as 'counter-discourse,' even when that counter-discourse takes the form not of the production of an essentialized and homogeneous native identity but a hybrid or syncretic one, necessarily constructs the postcolonial text as understandable only in relation to an assumed European referent. Ashcroft, however, contends that the counter-discursive literary text is never simply a response to the canonical text, reversing the imperial binary of civilized and savage, but a revision that exposes the cultural assumptions of those texts and so is transformative.[37] While I agree that many of the paradigmatic works of this sort do indeed expose the cultural assumptions of colonial authority and, further, that such cultural assumptions are necessary for the structures of material inequality and violence of the colonial project, it is not clear that exposing the binary thought of colonial knowledge, for instance, is necessarily transformative. Further, the value of the text – its 'resistant' or 'transformative' quality – is constrained by a reading practice that can only understand the text in relation to the authoritative and normative metropole.

Such a framework for analysing this literature also limits the (post)-colonial problem to the relationship between colonizer and colonized. For Arun Mukherjee, the idea that postcolonial writers write *back* to the *centre* overlooks a great body of work concerned more about class or family or the management of bodies by focusing on the way texts subvert or resist the colonizer.[38] The political significance of so-called postcolonial writing should not be limited to the way in which it responds to and challenges European forms, models, or representations of (post)colonial places and peoples. By first privileging particular literary texts that function to 'resist' colonialism, and then translating this organization of texts into a reading practice, postcolonial expression becomes synonymous with resistance. Further, what it means to resist is left unexamined. The postcolonial text as counter-discourse is resistant in so far as it is 'different.' As Stephen Slemon argues, 'Colonised societies have always been consigned to a modality of interpretation, comparison and representation that registers immediate experience not through an unproblematically reflective language but rather *against* the pattern of an-other culture, an-other sign.'[39] In many cases, anti-colonial nationalist identities were indeed posited through modern European discourses of identity or specifically against Europe. The tendency of postcolonialism to consign colonized societies to this 'modality of interpretation, comparison and representation,' however, occludes the problem of indigenous modes of domination as well as alternative modes of identity formation and limits the extent to which such constructions of identity can be assessed in terms of how they enable the transformation of structures of inequality that include, but are not confined to, specifically colonial political and economic structures.

Drawing upon Gauri Viswanathan's contention that English literary education in British colonies functioned to take the colonized further from themselves and their world to the self of the colonizing other and that other's world, Ngugi argues that decolonization requires the colonized to seize back control of the means of communal self-definition, including language and literary production.[40] As my analysis of postcolonial models of resistance in chapters 1 and 2 will show, postcolonial notions of resistance are either focused on deconstructing the categories of 'self' and 'other' assumed within such an argument or indebted to this oppositional binary. Indeed, in chapters 3 and 4, I will analyse Gandhi's notions of *ahimsa* (nonviolence) and *sarvadoya* ('the welfare of all') as well as South African initiatives towards reconciliation to conceptualize a notion of resistance, as transformation, that departs from postcolonial assumptions of resistance as opposition to colonial authority, self-affirmation through counter-narrative, or the deconstruction of colonial discourses of identity. However, I identify resistance as involving 'culture' in the sense that Ngugi uses: values, or ways of seeing and understanding. Resistance, in this sense, transforms the structure of power assumed within colonial discourse by recognizing, and fostering, an order in which the relationship between Self and Other is one of mutual interdependence rather than antagonism. I turn to Gandhi's analysis of power and his articulation of an ethics and politics of struggle as well as the South African project of reconciliation as ways of approaching and developing a conceptual framework for the sort of 'change' invoked in the work of Fanon or Ngugi, among many others.

The primary objects of my analysis of colonial power and the idea of resistance are narrative frameworks and cultural values that shape consciousness to look at the world (i.e., political and economic relationships) in a certain way. Here, I am at least implicitly drawing upon Shari Stone-Mediatore's writings on storytelling and resistance. Stone-Mediatore draws upon Hannah Arendt's examination of the 'structural affinity between political phenomenon and narrative that begins to explain the importance of narration to political thought.'[41] Her analysis of story as both meaning-making and social practices is particularly important in terms of the way in which narrative constructions of experience depend upon metaphors of actors and action units that are related together within a structure of beginnings and endings.[42] In part, then, I seek to deconstruct the narrative frameworks that inform postcolonial notions of resistance.

To do this, I also utilize Johan Galtung's theory of violence, which acknowledges the *experience* of suffering and harm that results from structural violence – or the violence of poverty, alienation, etc., that results from economic, political, and other social structures – and direct physical violence. When Fanon declares that decolonization is always a violent phenomenon, he seems to place the focus of both colonial power and anti-colonial opposition on the experience and use of direct violence. In chapter 3, I engage with Ranajit Guha's contention that the British colonial government was dominant but not hegemonic, relying upon the sword, or violence, to control the peoples of South Asia. While I do not want to ignore the significance of military conquest and repression or armed revolt, to focus *only* on these forms of violence simplifies the way in which colonial regimes asserted and maintained authority and the way in which the colonized subverted and challenged these regimes, or articulated alternatives to the structure of relationships and feelings of colonial order. In addition, to focus on direct violence – to the extent of marginalizing structural violence – as the South African Truth and Reconciliation Commission does, at least in its most public initiatives, masculinizes the experience of colonialism. In the history of colonial violence, such as that which Fanon maps, there is little room for the analysis of poverty, hunger, and ignorance – which Fanon names as the true problem of colonialism – specifically in terms of the stories of women's experience. I turn to Dangarembga's *Nervous Conditions*, Rao's *Kanthapura* (1938), and Magona's *Mother to Mother* because each of these novels foregrounds colonialism as manifested in forms of structural violence; as a result, each of these works engages with the intersections of forms of racialized and gendered oppression under colonialism, as well as the narratives, myths, and discourses that rationalize or legitimize this violence.

Galtung contends that forms of violence, from poverty to slavery to aerial bombardment, are not possible without 'cultural violence.' He defines cultural violence as those aspects of the discursive sphere, from language to religion to empirical science, that legitimize or explain warfare or structures of exploitation and marginalization. While he identifies rituals and symbols (such as the raising of national flags), forms of cultural production (such as literature), and language, among other aspects of culture, he does not identify these acts or processes as 'violent' in and of themselves; rather, he argues that the conceptual framework they instil or reinforce enables structural and direct violence.[43] For instance, the producers of 'colonial History' pretended that native resistance 'had not happened or was not worth mentioning, or, if that failed ... construe[d] it as out and out treachery (the Indian "Mutiny" of 1857) or an explosion of atavistic barbarity (the Mau Mau uprising in the 1950s).'[44] Native revolt reaffirmed the idea of the native's irredeemable savagery, at the same time that this perception of savagery justified the violent repression of the native as necessary and legitimate. While colonial discourse theory, I will argue, seems at times to elide the adversarial structure of colonial politics, oppositional models of resistance seem not to be able to conceive of politics as anything other than dualistic antagonism. Yet, the ideal of human interdependence, transcending or displacing this dualism, recurs in theories of liberation, from Fanon and Gandhi to Said and Gilroy. Hierarchical or binary thinking (i.e., patriarchy, racism) do not *explain* the structural violence of the exploitation of native labour or the direct violence of colonial conquest in a simple cause-effect relationship. It is not enough to change the story, nor is it possible without altering material relationships of power; cultural violence, according to Galtung, enables, and is reinforced by, forms of direct and structural violence.

The emphasis upon culture and narrative in postcolonial studies often seems to divorce the cultural from the material structures and experiences of colonialism, as if these modes are separable and hence require separate and distinct approaches to transformation. Hence, I seek to approach the 'discursive' sphere of colonial and anti-colonial thought in a way that relates it more closely to the material structures of exploitation and inequality than postcolonial discourse theory seems to do. Resistance, as the means of revolution, depends upon a narrative of conflict that seeks to reduce the actors of the conflict to two groups and assumes an, albeit amorphous, 'end' or a 'liberation from'; it is limited to the realm of critique and, hence, cannot 'imagine otherwise.' Both the examples of Gandhian thought and the idea of reconciliation, which I will develop in chapters 3 and 4, alter this narrative; resistance not simply deconstructs the binary framework and the linear structure of this narrative but transforms it. Rather than the particular *modes* (i.e., literature, language) of colonial cultural violence, in my formulation of a notion of resistance as transformation I am concerned with engaging with particular 'ways of looking at the world' (i.e., the superiority of European culture or the pre-eminence of economic development in the form of a capitalist ideology of production and value) that those modes impose or reaffirm. Such a notion of resistance is invested not in the ideas of opposition, or the production of counter-discourses, but in the transformation of structures/cultures of power. When Ben Okri states that people must change the 'stories' they live by in order to change the world in which they live, I interpret his use of 'stories' more broadly than particular historical or literary narratives as those discourses of identity and power through which subjectivity is constructed and within which action is understood.

In chapters 1 and 2, I analyse the two dominant conceptualizations of resistance within postcolonialism: resistance-as-subversion, and resistance-as-opposition. Resistance-as-subversion constitutes the disruption or modification of colonial modes of knowledge and authority. In contrast, resistance-as-opposition, though such approaches engage with colonial representation, relies upon a notion of opposition to colonial authority invested in the assumption of antagonism. I begin with an analysis of colonial discourse theory, for it has become (perceived as) the dominant framework for postcolonial studies. I then (re)turn to the work of Fanon, among other anti-colonial thinkers, in order to identify the way in which his materialist analysis was imbedded in reflection on discourse, narrative, and story. I return to Fanon's notion of a post-liberation 'new humanism,' and Said's development of this idea, as a way of foregrounding the idea of resistance-as-transformation, which I theorize in the latter half of the book. While I argue that this idea of 'transformation' has roots in the materialist critiques and humanistic ideals of anti-colonial thinkers such as Fanon, James, Memmi, or Césaire, and draws upon deconstruction-inspired critiques of colonial discourse, the ideas I derive from the work of Gandhi or through the idea of reconciliation are not easily recuperable within these critical perspectives.

In chapters 3 and 4, I challenge the idea that resistance constitutes a 'saying "no"' to power, whether in the sense that Ashcroft describes, Bhabha constructs as mimicry and hybridity, or Fanon identifies in the native's desire to overthrow the colonist. I am more concerned with forms of social and cultural 'resistance' that are performed as an affirmation of an alternative to the direct and structural violence of colonialism rather than merely a refusal or manipulation of, or protest against, colonial power. This is not to argue that such refusals or protest do not disrupt colonial power or constitute a form of resistance; rather, I seek to theorize an alternative approach to resistance that is consistent with the ideal of transformation and liberation that Fanon, Leela Gandhi, E. San Juan, Jr, or Paul Gilroy gesture towards. Gilroy contends that 'if we follow Fanon's example and work toward creative possibilities that are too easily dismissed as utopian, our moral and political compass might profitably be reset by acts of imagination and invention that are adequate to the depth of the postcolonial predicament he described.'[45] While neither of the examples I work through should be seen as 'models' of resistance in a positivist sense, they do provide examples of just such acts of imagination and invention.

Through an analysis of the role of Gandhi's philosophy of *ahimsa* and his conception of *sarvadoya* in the Indian independence movement and the role of the notions of *ubuntu* and reconciliation both in South Africa's anti-apartheid movement and in the post-apartheid Truth and Reconciliation Commission, I seek to identify an ethics and politics of transformation derived from (post)colonial experience. While the examples of Gandhian analysis and the South African reconciliation project are separated from one another in terms of time and place, and reflect differing experiences of colonialism, I turn to these two examples for a few reasons. As an analysis of resistance within postcolonial studies, a field that has from its inception been cross-cultural and comparative, it is important to develop an analysis that is consistent with this tradition. As well, both of the examples have a particular significance within contemporary, more ethical, formulations of postcolonialism, and continue to have an influence on political thought and action throughout the world; to cite but two examples: Arundhati Roy's analysis of contemporary manifestations of 'Empire' and the struggle for an alternative often invokes Gandhi's notion of *ahimsa* or nonviolence, while Edward Said relates lessons from the South African reconciliation project to the Palestinian struggle.[46]

Despite the immense significance that Gandhi's analysis and experiments with egalitarian alternatives have had on social movements around the world, it is only very recently that postcolonial critics and theorists have begun to examine his writings, rather than his function as a figure of the struggle, both discursively and politically. I seek to contribute to this analysis and evaluation of Gandhi's philosophical and critical thought rather than Gandhi the political activist. Similarly, the end of apartheid, the idea of a 'new' South Africa, and the project of reconciliation have had a profound impact on postcolonial thought. Each example figures 'liberation' as the transformation of relationships, as material experience, and ways of seeing the self and other. While a number of the critics of postcolonialism I have cited contend that postcolonialism fails to speak to contemporary concerns of power, exploitation, and injustice globally, I believe that the sort of analysis I undertake in this book contributes, in some small way at least, to the discussion about resistance that Arundhati Roy contends is so critical to contemporary global politics and culture.

1 Colonial Discourse/Power and 'Spectacular Resistance'

Deconstructing 'Barbarians': Colonial Discourse Theory

J.M. Coetzee begins his novel *Waiting for the Barbarians* (1980) with the interrogation of a suspected 'barbarian' spy by the 'Third Bureau' and rumours of an impending 'barbarian' attack on an administrative outpost of an unnamed and time unspecific Empire. In this allegory of imperial governance and culture, Coetzee portrays colonial confinement, both in terms of overt forms of repression – such as the imprisonment and torture of suspected 'barbarian' insurgents, as well as of the outpost's oppositional magistrate – and in terms of the way colonial discourse limits the imagination. The 'barbarians,' who the narrating magistrate characterizes as ignorant, slovenly, and cunning – yet somehow redeemable, if only they stay on the margins of 'civilization' – provide both a threat to the existence of the imperial settlers and the settlers' reason for being. An amateur archaeologist, the magistrate collects artefacts of the barbarians' ancient civilization, excavating ruins and collecting wooden slips marked with an indecipherable script: 'What an occasion and what a shame too to be here today! One day my successors will be making collections of the artifacts of these people, arrowheads, carved knife-handles, wooden dishes, to display beside my bird's eggs and calligraphic riddles. And here I am patching up relations between the men of the future and the men of the past.'[1] The magistrate collects artefacts of the barbarians' existence, for the presence of Empire is their doom.

While the magistrate is ambivalent about the barbarians, suggesting they are somehow noble, yet still savage, for the foot-soldiers and settlers the barbarians are not redeemable; they are a threat to the existence of the settlement and, hence, are the 'enemy.' Significantly, the discourse of the imperial project is distinctly militaristic. The narrative is driven by the perpetual threat of the 'barbarian' army's impending attack. As much as the Empire's project of conquest is ongoing, the presence of the settler is somehow normal; it is the native who is out of place, and whose existence threatens the settler's mission. Hence, it is necessary for the Empire to pre-emptively attack the 'barbarians,' not as a means of conquest, but as a means to provide 'security.' Ironically, then, the Empire's fear constitutes a projection of its own values and practices onto the other of its making; the colonial project is driven by the fear of an enemy that is a mimicry of the imperial self. In part, the magistrate's treachery against the state he is charged with administering is his recognition of the Empire's own 'barbarism.' Mocking the notion that the 'barbarians are at the gate,' the magistrate asks the military commander, Mandel, if he finds it easy to eat after conducting torture: 'I have imagined that one would want to wash one's hands. But no ordinary washing would be enough, one would require priestly intervention, a ceremonial of cleansing.'[2] Yet, while the magistrate is able to question just who are the barbarians in the conflict or shout 'no' during a public execution, his opposition is nonetheless confined by the binary thought of the Empire's militaristic discourse: 'Shall I tell you what I sometimes wish? I wish that these barbarians would rise up and teach us a lesson, so that we would learn to respect them.'[3] He rejects his own civilization in so far as it corrupts barbarian virtues and creates dependence, but his opposition maintains both the imperial dichotomy and the assumption that violence constitutes power.

The novel concludes with the magistrate returned to his post, the settlers working their fields with weapons at their sides, and children maintaining a row of scarecrow soldiers, meant to 'deceive the keen eyes of the barbarians' and hence prevent an attack.[4] Although Coetzee depicts people characterized as barbarians and there are reports of minor incursions by the barbarian army – damage to the irrigation embankment, for instance – the imagined threat of the barbarian army remains unfulfilled; indeed, the physical existence of such an army is ambiguous. The barbarians have little room to speak in this allegory; rather, they exist only as they are constructed within the colonial imagination, a function of the Empire's will-to-power. By constructing the barbarians as cunning, ruthless, and a threat to the Empire's security, the Empire rationalizes repression and coercion as tools of governance or the maintenance of 'peace,' and it produces its own identity.

Taking as its focus the production of colonial knowledge and identities, and departing from the 'realist' form that dominated African literature written in English during the 1960s and 1970s, *Waiting for the Barbarians* takes a significant place within the field of postcolonial studies as it emerged out of Commonwealth literature or world literature in English studies. Significantly, Coetzee's novel appeared just two years after Edward Said's foundational *Orientalism* (1978), a work that also examines the relationship between imperial knowledge/representation and material and political power. The appearance of *Orientalism* is widely regarded as marking the advent of postcolonial theory, and, as I alluded to in the Introduction, for critics such as E. San Juan, Jr, the field of postcolonial studies is often reduced to colonial discourse analysis, a critical project informed and guided by poststructuralism. Said's thesis, that through Orientalist discourse 'European culture was able to manage – and even produce – the Orient politically, sociologically, militarily, ideologically, scientifically, and imaginatively during the post-Enlightenment period,' was by no means completely original.[5] Indeed, for anti-colonial thinkers such as Frantz Fanon or, as I will argue in this chapter as well as chapter 3, Mohandas Gandhi, the understanding and critique of colonial knowledge, representation, or discourse was central to imagining political struggle and liberation. Nonetheless, *Orientalism* has had a profound influence across disciplines, and most particularly literary studies and history, this so-called 'discursive turn' particularly evident in the work of the Indian historical project of the Subaltern Studies collective.

In many ways, the work of the Subaltern Studies collective parallels the development of postcolonialism more broadly, originating with the analysis of colonial power and the illumination of forms of resistance – from literary counter-narratives to acts of native insurgency elided within colonial history – and moving towards an analysis of colonial historical discourses and the deconstruction of concepts such as 'power' and 'subjectivity.' The early work of the Subaltern Studies project provides a valuable critique of colonial and nationalist constructions of insurgency, as well as stories of subaltern opposition. Significantly, as well, these early Subaltern Studies essays were not limited to focusing only on structures of colonial power or opposition to colonial forms of control or governance. As much as the collective 'uncovers' local contexts and conditions of rebellion – against colonial agents, as well as indigenous landowners or *zamindars*, and 'traditional' structures of economics and politics – the collective reads these events in such a way as to produce a counter-narrative to the dominant nationalist or elite narratives of Indian history. The Subaltern Studies project, therefore, constitutes both a project of acknowledging subaltern opposition and subversion of structures of oppression and a project that critiques colonial and nationalist Indian historiography.

From this early interest in analysing specific historical events in order to challenge the dominant narratives of Indian history, members of the Subaltern Studies project have largely turned their attention to the cultural assumptions of the discipline of history itself. For some, Said's *Orientalism* is blamed for diverting Indian historiography's (more proper) Marxist trajectory of class analysis towards the study of discourse, representation, and power. This so-called 'discursive turn' is particularly evident in the contributions of Spivak, who first published in the collective's fourth volume. Influenced by both Marxism and deconstruction, Spivak regards the basic initial assumptions of the Subaltern Studies project to be suspect. While she notes that the early volumes of *Subaltern Studies* comprise mainly accounts of the 'failures' of the bourgeoisie to recognize the revolutionary potential of the peasantry and the 'failures' of trade union socialism or agrarian communalism to 'fully develop,' her concern is not with the limitations of such narratives but the conceptualizations of the actors taking part in these narratives.[6] Spivak argues that 'as long as notions of discipline and subjectivity are left unexamined, the subaltern will be narrativized in theoretically alternative but politically similar ways. Historians must face the contemporary critique of subjectivity.'[7] The Subaltern Studies project was envisioned as an interrogation of the way in which peasants are represented in, or written out of, colonial and nationalist histories of India. Nonetheless, the implication of Spivak's contention that the subaltern (and specifically the female subject) cannot speak within dominant discourses is that the reliance upon historical discourse for imagining the subaltern's agency or consciousness limits the way in which the subject, agency, and therefore resistance can be conceptualized and understood.

Critics such as Neil Lazarus, Sumit Sarkar, and O'Hanlon and Washbrook lament this shift from an analysis of the subaltern subject to the construction of subjectivity; Subaltern Studies 'turn' from an exploration of Indian history informed by Marxist analysis of material relations of power to approaches that are preoccupied with interrogating the 'foundationalism' of history or the subjectivity of the subaltern. While Sarkar, a former member of the collective, acknowledges that the project had to interrogate its own Marxist assumptions and confront the problem of European 'universalism' inherent in Marxist thought, he argues that discourse analysis deprives the colonial subject of autonomy and agency. Instead of creating a new Marxist reading practice, Sarkar argues that the collective swung from a 'simple emphasis on subaltern autonomy to an even more simplistic thesis of western cultural domination' and reduced all history into the simple problematic of colonial discourse/power.[8] Despite its early efforts to uncover the gaps and silences within colonial and nationalist historical narratives, Subaltern Studies, Sarkar contends, is now constrained by its preoccupation with critiquing colonial power-knowledge.

Although I am sympathetic to Sarkar's concern that Subaltern Studies, and postcolonial studies more generally, privileges analysis of the effects of colonial power at the expense of other forms and structures of difference and inequality – and indeed this concern is central to my articulation of resistance, as transformation – it is important to question this narrative of the Subaltern Studies group's 'discursive turn' in order to recognize the way in which this project has served to problematize not only nationalist and colonial historiography but the relationship between the material and the discursive itself. As Dipesh Chakrabarty reminds us in *Provincializing Europe* (2000), the impetus for the Subaltern Studies project arose in part from an unease with Marxist historicism, and particularly the representation of Indian peasants during the colonial era as somehow 'prepolitical.' The project, therefore, was never simply a project of recording a 'history from below'; rather, the counternarratives of Indian colonial history necessarily illuminated the limits of European notions of the political (i.e., the elision of relationships understood in terms of 'religion') and hence, as Chakrabarty argues, pluralized the history of power in a global context, separating it from a universalist narrative of capital.[9] Hence, the work of the Subaltern Studies collective has, from its inception, been concerned with the discursive framework through which history is represented and power is understood. As a result, I will return to the insights of this project, and particularly Ranajit Guha's adaptation of Gramsci's notion of hegemony as a form of dominance rather than an alternative to dominance, in chapter 3, relating it to Gandhi's critique of modernity.

Critics of postcolonial studies' preoccupation with colonial discourse analysis argue that discourse analysis marginalizes the material experience and inequalities of colonialism and elides the fact that colonialism is a conflict. Specifically, while Said's thesis in *Orientalism* has had a profound impact on the development of the field, it was not long before critics identified the way in which the influence of Foucault's formulation of power on Said's analysis forecloses the possibility of native agency and effaces oppositional voices. Indeed, Said acknowledges his failure to recognize the ambivalence of Orientalist discourse and the possibility of resistance to it, and departs from a strictly Foucauldian notion of the relation between power, knowledge, and discourse, most particularly in *Culture and Imperialism*. The voices of native opposition are also largely effaced in Coetzee's *Waiting for the Barbarians*, but, significantly, the representation of imperial discourse Coetzee provides illuminates the way it is 'constructed' as well as its ruptures. Further, the cultural construction of the 'barbarian' in *Waiting for the Barbarians* specifically places the barbarian in a relationship of conflict with Empire (between good and evil, civilization and savagery, survival and its threat) and rationalizes the Empire's will to dominate its 'others.' While the conflict is a material one, in this case focused on land and natural resources, it is understood, and, indeed, enacted, through language and story; the discourse of colonialism and its material structures enable one another.

Said's analysis of Orientalist discourse, the colonial discourse theory of Spivak or Bhabha, and the work of the Subaltern Studies collective as well, perform a vital function in uncovering assumptions about agency, autonomy, and subjectivity that limit our understanding of power and the possibilities for resistance. My purpose in this chapter is not to rehash the plethora of arguments for, against, and about colonial discourse theory, and particularly Bhabha's work. Rather, I am interested in exploring the way in which the concept of resistance figures in Bhabha's work, in particular, and how Bhabha has influenced the notion of resistance in relation to the postcolonial project. For instance, Hardt and Negri argue that by illuminating the resilience of 'difference,' in the form of mimicry, ambivalence, or hybridity, Bhabha's 'attack' on binary thought and essentialism constitutes 'a project aimed at social change and a claim about the real nature of societies.'[10] From this perspective, it is the postcolonial critic who 'resists' the oppressive structures of colonialism. My concern, here, is not specifically with the role of the critic, but I do want to affirm Bhabha's work as an examination of the way in which the nature of power is not so much 'new' as being analysed differently, perhaps more effectively.

My main concern in this chapter is to interrogate the sort of 'resistance' Bhabha imagines; for instance, the resistance that is evident in the space between colonial desire and the response of the native. The *failure* of the native to return the colonial gaze or to complete the narrative, which Bhabha characterizes as 'spectacular resistance,' constitutes resistance as subversion. The sorts of tools and language Bhabha provides can help illuminate the way in which more material forms of opposition, struggle, and protest can be seen as enabling, and enabled by, modes of discursive *refusal*, wherein the colonial narrative does not simply fail but is transformed by the colonized in politically meaningful ways. I examine the notion of resistance in Bhabha's work, then, to provide context for my analysis of a series of events in South Africa during the first decade of the twentieth century, in which segments of the immigrant Indian population organized to assert their 'rights' and to oppose policies that produced Indians as inferior and subordinate. The main forms of political opposition utilized by the Indian community, from advocacy to strikes to civil disobedience, largely conform to a notion of resistance as conscious and collective opposition. In addition to, or within, organized acts of non-cooperation and the political organization of the movement, however, are a series of acts that conform neither to dominant notions of resistance as opposition nor to Bhabha's 'spectacular resistance,' though I believe critical recognition of them is dependent upon colonial discourse theory, and particularly the critique of colonial power and the construction of colonial identities.

Homi K. Bhabha and Colonial Discourse/Power

In the introduction to *The Location of Culture* (1994), Bhabha distinguishes between postcolonialism as a field of study that authenticates 'histories of exploitation and the evolution of strategies of resistance' and cultures of postcolonial 'contra-modernity,' which are resistant in the sense that their cultural hybridity 'translates' and reinscribes the social imaginary of both the metropole and modernity.[11] This hybridity becomes operational in the sense that the native cannot return the language of authority without altering it. For Bhabha, this 'splitting' of the language of authority 'destroys the calculations of the empowered, and allows the disempowered to calculate strategies by which they are oppressed and to use that knowledge in structuring resistance. I have always believed that "small differences" and slight alterations and displacements are often the most significant elements in a process of subversion or transformation.'[12] In this explanation, Bhabha attributes to the native a form of agency; the disempowered 'calculate strategies' and 'alter' and 'displace.'

In his critique of *Orientalism*, Bhabha argues that Said's thesis misunderstands Foucault's concept of power: '"*Pouvoir/Savoir*" places subjects in a relation of power and recognition that is not part of a symmetrical or dialectical relation – self/other, master/slave – which can then be subverted by being inverted. Subjects are always disproportionately placed in opposition or domination through the symbolic decentring of multiple power relations which play the role of support as well as target or adversary.'[13] Drawing upon Foucault's understanding of power as omnipresent and diffuse, 'the multiplicity of force relations immanent in the sphere in which they operate and which constitute their own organization,'[14] Bhabha critiques Said's construction of colonial authority by challenging the construction of the 'subjects' or narrative-defined actors – colonizer and colonized – that take part in the colonial relationship. For instance, Bhabha turns instead to Henry Louis Gates, Jr, and Paul Gilroy, who 'propose forms of contestatory subjectivities that are empowered in the act of erasing the politics of binary opposition.'[15] Building on the work of Said and Fanon, Bhabha is concerned with interrogating the production of colonial authority through the construction of colonial knowledge. He challenges the assumption that colonial authority is based only upon material control and that colonial identity merely replicates these relations of power. As a result, he develops a theory of colonial subject construction that challenges assumptions about collective agency or change.

Bhabha rejects the assumption that colonial authority is homogeneous, total, and, as Fanon describes, completely destroys the indigenous culture. As a result, he contends that to conceptualize a binary relationship pitting the colonizer against the colonized (as distinct and homogeneous groups) misunderstands the relationship:

> Colonial authority requires modes of discrimination (cultural, racial, administrative ...) that disallow a stable unitary assumption of collectivity. The 'part' (which must be the colonialist foreign body) must be representative of the 'whole' (conquered country), but the right of representation is based on its radical difference. Such double think is made viable only through the strategy of disavowal ... which requires a theory of the 'hybridization' of discourse and power that is ignored by theorists who engage in the battle for 'power' but do so only as the purists of difference.[16]

Drawing upon, and responding to, Fanon's theory of the 'Manichean' colonial relationship, Bhabha challenges the basis of colonial difference (colonizer/colonized, white/black).

I am particularly interested in two aspects of the way in which Bhabha constructs hybridity and ambivalence as resistance. First, departing from colonial representations of power that construct an antagonistic colonial relationship wherein one actor dominates another – the 'oppressor' names, subjugates, and exploits the 'oppressed' – Bhabha constructs colonial power as a political and cultural structure in which subjects have varying positions or experiences of empowerment/dominance and disempowerment/exploitation. Second, Bhabha seems to conflate 'subversion' with 'transformation.' I believe that a significant distinction should be made between acts that *subvert* colonial authority and those that are *transformative*, though this is not to say that the two are not related and that subversive acts or processes, like those Bhabha describes, cannot be integral to more transformative acts, modes, or processes. Bhabha, however, seems to construct resistance as the failure or incompleteness of colonial authority, a concept of resistance that is too broad to have any political currency and forecloses the possibility of activism; while colonial power may never be total, this does not mean that it is not durable or oppressive.

Bart Moore-Gilbert criticizes Bhabha for giving too little attention to organized forms of resistance, from militant insurgency to non-cooperation to democratic political opposition. Nonetheless, he argues that Bhabha posits two forms of resistance in his work, one that constructs resistance as the impossibility of colonial authority and another that largely reinscribes modern notions of individual agency. 'Intransitive resistance,' or the ambivalence of colonial authority, is the rupture between the imaginary of colonial authority and the performance of colonial experience. This form of resistance is understood as a function of colonial discourse/power, which, Moore-Gilbert suggests, recuperates the resistance Said does not acknowledge in *Orientalism*, without reinscribing the sovereign subject of Fanon's later work.[17] Resistance is inherent within colonial authority in the sense that the ultimate success of colonialism's will-to-power – the production of the colonial 'other' into the 'same,' through, for instance, the project of civilization – would be the undoing of the colonizer's authority. In contrast to this 'intransitive' resistance, Moore-Gilbert argues that in 'Signs Taken for Wonders' and 'Sly Civility,' Bhabha postulates a form of 'transitive' resistance that recuperates native agency. Before analysing Bhabha's construction of a mode of 'transitive resistance,' as Moore-Gilbert calls it, I wish to briefly discuss Bhabha's theorizing of ambivalence and hybridity as forms of subversion.

Concentrating on what he calls the 'Third Space,' or space of enunciation 'in between' an event and its representation, Bhabha positions textuality and discourse as the fields within which colonial authority is both imagined and contested. He premises his critical perspective on the assumption that there is no knowledge outside representation: 'The dynamics of writing and textuality require us to rethink the logics of causality and determinacy through which we recognize the political as a form of calculation and strategic action dedicated to social transformation.'[18] Reading the textuality of colonial experience for its hybridity and ambivalence reveals spaces for resistance in the structures of colonial knowledge/power: 'If the effect of colonial power is seen to be the *production* of hybridization rather than the noisy command of colonialist authority or the silent repression of native traditions, then an important change of perspective occurs. The ambivalence at the source of traditional discourses on authority enables a form of subversion, founded on the undecidability that turns the discursive conditions of dominance into the grounds of intervention.'[19] Can, or should, the 'subversion' produced from the instability of colonial authority, due to hybridity and ambivalence, be recognized as resistance? Bhabha seems only to be illuminating the instability of the identities Said constructs in his theory of colonial discourse in *Orientalism*.

Bhabha's concern for identifying the ambivalence and hybridity of colonial discourse and the way in which they open up spaces in that discourse that may be read as subversion seems to homogenize all instances of colonial discourse or authority across time and space. His analysis concentrates upon an abstract individual subject who is without gender and exists outside material history or relations of power. Critics such as Young and Sharpe argue that by recognizing resistance as that space between the enunciatory present and representation, Bhabha privileges the act of 'reading between the lines' for forgotten or unacknowledged 'resistance,' and consequently disregards the plentiful documentary evidence of organized, oppositional military and political struggles.[20] I would add that such an approach also disregards the way in which subjects experience material conditions of labour exploitation, or access to resources, such as 'knowledge' or food, to return to Fanon's contention that the colonial problem is the problem of poverty, hunger, and ignorance. As I will argue below, however, Indian resistance in South Africa provides an example of the way in which the performance of an identity other than that permitted within colonial representations of the colonized at the very least complemented organized political struggle and *challenged* colonial authority in terms of the way in which both the colonizer and the colonized became aware of, and reacted to, the disruption of the assumptions of colonial difference. Yet, the form of resistance I will discuss through the example of Indian activism in early twentieth-century South Africa contrasts with the sort of resistance as subversion Bhabha describes. Bhabha's resistance seems only available as the performance of a hybrid subjectivity, which disrupts the binary structure and essential differences of the colonial imaginary, as if identity formation is not influenced by any other factors but the colonial will-to-power through representation.

Turning to the post-colonial nation, in 'DissemiNation,' Bhabha problematizes the work of theorists such as Hobsbawm and Anderson by identifying the ambivalence of concepts such as the 'people' and the 'nation.' He argues that the pedagogy of the nation is troubled by its performance: 'In the production of the nation as narration there is a split between the continuist, accumulative temporality of the pedagogical, and the repetitious, recursive strategy of the performative.'[21] Dipesh Chakrabarty has drawn upon this disjuncture between the pedagogy and performance of the post-colonial nation to identify the ambivalence of the Indian state's will to attain a national presence formulated within the model of European historicism and modernity. While the nation is premised on a historicist narrative of development – for instance, the 'development' of the peasant into modern citizen through institutions such as formal education – this historicist time is 'put in temporary suspension' each time there is a populist/political mobilization, or, indeed, each time an illiterate peasant votes.[22] Chakrabarty identifies the persistence of a plurality of registers of power, for instance, in terms of the way in which peasant kinship relationships or relationships with gods and the supernatural are classified as anachronistic within the pedagogy of the modern Indian nation but are nonetheless a reality of the Indian nation as performance. Chakrabarty does not postulate peasant actions as resistant, as opposed to anachronistic. Rather, he identifies the tension of the peasant as citizen within the history and nature of political modernity in the Indian nation.

Bhabha's discourse on the post-colonial nation has more often, however, served to present a critique of colonial or metropolitan constructions of racialized identity. Yet, his theorization of hybridity is limited by the boundaries of colonial discourse, as if colonial representation is, indeed, total. While he seems to discuss the constructs of the 'nation' and 'people' as broad and abstract categories, the closing of 'Dissemi-Nation' makes clear that the 'nation' to which he is referring is England, and more broadly the 'metropole,' wherein an imagined homogeneous (European) community is disrupted by the hybridity produced by immigration; the presence of a distinctly 'non-English' yet not quite 'other' Other subverts efforts to construct a distinctly 'English' national history. The discourse of the nation is destabilized by its own hybridity, and the ambivalence of the discourse of colonial difference, to which this troubling is attributed, is revealed by the immigrant subject's inability to enter modernity, or fulfil the historical narrative of modernity. As novels such as Hanif Kureishi's *The Buddha of Suburbia* (1991) and films such as Gurinder Chadha's *Bhaji on the Beach* (1994) reveal, however, the immigrant 'other' is not a threat by being out of place but by altering the place. Bhabha's construction of subversion paradoxically reinforces the European/native binary in that the colonized subject as subaltern, peasant, labourer, merchant, woman, etc., is virtually nonexistent in his work as he concentrates upon an abstract colonial subject in contact with the metropole.

Aijaz Ahmad points out that while we must reject the 'claims of Authenticity that come to us from so many religious and protofascist nationalisms of our time,' any understanding of hybridity must acknowledge that such a process of movement, transmutation, and hybridization of ideas, values, and norms is by no means new nor confined to relationships with(in) Europe.[23] While Bhabha's critique of the nation and the development of theories of hybridity in general provide insight into the limitations of colonial authority and our understandings of it, we must question the equation of hybridity with resistance to colonial authority. Hybridity, as Bhabha constructs it, is not specific to the colonial encounter. While Bangladesh, Tanzania, or Ethiopia are no less 'hybrid,' and their nationalisms are open to critique, the performance of this hybridity is not confined to contact with Europeans/the metropole. Bhabha describes how the concept of hybridity *subverts* colonial authority; colonial power does not function as it is supposed to function in dominant (anti)colonial discourses. However, Bhabha provides no indication of how hybridity may destabilize colonial power or transform the unequal relations of influence and access of colonial authority. This is precisely the sort of problem of appeals for an 'ethics of hybridity' or a 'postnational' identity, which do not seem to contend with unequal global power relations, relations that construct the hybrid or cosmopolitan as the experience of privilege (as opposed to the hybridity of the refugee). In addition, the hybridity of the colonial text or subject is only hybrid in relation to the imaginary of homogeneity and stability, as constructed within the historical narrative of the modern nation. Bhabha challenges colonial notions of modernity/tradition, authenticity, and the nation, but as Rey Chow warns, such a notion of hybridity revives 'an old functionalist notion of what a dominant culture permits in the interest of maintaining its own equilibrium.'[24] Bhabha's theory of hybridity and ambivalence does not account for the continuation of structures of material exploitation and subjugation, which suggest that power adapts to the subversions its ambivalence allows.

For Hardt and Negri, 'postcolonial theorists who advocate a politics of difference, fluidity, and hybridity in order to challenge the binaries and essentialism of modern sovereignty have been outflanked by the strategies of power.'[25] They argue that such theories have no utility in the context of 'the new paradigm of power.' I would argue, in contrast, that the value of these theories is not their construction of a politics of resistance (as subversion) but their illumination of colonial discourse/ power as more complex or ambivalent than Said's theory of Orientalism, or the Manichean discourse Fanon identifies in colonial and anticolonial thought that critics such as Parry, JanMohamed, and San Juan recuperate. Rather than dealing with an 'old paradigm of power,' colonial discourse theory challenges assumptions of the nature of colonial power, itself.

Critics such as JanMohamed and Moore-Gilbert argue that in articulating a theory of hybridity and in challenging binary oppositions, Bhabha collapses the colonizer and the colonized into a singular, hybrid 'colonial subject,' and that such a formulation ignores material relations of power.[26] Rather than collapsing colonizer and colonized into a single subject, however, Bhabha constructs all colonial subjects as being the product of colonial discourse. In *Black Skin, White Masks,* Fanon relates two instances of 'contact' that, as Bhabha describes, constitute 'myths of origin of the subject within the racist practices and discourses of a colonial culture.'[27] In one, a child fixes her gaze on the speaker and declares to her mother: 'Look, a Negro ... I'm frightened.'[28] In the other, the child in the Antilles is confronted with racial and cultural stereotypes in comics and other children's books in which 'the Evil Spirit, the Bad Man, the Savage are always symbolized by Negroes or Indians.'[29]

Since the stories are constructed so as to have the reader identify with the victor, Fanon argues that the child identifies with the white hero. Bhabha contends that the colonial subject – i.e., both colonizer and colonized – 'turns around the pivot of the "stereotype,"' and 'in the act of disavowal and fixation the colonial subject is returned to the narcissism of the Imaginary and its identification of an ideal ego that is white and whole.'[30] While Bhabha's analysis does not centre the material relationship of colonialism, his aim seems not to discount material relations of power but to analyse the way in which the actors that take part in these relations are shaped by colonial discourse.

In 'Signs Taken for Wonders,' in which he discusses colonial authority in terms of the 'colonial presence' or colonial identity, Bhabha writes: 'Such a display of difference produces a mode of authority that is agonistic (rather than antagonistic).'[31] For critics such as Benita Parry, Bhabha's contention that the colonial relationship should not be understood as antagonistic denies inscriptions of inequality and conflict in the material colonial world and thereby rejects 'that anti-colonialist tradition which perceived the struggle in terms that were antagonistic rather than agonistic, and construed the colonial relationship as generically ... one between competing political interests, forces, and goals.'[32] Drawing upon the OED definition of agonistic as a Greek athletic contest, or merely a game, and noting that antagonism specifies mutual resistance between two opposing forces, Parry poses the rhetorical question: 'In rejecting "antagonistic" in favour of "agonistic," is Bhabha, who reads social processes according to the rules of writing, positing colonialism as a competition of peers rather than a hostile struggle between the subjugated and the oppressor?'[33] Parry ignores the fact that 'agonistic' can also refer to various responses to conflict, from flight to fight to passivity, and hence the way in which the ambiguities of colonial power can be opportunistically exploited; I will return to this idea below and examine the distinction between a critical reading practice (i.e., colonial discourse analysis), which illuminates such moments and hence allows for the deconstruction of dualisms, and the way in which such acts can disrupt or enact an alternative to such dualisms.

I belabour this seemingly obscure point because it illuminates the way in which critics such as Parry uncritically assume the basis of colonial identity within the confines of an antagonistic colonial relationship as a battle between oppressive colonizer and subjugated colonized. The characterization of colonial authority as agonistic does not assume a 'competition among peers' or equal material relations between the colonizer and colonized. Rather, placed as it is within a discussion of the idea of the colonial presence as ambivalent – appearing to be original and authoritative, yet articulated as repetition and difference – the characterization of colonial authority as 'agonistic' suggests that colonial experience is hybrid, even contested, rather than stable or certain. As Bhabha acknowledges, to deconstruct a practice is not to dismiss its practical and functional power;[34] colonial discourse theory problematizes the discourses through which political action is imagined. The structure of colonial oppression does construct unequal subject-positions, but colonial power is *not* simply a binary relationship between oppressive colonizer and resistant colonized.

Parry's denunciation of any alternative to antagonism identifies a central tension within postcolonial theories of resistance. Her critique is informed by the assumption of an oppositional paradigm of power. I largely agree with her interpretation of colonial discourse theory as positing simply that power is never comprehensive and certain and that within the work of Bhabha, for instance, resistance is reduced to the ways in which colonial authority is subverted. Yet, to dismiss Bhabha ignores the way in which colonial discourse theory necessarily informs theories of anti-colonial resistance. For Parry or San Juan, the only alternative to such a construction of resistance as discursive subversion is a model that defines the conflict in terms of an antagonistic binary in which resistance is the conscious, sometimes collective, and to some degree organized act of a subjugated 'agent' in opposition to the agents or institutions of domination. As I will argue below, Bhabha's analysis of the production of colonial identities provides a way of understanding colonial power that allows for the recognition of forms of resistance that neither constitute merely the subversion of colonial authority nor are determined by colonial representations of difference.

The Limits of 'Spectacular Resistance'

Before turning to an analysis of Bhabha's 'spectacular resistance,' I wish to briefly discuss theories of 'everyday resistance,' as I believe Bhabha's notion of 'sly civility' provides an example of one such mode of resistance. Bill Ashcroft argues that while 'resistance has invariably connoted the urgent imagery of war ... the most fascinating feature of postcolonial societies is a "resistance" that manifests itself as a refusal to be absorbed ... In most cases this has not been a heroic enterprise but a pragmatic and mundane array of living strategies to which imperial culture has no answer.'[35] Everyday resistance constitutes neither dramatic, organized conscious opposition nor simply the ambivalence of colonial discourse. Prakash and Haynes, for instance, define resistance 'as those behaviours and cultural practices by subordinate groups that contest hegemonic social formations, that threaten to unravel the strategies of domination ... To use resistance in its more traditional sense would mean not to consider the very process by which power is often tested and eroded by the actions of the subordinate and by which it reconstitutes itself in response.'[36] Everyday resistance, therefore, can range from overt or apparently conscious acts, such as refusing to pay taxes, to more ambivalent forms of resistance, such as foot-dragging, pilfering, sarcasm, gossip, and rumour.

While Bhabha constructs 'spectacular resistance' through psychoanalytic and poststructural theories, the actual events/behaviours he uses as the basis of these theories are similar to the types of actions that are the object of the work of anthropologists such as James C. Scott. Everyday resistance is privileged as a form of insurgency that is more endemic to power than moments of distinct social unrest such as strikes, riots, or rebellions. Scott and the contributors to Prakash and Haynes's *Contesting Power: Resistance and Everyday Social Relations in South Asia* (1991) frame their analysis within the context of material relations of power that at times include colonial authority but are not limited to it. Nonetheless, Scott's theory of public versus hidden transcripts – in which, for instance, the native publicly shows deference to the landlord but privately refuses the landlord's demands – seems to describe the very same experience of power as Bhabha's example of 'sly civility' in which Indians accept Bibles but use them for purposes other than those intended by Christian missionaries. Indeed, Scott argues that the zone of struggle exists *in between* the public and hidden transcripts of native discourse, a construction of resistance not dissimilar to Bhabha's 'Third Space' of colonial discourse; while Bhabha recognizes resistance in the space created by the ambivalence of colonial power, Scott frames this in-between space as existing in the response to, or rather performance of, colonial authority.[37] For both Bhabha and theorists of everyday resistance, while resistance can be named as acts – sarcasm, sly civility, questioning – it may be conceptualized more accurately through the idea that power itself is unstable and provides spaces for its own subversion than through the acts of an 'agent' in opposition to power.

Like discursive concepts such as mimicry, ambivalence, and hybridity, Prakash and Haynes imagine resistance in a way that does not require native 'consciousness' or agency and does not limit it to oppositional strategies with an axis of power defined by the oppressive colonizer and the subjugated colonized. Indeed, Prakash and Haynes critique Scott's characterization of everyday resistance (i.e., tax evasion) as necessarily deliberate and his assumption of a self-determining subject: 'Scott ignores how such acts are necessarily conditioned by hegemony. At the very least, for instance, these acts are influenced by a logic that accepts the larger structures of landholding and political power as unalterable facts.'[38] Notions of everyday resistance identify the way in which authority is always contested and has to adapt. However, everyday resistance privileges primarily individual and unorganized acts, and therefore limits the possibilities for resistance to transform material relations or structures of power.

Ross Chambers argues that such behaviour 'consists of individual or group *survival* tactics that do not challenge the power in place, but make use of circumstances set up by that power for purposes the power may ignore or deny'; however, Chambers argues that such behaviour also 'has a particular potential to change states of affairs, by changing people's mentalities (their ideas, attitudes, values and feelings ...).'[39] As Frederick Cooper explains, small or individual acts may subvert a regime by raising the confidence of the people that power can be contested, allowing for the development of a spirit conducive to the mobilization of organized opposition.[40] Hence, these histories and theories of everyday resistance reveal the limits of dominance as well as the complexity of the experience of hegemony. These modes and practices of everyday resistance have been postulated as an alternative to a notion of resistance that does not account for the intricacies of hegemony, assuming, for instance, agency and conscious action that is not implicated within the discourse of colonialism and modernity. By examining and expanding upon Bhabha's notions of mimicry and sly civility, I seek to draw more closely the connection between these forms of resistance and the libratory politics of transformation evident in the work of Fanon or in the aims of revolution described by Williams.

In 'Signs Taken for Wonders' Bhabha explicitly characterizes the hybridization of the English book (the Bible) in its consumption by the Indian peasant as 'spectacular resistance.' Drawing upon Macaulay's 'Minute on Indian Education' and the British will to create an elite class of Indian middle (or mimic) men to manage the masses of the Indian population, Bhabha describes the experiences of one of the first Indian catechists, Anund Messeh, as he confronts a group of Indian peasants employed in reading and discussing the 'Book of God.' Messeh's presentation of the Bible and Christianity is questioned by his audience. For instance, Bhabha reports that members of the audience ask the young catechist how the word of God can come from a people who eat flesh.[41] Bhabha argues that the natives 'resist' efforts at conversion by appealing to their customary dietary practices. By rejecting Christian doctrine as it is presented to them, they are resisting both Christianity and colonial authority (the English as the representatives of God): 'When the natives demand an Indianized Gospel, they are using the powers of hybridity to resist baptism and to put the project of conversion in an impossible position.'[42] The subversive nature of the native questioning and interpretation of the Bible, Bhabha contends, effects a challenge to colonial authority, in that when faced with hybridity 'the *presence* of power is revealed as something other than what its rules of recognition assert.'[43]

The ambivalence of colonial authority allows for resistance, albeit a form of resistance that is not produced by oppositional politics. Bhabha argues: 'Resistance is not necessarily an oppositional act of political intention, nor is it simply negation or exclusion of the "content" of another culture, as a difference once perceived. It is the effect of an ambivalence produced within the rules of recognition of dominating discourses as they articulate the signs of cultural difference and reimplicate them within the deferential relations of colonial power – hierarchy, normalization, marginalization and so forth.'[44] While such a construction of resistance rejects the modern notion of individual agency, this is not to suggest that there can be no native agency at all: 'It is this liminal moment of identification – eluding resemblance – that produces a subversive strategy of subaltern agency that negotiates its own authority through a process of an iterative "unpicking" and relocating ... [Agency] requires direction and contingent closure, but not teleology and holism.'[45] Bhabha argues that resistance does not require 'intentionality' and should not be defined by an oppositional politics. He contends that colonial authority is challenged, instead, by the ambivalence of colonial power/discourse.

Critics such as Young and Moore-Gilbert critique this model of resistance as well as the example Bhabha uses to formulate it.[46] Moore-Gilbert, for instance, argues that 'the peasants' questions to the catechist are based as much on category mistakes or misunderstandings as on a considered challenge to his teachings.'[47] The peasants' unwillingness to translate their devotion to the Book into conversion to the values and rituals of the Christian church and their questioning of Anund Messeh's message disrupt the ability of the English to colonize their minds. To what extent, however, can we regard the peasants' interpretation of the Bible and Christianity through their own spiritual beliefs and practices as constituting resistance or a direct challenge to Christianity and, by association, colonial authority?

Bhabha historically contextualizes his reading of Anund Messeh's efforts to spread the Gospel in terms of the 1818 Burdwan Plan, commissioned by the Church Missionary Society, which Bhabha interprets as anticipating Macaulay's call for the production of a class of Indian teachers, translators, and compilers. Bhabha argues that the enunciatory conditions of an Indian educated in English and Christianity, proselytizing in rural villages, conceals the 'design of the Burdwan Plan to deploy "natives" to destroy native culture and religion.'[48] However, a distinction must be made between whether the Burdwan Plan was *designed* to *destroy* native culture and religion, as Bhabha argues, or to transform Indians into Christians in order to 'civilize' them, 'save' them, and/or better control them. The narrative of European responsibility, or benevolence, is significant, as it is distinct from contrasting initiatives that very much sought to destroy not only 'other' cultural practices but whole communities. Bhabha conflates colonialism as a structure of subjugation and economic exploitation with cultural change. I will return to postcolonialism's ambiguity as to the aim of colonialism and the object of resistance in chapter 2. The effect of the project of 'civilization' or 'uplift,' as much as it radically altered – and in a sense 'destroyed' – native culture, paradoxically served in some cases to produce a new communal identity, leading to organized opposition against colonial political and economic structures and the privilege and authority of the colonist; the idea of the Indian nation is paradoxically a product of colonialism and, seemingly, the only way to imagine liberation.[49]

Rather than exploring a story of a single meeting in which a catechist debates the 'English Book' with the people of a village, a more historical analysis of peasant responses to the Bible and the English language as they are introduced over time by colonial middle/mimic-men, such as Anund Messeh, would seem to provide a better way into the sort of theory of resistance Bhabha constructs and a better understanding of the extent to which colonial 'rules of recognition' were subverted. As it is, the story of Anund Messeh and the 'English Book' is ambiguous. While, in the moment, it marks the subversion of colonial rules of recognition, it may also mark the beginning of a form of cultural change. In his conclusion to the essay, Bhabha hints at the possibilities of such a broader historical analysis, juxtaposing an example of an Indian teacher begging for a copy of the 'Holy Scriptures' and an example of the way in which the Bible was being 'translated' into waste paper.[50] While I recognize the limitations of judging resistance by the response of those in positions of dominance, the clerical responses Bhabha attributes to this 'spectacular resistance' seem to affirm colonial authority and British racial superiority, in the minds of the British missionaries, at least. Bhabha quotes a J.A. Dubois, who, after twenty-five years of missionary work in India, wrote in 1815 that those who embrace Christianity never entirely renounce their 'superstitions.'[51] Jenny Sharpe questions the significance Bhabha and others place upon Macaulay's famous 'Minute on Indian Education,' arguing that English education was limited to a select elite and that general British colonial education policy emphasized vernacular education, as the Raj was primarily concerned with economic exploitation of the subcontinent and not cultural conquest.[52] As a result, Bhabha conflates the failure of the educated Indian class to become fully assimilated with the subversion of their message by the peasant masses.

Further, while Dubois seems to lament the fact that conversion was never total, Bhabha contends that the failure of mimicry was necessary for colonial authority. The 'mimic-man' – in the form of Anund Messeh, for example – fostered by the British was understood quite explicitly as a means of colonial control, both in terms of managing the indigenous population and in terms of reinscribing English identity. As Macaulay imagines it, the British colonial project in India sought to create an intellectual class 'Indian in blood and colour, but English in tastes, in opinions, in morals and intellect.'[53] In describing the way colonial authority constructs the native other 'as a subject of difference that is almost the same, but not quite,' Bhabha argues that the colonial desire for mimicry 'emerges as one of the most elusive and effective strategies of colonial power and knowledge.'[54] The proselytizing mission of Christianity or efforts to create an Indian intellectual class, in a distinctly European sense, can be seen as a function of colonial power in that such projects reinforced for the colonists the benevolence of the colonial project and the endeavour to fulfil the so-called 'white man's burden' by raising natives from their 'uncivilized' state. Further, the desire for mimicry reaffirmed British identity as a function of racial difference, measured against the necessary failure of the Indian or African to fully assimilate. Such projects undermined indigenous community structures and forms of autonomy that could have been utilized to oppose or subvert the material or economic program of colonization. As much as the desire for mimicry is a means of control, however, according to Bhabha, the ambivalent colonial demand for a difference that is not quite nothing or not quite total also provides the native a space in which to challenge colonial authority.

For mimicry to function as a means of colonial authority, the colonized must fulfil their role. The figure of Anund Messeh seems to be the perfect example of the way in which the native desires to be like the colonizer – in dress, manner, belief – thereby reinforcing the apparent benevolence of the colonizer while also reinforcing the colonizer's superiority; Anund Messeh can become *anglicized*, a functionary of English rule, but he cannot become English. The desire for mimicry, therefore, requires the native to 'satisfy the colonizer's narrative demand' to reaffirm British culture while not being able to become British. However, Bhabha argues that Anund Messeh's tale, when read as a 'masque of mimicry,' reveals a form of 'discursive warfare,' or 'spectacular resistance' within the agonistic space of colonial authority.[55] The refusal (or failure) of the Hindu peasants to satisfy the colonizer's narrative demand – their failure to return the colonizer's gaze in the image of the colonizer's desire – is, for Bhabha, an act of resistance. The act of accepting the Bible but using it for other purposes or interpreting its message in a way not intended by the colonizer constitutes what he calls 'sly civility.'

Bhabha constructs his theory of mimicry in psychological terms, arguing that the desire for mimicry reflects the colonizer's desire to be justified in their existence (in a colonized land). The colonizer is caught in the ambivalent position of recognizing the self as both father and oppressor; as a result, the native's 'refusal to return and restore the image of authority to the eye of power has to be reinscribed as implacable aggression, assertively coming from without: *He hates me.*'[56] As a number of critics have suggested, native hatred for the colonizer was not simply the colonizer's paranoia. Bhabha's musings on discursive power utilize few examples to develop these theories of mimicry as control and mockery as subversion. Does the example of Anund Messeh and the villagers reveal the difference between the native who fulfils the colonizer's desire for mimicry and those who refuse, or does it reveal two subjects with vastly different levels of experience with the colonizer?

The two central criticisms of Bhabha's idea of 'spectacular resistance' include the extent to which the native's refusal is conscious and the extent to which such a refusal destabilizes colonial power. Bart Moore-Gilbert, for instance, contends that 'if the resistance inscribed in mimicry is unconscious for the colonized ... it cannot function for the colonized as the grounds on which to construct a considered counter-discourse.'[57] Again, we must draw a careful distinction between the *failure* of colonial authority to function as it is represented (or the impossibility of mimicry as the colonizer desires it) and the *refusal* of the colonized. It is this distinction between *failure* and *refusal* that I wish to take up in the remainder of this chapter. For Benita Parry, one of Bhabha's most outspoken critics, while Bhabha's 'Third Space' allows him to recover an otherwise impossibly heard (as Spivak has argued) native voice in the colonialist text, 'native resistance is limited to its returning the look of surveillance as the displacing gaze of the disciplined.'[58] Through the example of the Indian struggle for political rights in South Africa, I wish to reformulate Bhabha's notion of mimicry to identify the transformative possibilities of the *refusal* to fulfil the narrative of colonial knowledge as an assertion of an alternative narrative.

Equal but Not White: Indian Resistance in Colonial South Africa

Mohandas K. Gandhi arrived in South Africa in 1893 as a young London-educated lawyer from India, and he was soon shocked by the racism he experienced. In his first visit to a South African court, he was forced to leave after refusing to take off his turban. Some weeks later, he was removed from a train for refusing to leave a compartment reserved for whites and was then beaten for the same offence. Gandhi quickly realized that not only was the treatment he received commonplace, but it was generally accepted as inevitable or normal by those classified as non-white. Gandhi's experience reflects the sort of failure inherent in the mimicry Frantz Fanon discusses in *Black Skin, White Masks*. Fanon describes how the black Antillean 'conducts himself like a white man,' but once he goes to France he learns that he can never escape his racial difference; regardless of his behaviour, the white population will always consider him a Negro.[59] Like Bhabha, Fanon theorizes mimicry and the experience of racial difference in psychological terms, but significantly, Fanon is concerned with the psychological effects on the native of the impossible desire to be the same as the European other.

In *An Autobiography: Or, The Story of My Experiments with Truth* (1927/9), Gandhi does not describe any specific incidents of racial discrimination during his time in London, but he does describe his infatuation with English style and manners. In contrast, when Gandhi begins practising law in the predominantly white urban culture of late-nineteenth-century Natal, he is immediately confronted with racism. Fanon suggests that the native's realization of the impossibility, in European terms, of his humanity results in feelings of inferiority. While it is important to acknowledge the difference in contexts between Fanon's observations of the black man's experience in France in the 1950s and Gandhi's experience as an Indian immigrant in a European African colony in the 1890s, as much as Gandhi is angry or hurt, he is deeply offended by the racism he experiences. Rather than an indication of his inferiority, Gandhi recognizes his experience of racism in Natal as indicative of the failure of the colonial project to fulfil its own ideals.

Gandhi initially registers his affront in the modes of his privileged English-educated class by writing a letter to the press about the first incident and a long telegram to the general manager of the railway pertaining to the second, and then initiates a political organization, the Natal Indian Congress. Gandhi's reaction to the abuse he experienced in his early days in South Africa reveals both the way he was enamoured with modern European culture and the way in which the assumptions of the discourse of the modern nation-state – development, citizenship, rights – shaped his perceptions of these experiences and his responses to them. Gandhi's experience of the inadequacy of these accepted modes of bourgeois political recourse would lead to a radical transformation of his lifestyle and the development of a mode of political action premised on a critique of modern thought. Gandhi's 'redemptive struggle for citizen rights' during this period reveals the way in which his thought was constrained by the conceptual and institutional framework of modernity. I want to examine the way Gandhi's loyalty to the British Empire and his personal interaction with colonial leaders provided a challenge to colonial authority/identity by assuming equal status with whites. Gandhi's political organizing in South Africa and his assertion of his rights as a citizen of the British Empire is not a story of subaltern resistance in the sense of the subaltern of the Subaltern Studies project; Gandhi was educated in England and as a lawyer was a member of a privileged class, who, at this stage, was actively seeking recognition within the framework of European modernity. However, Gandhi's interaction with the white emissaries of the State throughout this period of political struggle reveals a form of resistance that reflects that theorized by Bhabha, but which appears to be much more calculated and more linked to material relations of power than Bhabha's spectacular resistance.

Contributors to the Subaltern Studies project criticize Gandhi for not directly challenging colonial power. Guha, for instance, criticizes Gandhi for an 1899 article in which he praises the British Empire and characterizes Indians as subjects of the British Queen. Despite his sympathy for the plight of the Boers and the Zulus during the so-called 'Boer War' and 'Zulu Rebellion,' respectively, Gandhi helped form the Indian Ambulance Corps to serve with the British army in both conflicts. Guha uses this example, and the fact that Gandhi proposed that the Indians receive no compensation from the state for this work, to construct Gandhi as the consummate 'loyalist' or 'mimic-man,' fulfilling the duties of the subjugated under the illusory hope of gaining citizen rights: 'The so-called "earnest" loyalty was meant as a display to secure the white settler's and the imperial government's recognition of the sincerity and usefulness of Indian collaboration ... For the colonized, recognition of their services by the imperial overlords on any terms at all would have been a "privilege," that is, an honor done by the *master* to his *servant* by acknowledging the latter's servitude.'[60] Guha argues that this commitment to 'duty' to the British Queen, or the 'idiom of obedience,' was influential in creating the liberal nationalist, and decidedly 'non-radical,' character of Indian anti-colonial politics.[61]

It would be easy to concede Guha's criticism but to note that Gandhi's experience as a witness to British brutality precipitated his transformation from Loyalty to Dissent, literally prompting him to take vows of nonviolence and poverty and to wear the *lungie* or the clothing of the indentured labourer, shedding the physical and ideological garb of British modernity he had taken with a European education. Alternatively, one could argue that by focusing on the 1899 letter and Gandhi's role in the Boer War, Guha ignores numerous other possible examples of Gandhi's overt confrontation of British rule, both in South Africa and later in India. To focus on these examples of overt opposition, however, would ignore the way in which Gandhi's seeming mimicry of British ideals, this loyalty, failed to fulfil the master/slave relationship in the way Guha suggests, and indeed disrupted and challenged the authority of colonial identity in a way different from that theorized by

Bhabha. Guha contends that Gandhi was foolish to demand rights, for a colonial subject is not a citizen.[62] Gandhi's agitation for Indian rights in South Africa, however, reveals the way in which the conflicts resultant of such discursive forms of resistance – the demand to be recognized as citizen rather than inferior subject – were acknowledged in the moment, in contrast to being an effect of the postcolonial critic's rereading the past, and the way in which such discursive forms of subversion were integral to more confrontational modes of opposition.

In both *Satyagraha in South Africa* (1928) and his autobiography, Gandhi argues that despite his recognition that Indians are oppressed by the British as much as by the Boers, he recognizes his duty to the Empire as a British subject. One of the alleged causes of the Boer War was the British dissatisfaction with the Boer treatment of British Indian subjects in South Africa. In a debate over the role of Indians in the war, Gandhi argues:

> Our existence in South Africa is only in our capacity as British subjects ... Our rulers profess to safeguard our rights because we are British subjects ... If we missed this opportunity, which had come to us unsought, of proving the falsity of a charge which we believed to be false, we should stand self-condemned, and it would be no matter for surprise if then the English treated us worse than before and sneered at us more than ever ... And if we desire to win our freedom and achieve our welfare as members of the British Empire, here is a golden opportunity for us to do so by helping the British in the war ...[63]

Gandhi assumes that the performance of loyalty to the Empire will ensure that Indian grievances against the governments of South Africa would be redressed under British rule of a unified state. In fact, Gandhi notes that during the war Indians were treated well by the British and explains this treatment by contending that 'the knowledge that the Indians, forgetful of their wrongs, were out to help them in the hour of their need, had melted their hearts for the time being.'[64] While there were significant political and economic factors that contributed to the Indian expectations being disappointed – namely, the British desire to appease the Boer population and thereby avoid further war, and to appease white commerce, which felt threatened by Indian merchants – the British could not allow Indians equality under the law because Indians had been constructed as an inferior race. Indeed, the discursive construction of the 'Indian' is inseparable from these material and political concerns.

While Guha reads Gandhi's allegiance to Britain in terms of the Manichean or Hegelian loyalty of a slave to his master, Gandhi sought to transform the practice of British rule and attain for Indians a status equal to whites. He was, indeed, the consummate mimic-man, as Guha claims, for he *believed* that he was, or could be, *recognized* as an equal within the British Empire. Ashis Nandy argues that opposition to European colonialism derived from one of two ideological positions: (1) the acceptance of Western values, but the recognition that the West failed to live up to them; or (2) the repudiation of those values themselves.[65] At this point in what he would later call his 'experiments with truth,' Gandhi believed in the value of the British constitution as a means of organizing society but recognized the failure of the British to practise these values in their colonial projects.[66] In an 1858 proclamation, Queen Victoria states: 'We hold ourselves bound to the natives of our Indian territories by the same obligations of duty which bind us to all our other subjects, and these obligations, by the blessing of Almighty God, we shall faithfully and conscientiously fulfil.'[67] Gandhi (mis)understood this proclamation as acknowledging the equality of all British subjects, regardless of their racialized identities. He therefore measured the practices and policies of the colonies of South Africa as failing to live up to the spirit of the proclamation.[68]

Guha is critical of Gandhi's position, arguing that the condemnation of the British as 'unBritish' is based on the absurdity of accusing the English 'of deviating from norms which were displayed as ideals but prevented in fact from realizing themselves to any significant extent in the dominant idioms of political practice.'[69] In contrast, Bhabha argues that the 'form of multiple and contradictory belief that emerges as an effect of the ambivalent, deferred address of colonialist governance' reflects the way in which the 'Civilizing Mission' or 'White Man's Burden' is contingent upon the construction of the other in terms of its 'difference' or 'lack.'[70] I would argue that this 'split in enunciation,' like Bhabha's other 'in-between' spaces, does not merely reflect the instability of colonial power – and so resistance as a form of intrinsic subversion – but is a space in which more deliberate forms of resistance may germinate.

C.L.R. James hails the 1791 Haitian Revolution, under the leadership of Toussaint L'Ouverture, as the first successful slave revolt. The revolt was inspired by the ideals of the French Revolution – *Liberté, Egalité, Fra-*

ternité – and the failure of French colonists and slave-holders to fulfil these ideals. The Black Jacobins, as C.L.R. James calls Toussaint and his army, turned to force of arms to overthrow the rule of the slave-owners but, significantly, did not seek to exterminate, deport, or humiliate the French, or to separate the new nation of Haiti from the French Empire. In *Conscripts of Modernity*, David Scott contends that while *The Black Jacobins* presents a romantic narrative of vindication, with Toussaint as its hero, in the 1971 revision of the book James portrays Toussaint as a 'conscript of modernity' wherein the way in which his ideals, and the ideals of the Haitian Revolution, echo those of the French Revolution suggests not that Toussaint was inspired by those ideals but that he had little in terms of conceptual alternatives. The choices Toussaint made, Scott argues, were constituted by modernity and were partly constructed through its conceptual and ideological apparatuses.[71] For Scott, the conception of slavery as complete degradation and dehumanization allows for only one possible response, revolutionary overcoming.

In his discussion of violent rebellion in Algeria, Fanon seems to theorize the way in which the violence of revolts such as that in Haiti is necessary for the colonized to 'demand human behaviour from the other.' The importance of recognition and human connection, I believe, is central to the ideal of liberation Fanon assumes, and it is crucial to the form of resistance, as transformation, that I will argue for through the examples of Gandhian thought and reconciliation in chapters 3 and 4. For Gandhi, while in South Africa, the Indian attempt to fulfil their 'duty' to the Empire served as a means of making this demand and, I believe, exerting this demand in a way that confronted colonial authority despite the fact that Gandhi too could be seen as a 'conscript of modernity.' In the conclusion to *Black Skin, White Masks*, Fanon imagines resistance as the assertion of humanity: 'If the white man challenges my humanity, I will impose my whole weight as a man on his life and show him that I am not that "sho' good eatin'" that he persists in imagining.'[72] The native's obsession with vindication, or proving the stereotype wrong – like Gandhi's initiatives to promote 'hygiene' so that Indians would no longer be regarded by whites as 'dirty' – to some degree reflects the way in which the native is unable to escape the framework of colonial discourse. However, Gandhi's display of loyalty to the Empire – though it is an action constituted in and through the field of colonial power – reflects his belief in his equality with the British and so served as a test of Victoria's proclamation and British notions of their own authority.

Gandhi notes that the initial offer of the Natal Indian community to establish an ambulance corps during the Boer War was rejected by the British. In *Satyagraha in South Africa*, he writes: 'We encountered formidable difficulties in getting our offer favourably entertained. *The story is interesting but this is not the place to detail it.*'[73] I perceive in this omission a space of unacknowledged disruption of colonial power. Most accounts of the establishment of the Indian Ambulance Corps simply ignore, and hence reaffirm the silence of, these 'formidable difficulties,' explain the delay by appealing to the workings of the colonial bureaucracy, or suggest that the process was not difficult.[74] In contrast, D.G. Tendulkar suggests that the British administration initially refused the offer because they perceived Indians to be inferior: 'Gandhi was told: "You Indians know nothing of war. You would only be a drag on the army; you would have to be taken care of, instead of being a help to us." The common sneer prevailed that "if danger threatened the colony, the Indians would run away."'[75] A combination of British difficulties on the battlefield and Gandhi's relentless persistence to force the British to recognize the ability of the Indians led to the corps being established.

To a degree, Gandhi was purposefully seeking to overturn white stereotypes of Indians, in a similar way to Fanon's analysis. The Indian Ambulance Corps was a means of showing whites that Indians were not cowards and were capable of seeing beyond their own self-interest. Yet, while many of the English saw the contribution of the Indians as revealing that 'every Indian was as good a citizen of the British Empire as any one of them,' this goodwill deteriorated as the war progressed and British victory became ever more certain: 'Some of the colonists could not conceal their gall at any Indian trying to be the European's equal.'[76] Despite the failure of Indian participation on the side of the British to promote any changes in the Indian's position in South Africa, Gandhi again organized a medical corps to serve during the Zulu Rebellion of 1906 as a means of justifying the acquisition of citizen rights. Once again, however, the performance of the duties of a British subject did not translate into British recognition of Indians as citizens. Rather, the reward for Indian service during the Zulu Rebellion was a government ordinance that Gandhi recognized as constituting 'hatred' and, if not opposed, marking ruin for Indians in South Africa.[77] Significantly, Indian responses to this ordinance further challenged the colonial construction of Indian inferiority and provide further evidence of the sort of mimicry-as-resistance that I believe Indians performed through the ambulance corps.

The Transvaal Asiatic Ordinance legislated mandatory registration for Indians and required all Indians in the Transvaal to carry a pass; their failure to register or present their pass when asked resulted in imprisonment or deportation. Gandhi writes: 'I have never known legislation of this nature being directed against free men in any part of the world ... the Ordinance seeks to humiliate not only ourselves but also the motherland. The humiliation consists in the degradation of innocent men.'[78] Over the next few years, Gandhi would lead political opposition to government policies that required all Indians to register with their fingerprints, imposed a poll tax on Indians, limited Indian travel between the provinces, and declared null all non-Christian marriages. This struggle sought redemption for denied political rights, and by reacting to his perception of being not treated as a 'free man,' Gandhi realized that within modern thought he was, indeed, neither free nor a man. Hence, despite the importance of organized mass campaigns of non-cooperation and nonviolent civil disobedience during the period, it was as much Gandhi's acknowledgment of General Smuts as a peer rather than a superior that challenged colonial/white authority.

As leader of Indian opposition to the so-called 'Black Act,' Gandhi negotiated changes to legislation and the terms of the cessation of Indian *satyagraha* campaigns with General Smuts. Early in the campaign Gandhi acknowledged that 'it does not matter what General Smuts thinks today, but it will matter what he thinks a month hence, when we have shown that we are men. I do not have the slightest doubt that General Smuts has sufficient humanity in him to recognize our sincerity of purpose.'[79] By showing that the Indian community preferred imprisonment to the legislation, Gandhi believed that Smuts would have no choice but to recognize them as fellow human beings, and, hence, as citizens. He sought, then, to overcome the colonizer's conscience, rather than the colonizer himself through physical force. In his correspondence with Smuts, Gandhi is often polite but never reverential.[80] Following what Gandhi and the Indian community took to be a breach of faith on the part of Smuts, in which Smuts apparently reneged on a verbal agreement to amend the 'Asiatic Act,' Gandhi sent a letter to Smuts demanding the repeal of the act and asserting that if the act is not repealed, '"the certificates collected by the Indians would be burnt, and they would humbly but firmly take the consequences."'[81] While the 'bonfire of certificates' did blaze – a London newspaper compared the act to the Boston Tea Party – colonial authority was also challenged by the assumptions inherent in the letter, as opposed to simply the demands themselves or the political act of burning of the certificates.

Gandhi describes how he had not imagined the letter as an 'ultimatum' but that it was understood as such by members of the Transvaal government. He quotes Smuts as angrily declaring: 'The people who have offered such a threat to the government have no idea of its power.'[82] Reflecting on the letter, Gandhi argues that it was taken as an ultimatum and had such a pronounced effect on legislators and the white media because it prescribed a time limit for reply and because it was written in the language of one who is equal with the other. Gandhi writes:

> If the Europeans had considered the Indians to be their equals, they would have found this letter perfectly courteous and would have given it most serious consideration. But the fact that the Europeans thought Indians to be barbarians was a sufficient reason for the Indians to write such letter ... If there had not been behind the letter an iron determination to act up to it, it would have been held an impertinence, and the Indians would have proved themselves to be a thoughtless and foolish race ... When this letter was written, there was deliberate intention of claiming full knowledge and high prestige. Now as well as before the object aimed at was the repeal of the Black Act. But there was change in the style of language used ... When a slave salutes a master and a friend salutes a friend, the form is the same in either case, but there is a world of difference between the two, which enables the detached observer to recognize the slave and the friend at once.[83]

Gandhi's use of the master/slave analogy, here, contrasts with Guha's contention that the struggle for rights reinforces the master/slave dichotomy of the colonial relationship. Rather than simply *failing* to fulfil the colonizer's desire for a particular form of recognition, in the letter the Indian community *refuses* to perform their position as slave or inferior.

The development of *satyagraha* as a nonviolent form of confrontational politics is, in part, due to Gandhi's desire to refute European stereotypes of Indian difference, from lack of hygiene and cleanliness to the charge of barbarism. Such acts can be read, as Guha does, as attempts to appease the whites or fulfil their desire for mimicry. However, rather than becoming the 'other' of white desire, Gandhi and the other *satyagrahis* seek white recognition not of their impossible attempts to become white but of their equality, by 'imposing their weight as men' upon them. While the white population may have desired a recognizable Indian other who was 'the *same* but not quite,' this mode of colonial/racial authority is disrupted by the Indian assertion of their right to equal treatment under the law and their own demand, then, to be recognized as '*equal* but not the same/white.'

The motivation for raising the Indian Ambulance Corps in both the Boer War and the Zulu Rebellion was the belief that if the Indian community demanded rights as citizens it must perform the duties of citizens, assuming that status before it had been recognized by colonial authority. In his argument for the recognition of colonial authority as dominance without hegemony, Guha points to the fact that the colonial state, unlike the metropolitan state, is without citizens.[84] Similarly, Dipesh Chakrabarty argues that a cornerstone of imperial ideology was 'subjecthood but not citizenship, as the native was never adequate to the latter.'[85] As a settler state, however, colonial South Africa was a space in transition, a colony that desired to become a part of the metropolitan centre. Smuts biographer Kenneth Ingham notes that while Smuts recognized a place for Africans in a white South Africa, albeit an inferior one, he believed the presence of Asians *impeded* the development of a European civilization.[86] In a 1909 speech Smuts declares: 'Mr Gandhi has referred to Indians being in partnership with the white population of this country ... It is a claim ... which this white population will never allow (Sustained cheers).'[87] Indian assertions of their rights as citizens and the performance of the duties of the citizen call into question the idea of the nation that the colonists imagine.

Homi Bhabha reads white understanding of native resistance to colonial authority as being limited to the reinforcement of the stereotype of the native; the failure of the native to fulfil his role is recognized as folly, frenzy, or madness.[88] Resistance, in Bhabha's example, is the native's questioning of the Christian Bible. The Christian colonizer can understand these questions or the alternative uses the native has for the book only as indicative of the inability of the native to be civilized, proof of inferior status. In contrast, the Indian community's assumption of the inalienability of their rights as citizens could not be read by the colonizer as the Indians' fulfilment of their ambivalent, and impossible, subject position, their incontrovertible savagery. It constitutes not simply an act of 'subversion' of colonial authority that reinforces the stereotype of the other, their inferiority, but an active challenge to the assumptions of colonial authority. On one level, Indian persistence forced the South African government to *recognize* Indian concerns and *negotiate* with them, allowing for the years-long confrontation between 'Gandhi' and 'Smuts': 'The confrontation between Smuts, the acknowledged defender of white supremacy in what he deemed to be a white man's country, and Gandhi, the embarrassingly articulate reminder that the British Empire must, above all, stand for the equality of all subjects of the crown, had a telling impact on both their lives.'[89] Indian desire for equality, rather than sameness, challenged the legitimacy of white authority/identity itself.

In Fanon's description of mimicry from the perspective of the colonized, cited above, the native seeks to become the *same* as the other, and when he – the native of Fanon and Bhabha is always male – realizes that his skin colour makes this impossible, he is forced to recognize his inferiority within the system he has been acculturated to emulate. Similarly, the colonizer in Bhabha's theory of mimicry desires a colonized other who is the same but not quite/white. Mimicry reinforces the authority of the colonizer because of the impossibility of the other becoming the same; indeed, to do so would be to dissolve colonial authority. Bhabha defines the *failure* of the other to return the gaze, or to complete the narrative, as 'spectacular resistance.' While members of the Indian community, or at least Gandhi, seek vindication through their work in the ambulance corps, the aim of this work is not to ingratiate themselves to, or become, the English. Similarly, the 'ultimatum' does not simply reveal the Indian community's failure to complete the narrative of recognition that Bhabha describes. Rather, in both cases these actions alter the narrative framework of the relationship between the English and the Indians. The demand for citizen rights, while acknowledging difference, transforms the narrative from the impossibility of sameness to the demand – and in these two examples a demand that is both purposeful and grounded in material experience – for equality. This demand, overtly as a call for legislative recognition of equality rights, is accurately characterized by Guha as conforming to, rather than challenging, the liberal discourse of colonial authority; it did not challenge the structure but sought to change the position of Indians within that structure. Yet, the presumption of this equality in performance or behaviour undermines or threatens European authority.

This disruption of colonial authority/identity provides an example of the way in which concepts such as mimicry can be used productively to investigate the ways in which colonial authority can be disrupted or purposefully challenged. Does refashioning Bhabha's work in this way, however, avoid the central criticisms of Bhabha's discursive preoccupations? Is the sort of challenge to colonial identity and authority performed in the Indian Ambulance Corps or Gandhi's negotiations with Smuts 'resistance'? When Gandhi left South Africa in 1914, the government had abolished the poll tax and Indian marriages were recognized. For many Indians, however, the movement had not gone far enough to ameliorate their grievances, particularly in terms of trade and land rights. Indeed, the position of Indians in South African society would deteriorate drastically after the Great War. Neither the political campaign nor the presumption of equality led to the recognition of Indians as equal by the white population; rather, each instance of Indian imposition of their humanity – whether through the performance of citizen responsibilities such as the ambulance corps or the rejection of colonial authority through the burning of their certificates – was returned with more vociferous attempts by the state to control and subjugate them.

Many years after Gandhi left South Africa, Smuts would call him one of the most important men of his era and seemed to acknowledge a genuine, though dubious, respect for him as an individual.[90] While much has been made of the apparent mutual respect between Gandhi and Smuts, a close reading of their correspondence reveals instead mutual 'sly civility.'[91] In fact, Gandhi's contact with the leaders of South Africa seems only to have strengthened the dominant European culture's belief *in the need for* white supremacy. In a 1913 letter to Smuts, Prime Minister General Louis Botha refers to Indians as 'creatures': 'Dear Jannie, This morning I telegraphed you about Gandhi and others – whether we cannot arrest them again. I felt so irritated by their attitude, now again in Natal, that really one could take them by the throat.'[92] Bhabha's theorization of 'spectacular resistance' reveals the way in which native 'subversion' of the colonial demand reinforced the stereotype of the native and, hence, the colonist's contempt for an inferior race. In contrast, I believe the Indian community's various forms of *refusal* – which often took the form of an *assertion* of their humanity and equality – led the colonist to *hate* a group with which they understood themselves as being in competition or conflict. In this distinction between *contempt* for inferiority and *hatred* for an adversary, I see the possibility for a form of discursive resistance that is both transformative and linked meaningfully to material relations. Rather than revealing the way in which colonial authority was reinforced by, or adapted to, Indian resistance, *hatred*, or the increasing reliance on coercive modes of power to maintain white dominance, reveals the fragility of colonial authority and the impact these modes of discursive and material resistance had upon the government and the dominating culture, more generally.

As I will suggest in my discussion of the anti-apartheid struggle in chapter 4, diverse forms of opposition and resistance escalate conflict, making colonial power untenable and illuminating that power as injustice. While the Indian activism in South Africa did not escalate this conflict to such an extent, overt acts of refusal, such as the burning of passes, and more subtle challenges to colonial knowledge undoubtedly disrupted the functioning of colonial power and revealed the limits of this power to Indians, Africans, and Europeans alike. The examples of the Indian Ambulance Corps and the 'ultimatum,' however, as forms of resistance to colonial discourses of knowledge and authority, provide a significantly different challenge to colonial authority than does Bhabha's notions of hybridity, mimicry, and sly civility. Bhabha's 'spectacular resistance' provides no substantive account of how discursive 'resistance' alters or challenges colonial authority; indeed, it does not assume that such an alteration or challenge is a necessary component of 'resistance.' The Indian performance of a subjectivity other than that prescribed within colonial discourse constitutes not simply a 'failure' or 'refusal' to fulfil the narrative demand of colonial discourse, but an affirmation of a transformed narrative.

2 Opposition and the (Im)Possibility of Liberation

Opposition, Power, and Anti-Colonial Thought

For many critics of postcolonial theory, the emergence of colonial discourse theory has shifted attention away from the materialist concerns of the economic and political forms and effects of colonialism to concerns of discourse, language, and identity. Postcolonial theory has seemingly reduced colonialism to a cultural project, eliding its material impacts on colonized peoples and, more importantly, its role within the emergence of capitalism globally, both as an ideology and as a structure of material relationships. Significantly, the work of Frantz Fanon has been central to both the colonial discourse analysis of theorists such as Homi K. Bhabha as well as those who critique and challenge postcolonialism's seeming poststructural preoccupations, such as Benita Parry, E. San Juan, Jr, and Arif Dirlik. For instance, Fanon's interest in national and racial identity formation, mimicry, and marginalization has been recuperable as the core of colonial discourse theory. In contrast, for critics such as Parry and San Juan, the emphasis Bhabha places on Fanon's analysis of the individual's experience of colonialism in *Black Skin, White Masks* ignores his analysis of decolonization, nationalism, and revolt in *The Wretched of the Earth*. In this chapter, I focus on the way in which Fanon's oppositional politics has been recuperable for critics, both as a method of challenging, if not dismissing, postcolonial discourse theory and as a theory of social and political change.

I draw upon the work of Fanon, specifically, because of the impact he has had upon the field of postcolonial studies – in both its discursive and materialist formulations – but also because, like Edward Said, I believe that Fanon provides a provocative, albeit ambiguous, gesture towards a politics of liberation. I am particularly interested in how Fanon's ideal of liberation is imbricated within an assumption of humanistic ideals, and how this ideal of liberation has influenced the work of Said. In the wake of the poststructural critique of universalisms and narratives of emancipation, the faith in a (new) humanism that survives Fanon's (as well as Cabral's, Césaire's, or Senghor's) critiques of the deep contradictions between European ideals and practices has, in many ways, been lost. More importantly, because humanism has been discredited in this way, Fanon's critique of colonialism has often been too narrowly defined. Fanon's critique of colonial relations of power cannot be reduced to questions of identity nor, would I argue, to capitalism. Rather, Fanon theorizes structural *and* cultural change to a world economic and political order that produces inequality and suffering. Such an approach is crucial for transcending the limited notion of resistance I identified within colonial discourse theory as well as its alternative, the rhetoric and politics of opposition.

Postcolonial studies has been preoccupied with distinctly colonial formulations of power and the critical project of deconstructing colonial knowledge/power. As a result, other registers of power and forms of oppression, including European and indigenous forms of patriarchy and gender construction, class stratification, or religious and ethnic difference, have been marginalized. Indeed, by focusing on Fanon and Said, and by examining Gandhian notions of resistance and liberation as well as the concept of reconciliation, I reframe resistance as transformation in order to situate the critique of colonial power or capitalist relations explicitly in theories of liberation as alternative relationships.[1] In the first half of this chapter, then, I seek to contextualize my analysis of Fanon's theory of liberation by first examining the oppositional framework that I believe is indebted to his description of the Manichean relations of colonialism. Hence, it is necessary to briefly map the debate within postcolonial studies as to the value of conceptualizing power oppositionally. Next, I analyse critical responses to Tsitsi Dangarembga's *Nervous Conditions* to argue that postcolonial critics, even when they are overtly concerned with deconstructing or disentangling colonial discourse, rely upon an oppositional model of resistance. In the case of this novel, uncritical assumptions of oppositionality elide the way in which Dangarembga depicts multiple and conflicting structures of power within which the colonized/classed/gendered subject must navigate. The various ways in which the women of the novel experience and challenge oppression, I argue, reveal a colonial framework of opposition as both a problematic conceptual model of power and insufficient as a politics of resistance. I then turn to the way in which Fanon constructs the identity of the colonized in relation to 'resistance.' Rather than the collective identity of the native providing a framework for struggle against the colonist/other, Fanon conceptualizes the collective identity of the colonized as a manifestation of struggle. Fanon gestures towards a notion of liberation in his work that requires both the transformation of the binary and Manichean framework of colonial knowledge as well as social, political, and economic relations, not only within colonized spaces but more globally. Edward Said's treatment of liberation is indebted to Fanon, but Said too exhibits what I consider a tension between the politics of opposition, which informs strategies and tactics of social change, and an ethics of humanism that underwrites the hope of liberation.

As politically significant as the theoretical deconstruction of various essentialisms, and particularly race, have been, such hierarchical and binary frameworks had – and continue to have – significant political currency, both for the way in which they seem to explain material inequalities and the way in which they structure discourses of political struggle. If, as Laura Chrisman argues, colonialism must be understood as a product of struggle and contestation and anti-colonial movements as 'constitutive of, not merely constituted by, colonialism,'[2] the interrogation of colonial discourse must also engage with organized movements in colonized spaces that sought to evict the colonial interloper, protect societies from capitalist exploitation or Western culture, foster the emergence of capitalist structures, and/or build a 'national' community. Further, I believe it is also necessary to interrogate the politics of the oppositional discourses of power that critics such as JanMohamed, Parry, Ahmad, and San Juan (re)construct.

By critiquing postcolonialism as 'apolitical' and constructing a narrative of postcolonial studies in which postcolonial discourse is the result of a 'shift' or 'discursive turn,' these critics posit an alternative, original, and more genuine, oppositional theory of resistance in the work of anti-colonial writers such as Fanon, Cabral, Césaire, and James. Drawing on Fanon's conception of colonialism as a Manichean relationship, for instance, Abdul JanMohamed asserts that there is a 'Manichean world' that is manifested as a set of socio-political relations within which the colonizer and the colonized relate, and in which colonizers project upon the colonized their own anxiety, as settlers.[3] In other words, it is a form of cultural violence; Manicheism is a product of the colonial imagination that serves to rationalize and perpetuate the dominant position of the colonizer. As a cultural imaginary, this relationship between colonizer and colonized can be deconstructed by the critic; yet, this oppositional discourse nonetheless functions to construct and maintain authority. While, as Anthony Kwame Appiah reminds us, the presence of Europeans and the direct influence of European culture was marginal to the daily lives of the vast majority of people living in Africa and India during direct British colonial rule, the eviction of the settler and the liberation from European control shaped narratives of African and Indian national identity and independence, or at least those narratives that have been recuperated within postcolonial studies.[4]

Benita Parry suggests that Bhabha's selective reading of the work of Fanon constructs a critical Fanon that is congenial to his deconstructive preoccupations. She further argues that Bhabha disregards the process of resistance 'initiated by Fanon's oppositional discourse when the definition colonizer/colonized conceived under the old regime of thought, is displaced by a different usage of the same term, one invoking *implacable enmity* both as analysis of a political condition and as a galvanizing political slogan.'[5] Parry's critique of the deconstructive preoccupations of colonial discourse theory assumes that resistance is necessarily *antagonistic*; it takes the form of counter-discourse, relies upon the 'implacable enmity' between the contesting subjects of the *colonial* relationship, and maintains the assumption of the colonized subject's agency *as opposition* to colonial authority.

For many critics of colonial discourse theory, the deconstruction of oppositional binaries of power, by definition, negates the possibility of resistance as it is understood within the rhetoric of anti-colonial struggle. San Juan, for instance, explicitly differentiates his object of analysis from that of postcolonial theory, postulating the 'Third World' as a trope or site of dissent rather than a geographic space: 'I am referring to all places in which *an actual movement of resistance or opposition* to imperial domination exists.'[6] Indeed, he claims that postcolonial theory is especially problematic 'for people of colour seeking to affirm their autochtonous traditions of resistance.'[7] Within such a formulation, however, the 'Third World' subject is defined, and contained, by its position *against* an oppressive 'other.' Although San Juan draws upon a notion of social and political transformation – citing James, for instance, to figure resistance as the production of new cultural forms or the subversion of imposed modes – throughout the book, he privileges organized, violent movements as 'resistance.' In his discussion of Fanon's 'Concerning Violence,' San Juan contends that Fanon argues that the process of armed struggle has a pedagogical effect wherein it enacts a form of participatory democracy and demystifies all state authority.[8] Parry's or San Juan's concerns emphasize the way in which academic deconstruction of colonial knowledge erases the dichotomous axes through which colonial life was organized; colonialism must be understood as Manichean or antagonistic because it was experienced this way. However, Appiah argues that by understanding colonialism *only* as antagonism and (post)colonial culture as simply the product of marginality, postcolonial critiques that assume the Manichean framework of Fanon's description 'ignore the reciprocal nature of power relations ... and neglect the multiform varieties of individual and collective agency available to the African subject.'[9] For Appiah, the deconstruction of the Manichean binary is not apolitical; rather, it is the Manichean framework that forecloses the possibility of action in the 'real world of politics.'[10]

As I will argue in my treatment of Gandhian thought and South Africa's project of reconciliation, to deconstruct the Manichean framework of colonial relations is not to deny the way in which this antagonistic dualism shaped colonial experience. If, as I interpret Jan-Mohamed, we must understand Manicheism as a form of cultural violence (i.e., a discourse or narrative that legitimizes the violence of colonial exploitation and repression), then neither its deconstruction nor its affirmation as a rhetoric and politics of struggle, I would suggest, can dismantle the oppressive relations of power it justifies. However, these relations of power are experienced through a particular narrative that limits both the possible actors in the conflict and the kinds of agency that these actors may have. This Manichean or oppositional framework limits the possibilities for resistance, reinforcing colonial identities that anti-colonial thinkers such as Fanon suggest must be both deconstructed and transformed as a project of decolonization and liberation.

Bill Ashcroft argues that any discussion of resistance within postcolonial studies must engage with the problem of whether or not a history of resistance as armed or ideological rebellion 'leaves in its wake a *rhetoric* of opposition emptied of any capacity for social change':[11]

> Resistance which ossifies into simple opposition often becomes trapped in the very binary which imperial discourse uses to keep the colonized in subjection ... The most tenacious aspect of colonial control has been its capacity

to bind the colonized into a binary myth. Underlying all colonial discourse is a binary of colonizer/colonized, civilized/uncivilized, white/black which works to justify the *mission civilatrice* and perpetuate a cultural distinction which is essential to the 'business' of economic and political exploitation.[12]

Armed or ideological 'rebellion' requires an other to defeat, evict, and/or destroy. In the teleology of revolution Fanon describes, this other is the settler, the colonist; yet, as Fanon emphasizes in his critique of national consciousness and his gestures towards a notion of liberation, 'true liberation' requires the transformation of a variety of social, cultural, political, and economic structures. While San Juan, through the work of Fanon and James, among others, privileges a politics of violent opposition born out of the Manichean framework of colonial knowledge, as I will argue below, I believe that Fanon and Said imagine liberation as effecting an alternative to the binary framework of colonial discourse and anti-colonial rhetoric, and hence the epistemological locos of Western reason and humanism.

In *Culture and Imperialism*, Said describes the way in which the colonized transforms the colonial experience into a 'battle' that forces the colonizer to see himself on the 'other side.' Said argues that when the colonized initiates this struggle, 'there are now two sides, two nations, in combat, not merely the voice of the white master answered antiphonally – reactively – by the colonial upstart.'[13] Yet, while Said defines resistance as necessarily oppositional, he also acknowledges the failure of the post-colonial nation to challenge the structures of colonialism. For instance, he recognizes the way in which writers such as Fanon warned of the dangers of an essentialist basis to anti-colonial agitation.[14] Further, he is careful to specify that he considers the work of Fanon and Cabral as a theory not just of opposition but of decolonization or liberation, which transforms social structures/consciousness as well; he argues: 'At its best, the culture of opposition and resistance suggests a theoretical alternative and a practical method of reconceiving human experience in non-imperialist terms.'[15] In *Culture and Imperialism* Said takes as his objects of study works of cultural resistance; the 'ideological and cultural war' to which these texts contribute takes place within a teleological model of revolution. Echoing the historical narrative of anti-colonial agency that Fanon describes, Said reinforces this narrative as a theory of anti/post-colonial struggle.

While Said maintains this notion of conflicting sides, he imagines postcolonialism, and specifically *Culture and Imperialism* itself, as an attempt to 'formulate an alternative both to a politics of blame and to the even more destructive politics of confrontation and hostility.'[16] In the latter part of this chapter I will return to what Said has to say about an alternative to what he calls a 'politics and rhetoric of blame,' for I believe that such an alternative has a profound potential not simply for understanding the past but for cultivating social, political, and economic change. However, Said's critique of this 'rhetoric of blame' is constrained by an oppositional politics consigned to a teleological model of change originating with the idea of 'two sides' manifested in 'battle.' As I will argue in my treatment of *Nervous Conditions*, all protests *against* figures of authority are not necessarily transgressive. As a result, I believe we need to examine the 'politics' of reading the colonial relationship as 'antagonistic' and resistance as the product of 'implacable enmity,' not in an effort to disregard the very real material and social differences among colonial subjects, or the way in which narratives of antagonism shape experience and political action, but to interrogate whether such a politics is helpful in understanding how these differences can be transformed.

Tsitsi Dangarembga's *Nervous Conditions*: (Re)Reading Opposition

Tsitsi Dangarembga's *Nervous Conditions* has taken a prominent place in the canon of postcolonial literature and has received much critical attention, specifically in terms of the way it depicts and performs 'resistance.' As Deepika Bahri argues, by telling the stories of Zimbabwean women and girls, Dangarembga provides a counter-narrative to male-centred and bourgeois narratives of the nation, and by representing women of different ages, classes, and educational backgrounds, she challenges composite and reductive sketches of the Third World woman.[17] Dangarembga's narrator Tambu begins her story by constructing a taxonomy of women's responses to oppression that frames the narrative. She introduces the main women characters of the novel by explaining that the story she has to tell is about the 'rebellion' of her cousin Nyasha, the 'entrapment' of her mother and her aunt Maiguru, and the 'escape' of both herself and her mother's younger sister Lucia.[18] Hence, the central female figures of the novel are introduced to the reader in terms of the way in which they negotiate their roles as African women in a male-dominated society colonized by a European power. In many ways, this taxonomy of responses to oppression has shaped readings of the novel.

By analysing the critical reception of the novel – and particularly the critical focus upon Nyasha's experience of anorexia and bulimia as a form of resistance (as opposition) to patriarchal and/or colonial power – I want to examine the way in which resistance – as acts, subject-positions, figures – has been constructed through the metaphor of opposition. I believe that analyses that construct resistance in this way cannot account for the complex web of power Dangarembga constructs. *Nervous Conditions* reveals the 'multi-form varieties of individual and collective agency' Appiah argues are available to the African subject. In response to critical responses to the novel that focus on Nyasha's 'opposition,' I seek to examine how the responses and experiences of the other women in the novel do not necessarily provide routes to, or processes of, 'liberation' but do problematize the notion of resistance as opposition.

Readings of resistance in *Nervous Conditions,* because they are shaped by the taxonomy Dangarembga's narrator provides, reinscribe binary relations of power in which resistance is only understandable as opposition to, or the *negation* of, figures and signs of oppression. In particular, critical responses to the novel focus upon Dangarembga's depiction of Nyasha – one of five women described in Tambu's opening taxonomy – and specifically the way in which Nyasha's body becomes a space upon which patriarchy, colonialism, and/or modernity are enacted and a space in which 'rebellion' to these forms of oppression can take place.[19] Nyasha's conflict with her father develops throughout the novel, culminating in her purging after meals and her physical and emotional deterioration. For Bahri: 'Nyasha's diseased self suggests the textualized female body on whose abject person are writ large the imperial inscriptions of colonization, the intimate branding of patriarchy, and the battle between native culture, Western narrative, and her complex relationship with both. Not surprisingly, Nyasha's response to this violence on the body is not only somatogenic but it is to manifest specifically that illness which will consume that body.'[20] Nyasha's body, then, is a text on which we can read the multiple modes of power of colonial Rhodesia, and the illness that consumes her body can be seen as the *effect* of these conflicting forms of oppression.

Yet, while Bahri constructs Nyasha's illness as an *effect* of her experience of oppression, she also describes it as a form of resistance. She contends that 'the usually appearance-centred practices of anorexia and bulimia become narrativized as artful, if grotesque, protest that will prevent Nyasha's maturation into full fledged commodified "womanhood,"' and that 'Nyasha's *war* with patriarchal and colonial systems is fought on the turf of her own body, both because it is the scene of enactment of these systems and because it is the only site of resistance available.'[21] So while Nyasha's anorexia and bulimia are interpreted as the effect of a battle between competing discourses of femininity and racial identity, her illness is also read as a form of resistance *against* patriarchal and colonial systems. Biman Basu reiterates Bahri's suggestion that because the female body is disciplined by both patriarchal and colonial authority, it is the material and corporeal space in which resistance can take place. As a result, Nyasha's 'disgorging that which is forcibly inserted into her body, initiates a counter-movement to the prevailing syntax of the narrative ... it is Nyasha's violent rebellion that initiates the lines of flight from the territorialized body of the colonized native.'[22] However, does Nyasha's subversion of her father's demands for her to eat – her saying 'no' to authority – constitute resistance to colonial and/or patriarchal oppression?

I find the association of Nyasha's illness with warfare particularly problematic as a model of resistance and incongruent with the narrative Dangarembga constructs. Janice E. Hill, for instance, argues that Nyasha's opposition to her father's authority reflects the armed struggle of ZANU and ZAPU guerrillas against the colonial government of Rhodesia.[23] If *Nervous Conditions* provides a counter-narrative to the nationalist, and particularly masculine, literature of African anti-colonialism and disappointed independence, recuperating Dangarembga's narrative into such a discourse of militant nationalism, and constructing Nyasha as a metonym of organized political struggle, seems to undermine the feminist politics of the text. The tendency of critics of *Nervous Conditions* to focus upon Nyasha's violent experience-of as response-to oppression and to incorporate her illness into narratives of collective violent rebellion, or warfare, ignores the fact that this violence is directed at her own body rather than that of an other; while anorexia and bulimia are performed as an act of control or power, they are also a form of self-destruction rather than 'rebellion.' Further, such readings uncritically reinscribe violent rebellion as 'genuine' or 'true' resistance. Constructing resistance as 'rebellion,' or the act of saying 'no,' seems to occlude the possibility of transforming the web of power within which the women exist.

On one level, to see Nyasha's self-destructive illness as a mirror of the contemporaneous Zimbabwean struggle for independence, as Hill does, reveals a wilful disregard for Zimbabwean history. The violence that wrested political control of the colonial Rhodesian state away from the white minority did not end with independence; the two major opposition militants/parties, ZANU and ZAPU, turned their guns towards one another, the conflict raging throughout the 1980s. Further, guerrilla warfare in Zimbabwe, and the political culture it has produced, has by no means cultivated a healthy social or cultural national 'body.' Readings that parallel the violence perpetrated by Nyasha against her own body with the colonial violence perpetrated against a collective African body *and* violent opposition in response to colonial oppression at least implicitly rely upon Fanon's assertion that decolonization is necessarily a violent phenomenon and that this violence is cathartic or humanizing.

Yet, Fanon's argument for the necessity of violence is undermined by his association of violent rebellion with the native's desire to replace the settler: 'The native is an oppressed person whose permanent dream is to become the persecutor. The symbols of social order – the police, the bugle calls in the barracks, military parades and the waving flags – are at one and the same time inhibitory and stimulating.'[24] Violence, then, is closely associated with the symbols and structures of European power. Fanon acknowledges the cycle of violence in Algeria and underscores the way in which violence is both a tactic and an ideology for the colonized, but one, significantly, that is 'furnished by the settler.'[25] Like the violence of guerrilla warfare, which is described by Fanon as a mode of communal self-definition, the violence that debilitates Nyasha is presented as a means of individuation (and, I would suggest, alienation) that escapes the constraints of the representation of the native imposed by dominant colonizing others.

Tambu expresses some ambivalence towards Nyasha's rebellion, suggesting that it 'may not in the end have been successful,' a sentiment echoed by a number of critics.[26] While Nyasha's rebellion may not have been 'successful,' it is nonetheless accepted that her acts of rebellion are, indeed, 'resistance,' and acts of self-determination. For instance, Saliba argues that 'this fighting back is part of the process of claiming a "self,"'[27] and Sue Thomas contends that anorexia and bulimia are 'a critical and highly ambiguous attempt at self-determination.'[28] Since the body is where colonial and patriarchal authority is performed and it is the only space over which the colonized woman has any measure of control, for these critics, Nyasha's act of starving herself is recognized as the performance of a specifically anti-colonial and anti-patriarchal agency. Reading Nyasha's illness within such a narrative of resistance as oppositional violence, however, problematizes the feminist politics of the novel. As Nair acknowledges, the narrative of liberation through violent revolution affirms a 'scenario of macho revolutionary process of individuation.'[29] Conferring a cathartic potential upon violence reinscribes a masculinist form of nationalism. Further, to recognize Nyasha's self-destructive acts as, albeit 'ambiguous,' attempts at self-determination seems too positive an assessment of the function of this resistance in effecting her empowerment or transforming the structures of power that marginalize and alienate her.

Nyasha's ideal of a slender body reflects her assimilation into European values *as well as* her rejection of Shona patriarchy. While the violence of anorexia and bulimia is directed at her own body and psyche, her violent outburst at the end of the novel, precipitating her psychiatric treatment in Salisbury, is directed at symbols of European cultural domination in the form of English history books *and* its other, the clay pots, as markers of traditional culture. Her destruction of the history book is a form of rebellion against the epistemological violence that subsumes Shona culture into the 'body' of English History; yet the destruction of the pots seems to be a rejection of an essentialized past or tradition constructed to counter that History, a counter-discourse in which women's bodies and labour are also controlled and exploited. Nyasha rejects the modern (European)/traditional (native) binary as a framework for understanding and expressing herself, in part, at least, because for the African woman, 'tradition,' in the form of the private, domestic space, does not provide relief from the public, or societal oppression of colonial rule; rather, 'tradition' and 'modernity,' though different, both enact the subjugation of women.

Following their sojourn in England, Maiguru and Nyasha are represented as out of place and uncomfortable within the social space of the homestead, a space in which men gather to make decisions that affect the lives of women and in which much of the labour of daily living is conducted by women. Bahri argues that 'Nyasha's attraction to the Western ideal of femininity must be mediated, then, by her understanding of the exploitative usurpation of the healthy African female body' within the social space of the traditional 'homestead.'[30] Nyasha's repeated references to her desire for a slim figure and her warning to Tambu not to get fat seem to reflect on one level the active subversion of Shona cultural ideals of a strong, large, and healthy female body and her father's specific demands for her to eat and gain weight. Readings of this disease and the discontent with 'traditional' modes of gender relations and lifestyle expressed by Maiguru and Nyasha and learned by Tambu in her formal European education are used to support the feminist politics of the novel. For instance, Basu characterizes wearing short dresses, smoking cigarettes, and going dancing as other ways in which Nyasha enacts her resistance.[31] Here, then, the practice of European modernity, or specifically Western and bourgeois gender roles and values, becomes not a form of mimicry but of 'resistance.'

The association of Nyasha's illness with her own assertions of femininity – the idea that 'angles are more attractive than curves,' the links between the most extreme stages in the illness and Nyasha's desperate desire for a 'svelte and sensuous' figure[32] – reveals the way in which Nyasha has internalized Western values and norms related to beauty and gender if only as the means to enact control. Patriarchy cannot be understood as another form of oppression that affects the female African subject, *in addition to* colonialism, but a form of control that, although exhibiting different and perhaps conflicting forms and symbols, is inflected through Shona culture (which becomes synonymous with the traditional, domestic, or rural) and colonial culture (which becomes synonymous with the modern, foreign, or institution of formal education). While Nyasha's refusal to be the decent daughter her father demands subverts his individual authority as father, her emotional and physical self-destruction is hardly emancipatory; rather, it *is* her experience of oppression and, just as importantly, her hybrid cultural experience.

E. San Juan, Jr, contends that hybridity may describe experience but that it masks the 'central issue': 'What is the actual alignment of power relations and political forces in which we find ourselves imbricated?'[33] Many critics recognize Nyasha's hybrid cultural experience yet characterize this hybridity as an experience of multiple forms of oppression. For instance, Therese Saliba contends that Nyasha's anorexia and bulimia 'serves as an internalization of and resistance to sexual oppression and colonial domination, and is symptomatic of the Western and class privileges she experiences as a cultural hybrid.'[34] Saliba characterizes patriarchy as an 'internal' form of oppression while colonialism is 'external.'[35] Rather than being a product of, simply, *multiple* forms of oppression, however, I would argue that Nyasha's illness – if we are to see it as the product of the power relations in which she is imbricated – seems rather to be the result of multiple and *conflicting* forms of oppression. For instance, in one of her letters to Tambu after Tambu left for Sacred Heart School, Nyasha describes the sense of isolation she feels:

> [The other girls at school] resent the fact that I do not read their romance stories ... If only they knew that when I was ten my mother used to scold me very severely indeed for sneaking them down from the bookshelf ... they do not like my language, my English because it is authentic and my Shona, because it is not! They think that I am a snob, that I think I am superior to them because I do not feel that I am inferior to men ... And all because I beat the boys at maths! I know that I should not complain, but I very much would like to belong Tambu, but I find I do not.[36]

Nyasha's sense of trauma seems to reflect the alienation she feels not only as a 'victim' of the oppression of patriarchy (men over women) *or* colonialism (as Western modernity over Shona tradition) but also as a result of existing in a space of intersection where various axes of power conflict and/or reinforce one another, including Western and Shona patriarchy, racial hierarchies, and material privilege.

When Tambu next returns home she finds Nyasha looking 'too svelte,' and one night Nyasha experiences a breakdown that finally alerts her parents to the severity of her trauma. Before shredding her history book between her teeth and breaking her mirrors and the clay pots, Nyasha wakes Tambu to warn her of her self-destructive desires:

> 'I don't want to do it, Tambu, really, I don't, but it's coming ... They've done it to me,' she accused, whispering still. 'Really, they have.' And then she became stern. 'It's not their fault. They did it to them too. You know they did,' she whispered. 'To both of them but especially to him. They put him through it all. But it's not his fault, he's good.' Her voice took on a Rhodesian accent. 'He's a good boy, a good munt. A bloody good kaffir ... They've deprived you of you, him of him, ourselves of each other.'[37]

In this frenzied monologue, 'they' becomes an amorphous marker of the oppressor, yet it is a signifier that displaces her trauma; there is no single, identifiable oppressor – a 'they' – to blame, hold accountable, or chase away.

One way to account for Nyasha's sense of alienation and the physical illness and psychological breakdown it manifests is to recognize the way in which she is necessarily implicated in the structures of power within which she is located. As Bahri argues:

> Her 'anti-colonial' war ... is complicated by her own collusion with the corrupt system she is fighting – her unwillingness to relinquish the accent

acquired from her brief stay in England, her criticism of the racist dominion of colonizers while remaining standoffish with her compatriots at school, and the lack of effort at regaining her native language or contact with homestead relatives – visible to Tambu but unacknowledged, or unknown to her except in her sense of herself as 'hybrid,' is also a factor in the war of ideas and values being narrativized on her corporeal bodily space.[38]

Bahri complicates the oppositional binary of domination by illuminating the ways in which Nyasha is complicit within various systems of oppression. However, she contends that Nyasha's unwillingness to redevelop her Shona language skills reflects complicity in the corrupt system of British colonialism or European cultural intrusion, thereby seeming to recuperate an oppositional framework pitting English against Shona, modernity against tradition.

While critics such as Uwakweh and Saliba have constructed Nyasha's anorexia and bulimia as resistance to show that she is not simply a 'passive victim' of patriarchal and colonial oppression,[39] placed within the context of women's various experiences of and responses to multiple and conflicting forms of oppression in the novel, I find it difficult to read the destruction of Nyasha in body and spirit as an act of resistance. Further, the question of this rebellion's 'success' reveals the ambivalence or ambiguity that surrounds what it means to successfully resist. Therese Saliba contends that during her breakdown, Nyasha 'rejects colonial history, which has fragmented her culture and, along with the Shona patriarchal traditions, has scarred her flesh, and she refuses her material privileges gained by colonialism's capitalist system.'[40] Can Nyasha, however, genuinely reject these influences or refuse these privileges without ceasing *to be* – without wasting away to nothing? For Bahri, Nyasha's self-destruction is the attainment of a 'body without organs': 'The woman that dies is the abject self that has never enjoyed the luxury of self-determination, that is no real woman but an insubstantial changeling who functions as token and currency in the labor and matrimonial market. Nyasha's pathological persona enacts a multi-pronged assault on a complex and interwoven system that involves the body and the mind, patriarchy and the female body, colonialism and history.'[41] Nyasha's wasting away constitutes a saying 'no' to her father; it is an active rejection of her father's demands and an active subversion of Shona patriarchy, but it is also woven within a web of systems of power and it is indebted to European cultural values.

Nyasha's trauma reflects the impossibility of performing the narratives of identity marked by colonial 'knowledge' or Shona patriarchy. While these narratives explicate specific relations of power, they cannot account for the complexity of the way in which these narratives interrelate and conflict in the experience of the individual. The violence of the conflict that takes place upon Nyasha's body is neither cathartic nor liberating. Rather, Nyasha's violent act seems to be the most dramatic manifestation of the dehumanization of oppression.[42]

Although Dangarembga's explicitly anti-patriarchal or anti-colonial rhetoric in the novel's introduction and Nyasha's thoughtful critique of her experience of colonial and patriarchal power frame power and resistance in the novel oppositionally, critical readings of *Nervous Conditions* nonetheless impose on the novel a model of resistance that is discursively insufficient and politically unproductive. Tambu suggests that Nyasha's rebellion may not have been successful. Without dismissing the politics of Nyasha's actions – from the destruction of the signs of the binary framework of European domination and nativist counter-discourse to the destruction of her own physical body – in these acts of desperation Nyasha performs the ambivalence and ambiguity of power in the colonial space. Dangarembga provides no clear narrative of emancipation, but neither does she construct her characters as hopelessly passive or victimized. By illuminating the complex web of power within which her characters exist, including colonial rule, modernity, patriarchy, and Shona cultural practices, Dangarembga reveals the way in which oppositional resistance against any one field of power often reinforces another. While the novel does not posit a model of resistance as transformation, it does problematize oppositional models of resistance.

Two of the three possible responses to oppression in Tambu's taxonomy, 'rebellion' and 'entrapment,' frame oppression oppositionally, in this case defining how women are oppressed in a patriarchal system informed or reinforced by colonial authority. The emphasis upon rebellion in critical treatments of the novel, however, suggests that rebellion is the only alternative to passivity. Resistance, therefore, is defined as a negative reaction: Nyasha reacts *against* her father's authority and *against* 'traditional' constructs of femininity. Yet, as Nyasha realizes in her tirade against 'them,' her parents are as much a product of the interconnected systems of colonialism, modernity, and tradition as she is. There is no political utility in opposing the *figures of authority* within these structures; there is no 'them' to rebel against. As a result, the conflict becomes physically manifested in the space of Nyasha's own body. In Nyasha's attack on her European history text and the clay pots, she seems to be disrupting both poles of the binary between colonizer/colonized, modern/traditional. An oppositional conceptualization of resistance allows Nyasha's subversion of her father's demands to be characterized as resistance, though that subversion reinforces particularly modern or Western structures of identification.

The third reaction to colonialism and patriarchy in Tambu's taxonomy is 'escape.' Escape, as it is constructed within the novel, seems to figure the sort of resistance Ashcroft conceptualizes in the idea of saying 'no.' In some ways, the example in chapter 1 of the work of Gandhi and other Indians in South Africa reflects the way in which South African Indians were able to 'escape' the discursive constructions of their subjectivity, thereby challenging colonial authority, though by no means significantly altering the material or political structure that reinforced white privilege and dominance. While escape may constitute a space negotiated by the oppressed, which disrupts the oppositional binary of their oppression – and in this way perhaps we should construct Nyasha's response as one of attempted 'escape' rather than 'rebellion' – neither Lucia nor Tambu finds space outside patriarchy or colonialism or 'escapes' these structures of power. Each woman escapes the patriarchal authority of the homestead in terms of specific relationships; for instance, Tambu escapes the authority of her father, the lingering presence of her gendered 'difference' from her brother, and the communal expectations of gender roles. As evidenced by Maiguru's feelings of 'entrapment,' however, the movement away from 'traditional' gender constraints facilitates an alteration in subject-position but not an 'escape' from patriarchy; the structure is left unchallenged and continues to shape and limit in different ways.

Further, Lucia and Tambu's escape marks a form of 'upward mobility' in material or class terms, from the traditional homestead to the modern school. Lucia, for instance, escapes from the responsibilities of the woman within a subsistence economy into waged labour at the school; her move to the school is facilitated by her willingness to sell her labour, a labour that in the homestead is an obligation of her gender. Similarly, the emancipation for which Tambu longs, and ultimately receives, is the escape from the homestead:

> How can I describe the sensations that swamped me when Babamukuru started his car, with me in the front seat beside him, on the day I left my

home? ... When I stepped into Babamukuru's car I was a peasant ... It was evident from the corrugated black callouses on my knees, the scales on my skin that were due to lack of oil, the short, dull tufts of malnourished hair. This was the person I was leaving behind ... At Babamukuru's I would have the leisure, be encouraged to consider questions that had to do with survival of the spirit, the creation of consciousness, rather than mere sustenance of the body.[43]

This migration from the mental and material limits of the homestead to the 'limitless horizons' outside the homestead reveals the binary structures of patriarchy and colonialism as essentializations. As a result, direct opposition by those figured as oppressed against figures or symbols of oppression is problematic. Patriarchy functions differently in different spaces, and it is experienced within the emergence of modern and capitalist relations of power and identity as it is within 'traditional' Shona culture.

For a number of critics, Tambu's education, at the very least, allows for a particularly feminist emancipation. For instance, Supriya Nair argues that Ngugi's critique of colonial education in *Decolonizing the Mind* disregards the way in which the education of girls, such as Tambu, is an anomaly, and therefore provides a significant intervention into the way in which local patriarchal structures collude with colonial authority to reinforce the subordinate status of the colonized woman.[44] Further, Nair contends that 'although Tambu is aware that her foray into colonial education is also a death of sorts, it is a death she welcomes because, she believes, her incarnation will emerge with more power than she has as a poor, uneducated, African girl.'[45] The novel and criticism of it reveal the way in which various forms of control and privilege intersect, and at times become muddled in critical interpretations of resistance and power. For Basu, Tambu's appeal to consciousness as a product of education, and specifically the consciousness of patriarchy she attains through education, does not alter her subjection: 'If power is apprehended not *negatively* as repression, prohibition, or objectification but *positively* as producing subjects, the narrator's rhetoric of consciousness signals this subjectification and serves to elide the materiality of her contradictory position.'[46] As problematic as both Tambu and Nyasha recognize education to be, for both it is a significant means of negotiating a place of privilege within a patriarchal world and, just as significantly, as a potential remedy to material hardship.

Tambu characterizes her move to the mission school as her 'reincarnation,' a rising from the death-like experience of the homestead, 'freed from the constraints of the necessary and the squalid that defined and delimited our activity at home.'[47] Yet, Tambu's embrace of formal education is not indicative of a total rejection of 'tradition' within a simplistic modern/traditional binary. Tambu's consciousness of 'other struggles to engage in besides the consuming desire to emancipate myself and my family'[48] – a realization she attributes to the influence of Nyasha's continuous questioning – is manifested most significantly in her refusal to attend the Christian wedding ceremony of her parents. Tambu's stubborn refusal to attend the ceremony takes the form of literal 'escape,' first as her disappearance to the girls' hostel and then as a feigned illness. Babamukuru considers her ungrateful and disrespectful, a 'bad child' because she does not follow his orders. Tambu's unwillingness to go to the wedding, however, is not inspired by the desire to refuse Babamukuru, as a figure of oppression in the domestic sphere, but by her belief that the Christian ceremony demeans her parents' relationship: 'A wedding that made a mockery of the people I belonged to and placed doubt on my legitimate existence in this world.'[49] Tambu's ambivalence towards her home – a place she sees herself as 'too civilised' to return to, yet the place where she belongs[50] – reflects the ambivalence of modernity within (post)colonial experience.

Tambu's 'escape' reveals 'modernization,' 'Westernization,' and 'colonialism' as concepts that are not synonymous and as concepts that are always being negotiated. Tambu recognizes formal education – one marker of modernity or Westernization – as the way to 'freedom.' On one level, formal education facilitates her 'emancipation' in the terms of the modern individual, but as the experiences of Maiguru and Nyasha reveal, this emancipation is also experienced as alienation. Such a notion of emancipation is predicated on the idea of the bourgeois individual subject, rather than a notion of the subject within the community. However, Tambu's access to education also suggests the possibility of material emancipation from poverty. Indeed, she defines education specifically in material terms as the antithesis of the flies, empty stomachs, dirt, and disease of the homestead.[51] How can an oppositional framework allow for resistance to poverty, or liberation from poverty? Readings of the novel that focus upon 'patriarchy' and 'colonialism' tend to ignore the way in which these discourses are imbedded within material structures of inequality. The oppositional framework through which resistance is read in the novel limits the possibilities for imagining social change. Dangarembga's representation of complex and intersecting relations of power undermines oppositional discourses of resistance that construct experience within binary frameworks. The various ways in which the women of the novel experience, subvert, and seek to challenge oppression reveal a politics of opposition both as a problematic conceptual model of power and insufficient as a politics of resistance. Significantly, Dangarembga concentrates on the negotiations of power by individuals and reveals the way in which the overlapping structures of power impede the formation of 'communities' in opposition. It is this idea of the (resisting) community that has been the basis of anti-colonial notions of (national) liberation.

Resistance and Identity

Albert Memmi argues that because the peoples of South Asia and Africa were oppressed as groups, they necessarily had to adopt a nationalist or identity-based form of opposition that excluded the colonizer.[52] Anti-colonial intellectuals such as Léopold Senghor, who argued for a pan-African solidarity through the notion of *negritude*, imagined a collective African 'people.' For Senghor, the 'sum of the cultural values of the black world' could be used as 'an instrument of liberation' from colonial oppression.[53] As numerous critics – both contemporaneous with Senghor and since – have argued, notions such as *negritude* rely upon problematic notions of the 'masses' and 'pure culture' and reinscribe the binary framework of colonial knowledge. For instance, in *Black Skin, White Masks* and *The Wretched of the Earth*, Fanon critiques forms of nationalism that depend upon the construction of a shared ethnicity/race as a 'national' cultural past. In contrast, Fanon defines the national culture of the colonized not as pre-existing colonization but as a product of the violent struggle against colonial occupation. Such a critical stance relies upon the binary framework of colonial authority, in terms of colonialism as a conflict, but it does not reinforce or valorize the colonized as a product of difference in the way that the notion of *negritude* does. National identity is neither some pre-existing essence to which anti-colonialism is a struggle to re-establish, nor is it simply the manipulation of an identity produced as colonial knowledge; rather, for Fanon, national identity is produced through/as struggle.

Fanon describes colonialism as not merely physical coercion and material exploitation but a product of knowledge and representation. He argues that 'the settler paints the native as a sort of quintessence of evil ... he represents not only the absence of values, but also the negation of values.'[54] For Bhabha, Fanon's analysis of the colonial construction of identity and the psychological trauma it produces provides a source for his own discursive analysis of colonial authority. In contrast, for Parry, Fanon's conceptualization of colonialism as a Manichean struggle provides a 'radical tradition'[55] – rather than simply a theoretical framework – in which to base her own critique of colonial discourse theory. Frantz Fanon and his work have become a contested space through which contemporary postcolonial critics seek to understand the moment of, as well as construct an 'originating' narrative for, decolonization.

The fraught status of Fanon's work in postcolonial studies is particularly evident in discussions of violence and revolution. Postcolonialism has historically focused upon the cultural manifestations of colonial domination and resistance, and at times critics posit the terrain of culture as a more significant, and indeed separate, 'battlefield' for the colonial project than either the economic or military spheres. Nonetheless, implicit in much of this work is the assumption that if military rebellion is not the primary means of decolonization, it is at least a necessary stage in the process of decolonization. Although Said is critical of what he calls the 'politics of blame,' which underpins any antagonistic and violent conflict as well as historical representations of it, like many other critics he takes Fanon's writings on violence at face value, contending that in 'Fanon's world' the epistemological revolution in which the native becomes conscious of his subject-position and demands an end to colonial domination allows for the crucial stage of violence as a 'cleansing force' to commence.[56] However, Fanon's treatment of violent resistance in *The Wretched of the Earth*, like much of his writing, is ambivalent.

The idea that Fanon's *description* of colonial power and revolution provides some sort of genuine or original theory of opposition becomes untenable if we read Fanon's work, as Ato Sekyi-Otu suggests, as a dialectic dramatic narrative.[57] Sekyi-Otu characterizes Fanon's oeuvre as a dialectic of experience 'because it narrates the generation of relations infinitely more complex than the "mass relationship" or "simplifying" logic of the colonizer-colonized opposition.'[58] I have been careful thus far to refer to Fanon's 'description' of colonialism, violence, or revolution, rather than reaffirm the idea that Fanon provides an explanatory narrative of decolonization or theorizes power. The description Fanon provides is discontinuous and paradoxical. As Sekyi-Otu suggests, in *The Wretched of the Earth* the text acts 'as an interlocutor of its own representational claims, questioning its own depiction of history as the radical reversal of a brute facticity by the abrupt intervention of a collective will – history as an act without a process, an instantaneous event unconstrained by any determinate antecedents save for the grim confrontation of two "species" of humanity, the colonizer and the colonized.'[59] Fanon's analysis of anti-colonial violent opposition, therefore, cannot be read at face value but must be interpreted in the context of what Sekyi-Otu describes as its 'scene of immediacy.'[60]

In *The Wretched of the Earth,* Fanon asserts that violence provides the native the possibility of overcoming the subject/object relationship of the Manichean world-view. Fanon's construction of individual subjectivity and collective identity is embedded within a descriptive yet universalizing narrative of native consciousness.[61] It is difficult, however, to characterize the narrative of anti-colonial opposition Fanon describes as an unproblematic theory of violence as a 'cleansing force.' He contends that the mind of the native has been colonized; the religion of the colonialist bourgeoisie paralyses the colonized by teaching forgiveness and meekness, and 'in the innermost recesses of their brains the settler's tanks and airplanes occupy a huge place.'[62] Consequently, it is only violence that can *free* their minds.

Fanon's description of the cathartic nature of violence seems much more a description of political rhetoric or ideology derived from the immediacy of the Algerian experience than a committed philosophy of social change. Indeed, the contention that 'violence is in action all inclusive and national'[63] is neither developed nor supported by Fanon; rather, it is troubled by his assertions in the final chapter of *The Wretched of the Earth* that the war of national liberation in Algeria was 'a favourable breeding ground for mental disorders.'[64] The violence of revolution is traumatic and debilitating, at least for the individual, more than it is liberating. Further, Fanon also acknowledges that this violent antagonism locks the native into imperial ideology. While he critiques the way that the compromises of the 'nationalist bourgeois' forge a nation-state within a Western-dominated capitalist system, violent antagonism reinforces the racialized identity politics of colonialism. Fanon characterizes the native's challenge to the colonial world as 'not a treatise on the universal, but the untidy affirmation of an original idea propounded as an absolute.'[65] Drawing upon his experience of the Algerian Revolution, Fanon foresees a cycle of violence;[66] the violent revolutionary ethic and the culture of violence and fear it produces cannot escape the 'misadventures,' to use Sekyi-Otu's translation,[67] of the binary thought of colonialism that nationalist consciousness replicates.

Hence, there is a disconnect between the ideal of liberation Fanon gestures towards and the process of decolonization he describes. Violent revolution will not free the new African state from the influence of imperialism, Fanon observes, and so the 'atmosphere of violence' will continue to dominate national life.[68]

In *The Wretched of the Earth*, Fanon describes the way in which the African peasant's desire for the settler's farm – as opposed to the settler's status – a desire that can only be fulfilled through violence, is appropriated by the African bourgeois class as a desire for status and transformed into a project of nationalization. It is this class that constructs the eviction of the colonizer as a project of a 'national' people. The peasant's desire for self-sufficiency and self-determination is appropriated by the nationalist movement and translated into a mode of imagining a national community. Fanon argues that 'dreams are encouraged, and the imagination is let loose outside the bounds of the colonial order; and sometimes these politicians speak of "We Negroes, we Arabs," and these terms which are so profoundly ambivalent take on during the colonial epoch a sacramental signification.'[69] Despite Fanon's privileging of violence as a cleansing force, the concerns he raises in *The Wretched of the Earth* that the bourgeois class seeks merely to replace foreign rule while maintaining the structures of imperial order are true as much for Africa's violent revolutions as for the 'passive revolutions' conducted by elite classes who won national independence through negotiation.

Indeed, it is this limited construction of national liberation within the boundaries of colonial identity politics and the modern nation-state that seems to account for the expressions of disappointment with the post-colonial state in the years just after independence. Fanon critiques the construction of national liberation as merely the eviction of foreign rule:

> The people who at the beginning of the struggle had adopted the primitive Manicheism of the settler – Blacks and Whites, Arabs and Christians – realize as they go along that it sometimes happens that you get Blacks who are whiter than Whites and that the fact of having a national flag and the hope of an independent nation does not always tempt certain strata of the population to give up their interests or privileges ... This discovery is unpleasant, bitter, and sickening: and yet everything seemed to be so simple before: the bad people were on one side, and the good on the other.[70]

Nationalization, Fanon argues, constitutes the transfer into native hands of the structures of privilege and subjugation of the colonial era rather than the transfer of the whole economy into the service of the 'masses.'[71]

National independence does not equate with the peasant's independence, for instance, in terms of fulfilling the peasant's desire for the settler's land. The struggle to end poverty, hunger, illiteracy, and ignorance, which Fanon argues must be the focus of the struggle – rather than national sovereignty – becomes merely the rallying cry of 'development' for the new national leaders:[72]

> [The bourgeoisie] have come to power in the name of a narrow nationalism and representing a race; they will prove themselves incapable of triumphantly putting into practice a program with even a minimum humanist content, in spite of the fine-sounding declarations which are devoid of meaning since the speakers bandy about in irresponsible fashion phrases that come straight out of European treatises on morals and political philosophy.[73]

Fanon predicts popular dissatisfaction with the national project – or its failure – due to the way in which not just the imagined national community but the nation as a social and political structure is reduced to a question of race.

Fanon argues that peasants and labourers are not so much concerned with placing themselves within a 'black' community or a 'Negro' history, but with ending their material oppression: 'For the Negro who works on a sugar plantation in Le Robert, there is only one solution: to fight. He will embark upon this struggle, and he will pursue it, not as the result of a Marxist or idealistic analysis but quite simply because he cannot conceive of life otherwise than in the form of a battle against exploitation, misery and hunger.'[74] Fanon constructs the self-actualization of the 'native' not as a consequence of (or following) acts of violence perpetrated against the colonizer but *through* these acts. While he presents native rebellion within the framework of the native's desire that the 'last shall be first and the first last,'[75] he represents the native as not seeking to *struggle for life*, but as conceiving of *life as struggle*. The struggle for freedom ruptures the native from his cultural past – a past in which violence was played out in 'symbolic killings' and 'fantastic rides' – and shapes his identity: 'After centuries of unreality, after having wallowed in the most outlandish phantoms, at long last the native, gun in hand, stands face to face with the only forces which contend for his life – the forces of colonialism.'[76] The national community of the colonized does not exist just as a construction of colonial discourses of difference. Nor can national identity be grounded in a pre-colonial 'shared' language, values, or cultural past, as Senghor in his early articulations of *negritude* would have it. Rather, the colonial subject is produced within these relations of power and specifically through the struggle against colonial authority.

Resistance, as opposition to, or struggle against, the settler, therefore, does not constitute the means of *achieving* self-determination for a pre-colonial 'people' or a national community defined by/through colonial knowledge, but the means of *producing* that national community. While Fanon describes this as a predicament that must be overcome in the next stage of decolonization, other anti-colonial critics seem to affirm the nature of the collective as produced through/as struggle against the colonial occupier. Ngugi wa Thiong'o, for instance, constructs Kenyan cultural identity as synonymous with 'resistance.' The history of the 'people' is a history of opposition to (neo)colonialism – Mau Mau insurgency, for instance – rather than an idealized pre-colonial history.[77] Similarly, Amilcar Cabral frames political struggle as a determining factor in the constitution of national identity. Cabral contends that armed struggle is not merely a means of achieving liberation from colonial rule but a central means of constituting the 'nation.' Arguing that armed struggle is necessarily democratic, self-reflective, popular, and constructive, Cabral argues that 'the armed liberation struggle is not only a product of culture but also a *determinant of culture.*'[78] Further, he contends that 'the armed struggle for liberation, in the concrete conditions of life of African peoples, confronted with the imperialist challenge, is an act of insemination upon history – the major expression of our culture and of our African essence. In the moment of victory, *it must be translated into a significant leap forward of the culture of the people* who are liberating themselves.'[79] I will return to this idea of a 'leap forward' throughout the remainder of this chapter.

Constructions of cultural identity and resistance such as this exhibit a paradox: the national community is produced through the act of resistance – the African essence *is* violent struggle against the colonizer – but the logic of resistance nonetheless assumes that this community somehow pre-exists resistance. In other words, the community that the struggle purportedly aims to liberate is a product of that struggle. Benedict Anderson asserts that the imagined community is something that makes possible the willingness of millions to kill and die;[80] in contrast, in the colonial context, the act of killing and dying and the larger framework of resistance as opposition constitute the cultural production of the national community. What are the implications of recognizing how 'national' identity is imagined as a 'return' to an ante-colonial foundation, yet is an act of creating a community, one that is produced through a shared history of subjugation and struggle?

The oppositional nature of such a 'culture of opposition and resistance' reinforces colonial discourse in a similar, but certainly not identical, way as 'nativist' forms of nationalism that have been critiqued by postcolonial theorists. In many ways, postcolonial studies has developed as a project to uncover a history of cultural and material 'resistance' to European colonialism and to not simply deconstruct but humanize a colonized subject constructed as 'primitive,' 'uncivilized,' or 'barbaric' within the colonial project. Most often, acts of what the Subaltern Studies collective (re)describe as peasant insurgency in European colonies were not recognized by the colonists as political acts of rebellion against their rule but as evidence of the 'native's barbarity.' In contrast, anti-colonial thinkers such as Albert Memmi assume that the colonized takes up arms, or rebels, because 'this is the only action that the colonizer understands.'[81] Silenced, debased, and denied in a multitude of other ways, the colonized can seemingly only gain the recognition of the colonizer through combat. Memmi argues: 'After having been rejected for so long by the colonizer, the day has come when it is the colonized who must refuse the colonizer.'[82]

However, like Fanon, Memmi also constructs this act of rejection within a teleological narrative of the colonial experience. While he argues that mimicry precedes revolt,[83] his description of the psychological conditions for revolt suggests that as much as rebellion enacts a breach of colonial order – a re-conception of life outside the terms of imperialism – it may also be regarded as a form of assimilation, or mimicry: 'At the height of his revolt, the colonized still bears the traces and lessons of prolonged cohabitation ... The colonized fights in the name of the very values of the colonizer, uses his techniques of thought and his methods of combat.'[84] Obviously, warfare was not introduced to South Asia and Africa by European colonists. Nonetheless, opposition against the colonizer, in the form of an organized violent struggle that appropriates the methods of colonial authority and seeks the hallmarks of European modernity – sovereignty, property, nationhood, citizenship, rights – rejects the figures of colonial oppression but adopts the principles and practices upon which that oppressive order is based. If the national community for which the struggle takes place is a product of that struggle, the expectations of the anti-colonial national project cannot but be undermined; the nation exists as a 'people' only in so far as it reflects a community in opposition.

Ahmad argues that because no culture is homogeneous and because of the varying axes of privilege and power within any society, 'the totality of an indigenous culture can hardly be posited as a unified, transparent site of anti-imperialist resistance.'[85] Further, the production of culture as shared struggle limits the possibilities for the sort of 'leap forward' towards liberation that Cabral suggests. For instance, Ashis Nandy argues that when a violent and oppressive society with its special brands of victimhood and privilege collapses, 'the psychology of victimhood and privilege continues and produces a second culture which becomes, over time, only a revised edition of the first.'[86] As Fanon acknowledges, it is difficult for a community imagined through oppositional violence to avoid a cycle of violence, repression, and distrust without dramatic cultural and material transformation, or reconciliation. To return to Ashcroft's formulation of resistance as a 'saying no' or negation, if identity is based on a negation, on being against, what sort of liberation is possible? As Albert Memmi describes, liberation requires that the colonized free themselves from the conditions of their struggle.[87] These conditions are both material and discursive. As I will argue in chapters 3 and 4, however, I believe that Gandhi's writings on colonialism, resistance, and justice and the South African reconciliation project reveal how the transformation Fanon and Said identify as 'liberation' is not a step that *follows* the anti-colonial struggle but is, itself, resistance.

Liberation: Transcending Opposition

Guha's contention that the central problematic of the historiography of colonial India is the 'historic failure of the nation to come into its own' constructs the 'nation' as the only, or primary, means of imagining community and liberation. Yet, the nation is an ambivalent sign in discourses of liberation; it signifies a great diversity of sometimes contradictory perspectives and hopes. Liberation, as the 'nation,' signifies at different times and in different contexts liberation *from* foreign rule, capitalist exploitation, economic and technological underdevelopment or poverty, and/or 'primitive' modes of governance. Fanon argues that 'nationalism is not a political doctrine, nor a program,'[88] but the ideological assumption of liberation as nationalism, as fraught and diverse as it may be, imposes a defining framework for analyses of liberation. Within postcolonial discourses, the nation-state is synonymous with both liberation and its deferral. On the eve of India's national independence, Jawaharlal Nehru declared that 'a moment comes, which comes but rarely in history, when we step out from the old to the new, when an age ends, and when the soul of a nation, long suppressed, finds utterance ... The achievement we celebrate today is but a step, an opening of opportunity, to the greater triumphs and achievements that await us.'[89] Achievement of nation status marks a new beginning for India. The nation seemingly provides the possibility for the liberation of the 'Indian mind' from colonial constructions of difference as inferiority, and the liberation of productive forces for the benefit of all. The nation does not fulfil that 'great leap' from resistance to liberation, but it is the space within which this leap is imagined to occur.

What does this leap entail? What is imagined as liberation? Fanon's description of decolonization, like the anti-colonial critiques of many other anti-colonial thinkers, begins by focusing upon the presence of the colonist; the struggle is waged against the oppressive and exploitative practices of colonialism. Yet, liberation seems to allude to the fulfilment or process of a struggle that is much broader. While postcolonial criticism has been concerned primarily with the relationship between the colonizer and the colonized and the methods and discourses of colonial knowledge and authority, the aim of anti-colonial struggle, as Fanon describes it, is the alleviation of material exploitation and the establishment of sovereignty over social and material development. The experience of the post-colonial nation, however, reveals the way in which national identity became conflated with, and a replacement for, the alleviation of poverty; the figure of the European was identified as the source of the problem, rather than structural inequality, namely capitalism.

Critics such as Guha and many of the contemporary critics of postcolonialism I have drawn upon ground their critique of colonialism, and, indeed, postcolonial theory, in an anti-capitalist, if not Marxian, framework. Benita Parry, for instance, counters the charge that anti-colonial resistance was primarily reactive and failed to effect an epistemological break with dominant forms of knowledge by arguing that Marxist-inspired movements imagined liberation as not simply the eviction of foreign rule but the complete destruction of capitalism.[90] While Parry points to Cabral's contention that the goal of the organized anti-colonial movement in Guinea and Cape Verde was the '"destruction of the capitalist structure,"'[91] it is important to recognize that Cabral's work, as much as it was framed within a specifically anti-capitalist ideology, was very much grounded in the modern concepts of progress and development, as is Marxism more generally. Cabral argues that 'the chief goal of the liberation movement goes beyond the achievement of political independence to the superior level of complete liberation of the productive forces and the construction of economic, social and cultural progress of the people.'[92] Similarly, Césaire argues that European colonial occupation of Africa and Asia impeded a 'movement of Europeanization' already in progress: 'The proof is that at present it is the indigenous peoples of Africa and Asia who are demanding schools, and colonialist Europe which refuses them; that it is the African who is asking for ports and roads, and colonialist Europe which is niggardly on this score; that it is the colonized man who wants to move forward, and the colonizer who holds things back.'[93] Césaire claims that pre-colonial African society was not simply ante-capitalist but anti-capitalist: democratic, communal, and cooperative.[94] For Césaire the problem of colonialism is European control, which impedes Africa's 'progress' into modernity.

For Fanon, Cabral, Memmi, Césaire, and, as I will argue in chapters 3 and 4, Gandhian thought and many articulations of the South African struggle as well, anti-colonial liberation is imagined in material terms; or, cultural and national liberation is imbedded in notions of liberation from material domination and exploitation. However, the material aspects of anti-colonial national liberation in the work of such anti-colonial critics as Cabral and Césaire cannot be simplistically separated from the way in which this notion of national liberation is imbedded within European knowledge systems. For critics such as these, while national liberation may be imagined in anti-capitalist terms, it also seems to signify the completion of the unfinished business of (colonial) modernity: freedom, citizenship, formal education, progress, development. The way in which the rhetoric of these values is imbedded in a specifically capitalist culture, however, became quickly evident in the post-colonial 'nation.' Nehru's program of planned development, for instance, while it provided a form of economic progress, was not independent from international economic forces and was neither 'non-coercive' nor 'egalitarian.' As much as such social goals were evident in the rhetoric of resistance of an Indian National Congress, Kwame Nkrumah in Ghana, or a multitude of other anti-colonial movements, parties, and leaders, the transformation from colonial order to anti-capitalist nation, and the revolutionary movement from an anti-colonial movement to a liberation movement, was not easily made. As Hardt and Negri observe, with the establishment of the nation-state, the 'revolutionaries got bogged down in "realism."'[95]

Fanon delineates a multitude of objectives for anti-colonial opposition or resistance. At the most basic level, the native desires to evict the settler from the occupied land and the anti-colonial movement seeks to force an end to colonial rule. A more complete form of liberation, on the other hand, entails 'the total destruction of the colonial system, from the pre-eminence of the language of the oppressor and "departmentalization," to the customs union that in reality maintains the former colonized in the meshes of the culture, of the fashion, and of the images of the colonialist.'[96] While Fanon analyses the construction of colonial identities and mentalities, ultimately, he argues that the overriding concern of the colonized masses is to alleviate hunger, poverty, and ignorance. Rather than simply a counter-discourse of colonial knowledge, nationalism may be seen as a function of this primary desire for an end to poverty as it appears as the only framework through which to imagine an end to colonial exploitation.

However, Fanon argues that simply wresting control of the means of production away from the colonial ruler will not provide the material or psychological liberation the colonized desire. For instance, he contends that newly independent post-colonial nations continue to function within a world economic system dominated by capitalism and the West/North; hence, they are dependent upon foreign investment and the structures of trade organized during the colonial period. Because the economies of Africa, South Asia, and the Caribbean were never fully capitalist themselves, the new post-colonial governments are obliged to maintain the economic relationships created by the colonial regime; having wrested control over the means of production, the post-colonial nation's emergence into modernity is only possible by furthering the exploitative forms of industry and export developed by the colonizer.

In *Black Skin, White Masks*, Fanon argues that the black man must come to consciousness that the apparent dilemma of either 'turning white' or being invisible misrepresents the colonial problem: 'My objective, once his motivations have been brought into consciousness, will be to put him in a position to *choose* action (or passivity) with respect to the real source of the conflict – that is, toward the social structures.'[97] Fanon abstractly calls for the 'restructuring of the world' in that work, but in *The Wretched of the Earth* he begins to imagine what such a restructuring must entail. Where in *Black Skin, White Masks* Fanon is indebted to an individual and psychological framework of analysis that focuses upon agency, will, and consciousness, in *The Wretched of the Earth* he confronts the dominant discourses of struggle, including the framework of Manichean conflict and the narrative of the nation. In this work, the project of decolonization is necessarily transnational, requiring a restructuring of the global economic system in order to redistribute wealth.[98] As a result, the liberation of the post-colonial state cannot be separated from the transformation of international relationships.

Fanon characterizes Europe as 'the creation of the Third World'; its wealth is a product of the resources – diamonds, oil, cotton, wood, human labour – of colonized spaces.[99] Hence, Western projects of development in the Third World cannot be understood as 'aid' or 'charity' but the responsibility of the imperial states to pay a just reparation: 'This help should be the ratification of a double realization: the realization by the colonized peoples that *it is their due*, and the realization by the capitalist powers that in fact *they must pay.*'[100] Reparations, in the form of aid, and as a model of redistributing wealth, do not necessarily effect the sort of radical structural change that Fanon seems to imply, but they do, when understood as reparations rather than charity, require a radical change in the narratives that govern global relationships. Material redistribution in such a model requires recognition not only of the Other as human but also of the history of exploitation and the politics of privilege. Implied in such a redistribution of wealth is the end to the (neo)colonial relationship in which the material resources of Africa and other formerly colonized spaces are no longer produced, distributed, and consumed in a structure of global economic relations that benefit Europe and North America.

Without a fundamental transformation of the way in which Africans and Europeans, for instance, perceive their relationship to one another, not only will pan-Africanist notions of nationalism lead up a 'blind alley' but so too will political formations, including socialism, which wrest control of wealth within the post-colonial economy without transforming the global relationships of industrialism. Fanon argues:

> What [the Third World] expects from those who for centuries have kept it in slavery is that they will help it to rehabilitate mankind, and make man

victorious everywhere, once and for all. But it is clear that we are not so naïve as to think that this will come about with the cooperation and the good will of the European governments. This huge task which consists of reintroducing mankind into the world, the whole of mankind, will be carried out with the indispensable help of the European peoples, who themselves must realize that in the past they have often joined the ranks of our common masters where colonial questions were concerned. To achieve this, the European peoples must first decide to wake up and shake themselves, use their brains, and stop playing the stupid game of Sleeping Beauty.[101]

Significantly, Fanon is not simply discussing economic redress in this passage. Rather, he is arguing that the material inequalities of the world system must be acknowledged as a cultural phenomenon as well, which requires the fundamental transformation of human relationships, both materially and discursively. Decolonization requires the redistribution of wealth, if not structural changes to the global economy; yet, this argument for material transformation cannot be articulated without appealing to the requirement of recognizing the Other as human, in a way that is much different than the sorts of vindicationist narratives Scott critiques, in which the rhetoric of humanism becomes a form of oppression compelling the native to desire a recognition from the colonizer that can never be achieved.

In the conclusion to *Black Skin, White Masks*, Fanon positions himself in the present looking towards the future. He argues, for instance, that the fact of ancient African civilizations provides no solace to contemporary child labourers in Martinique or Guadeloupe. As a man of colour, he declares that he wishes only that 'the enslavement of man by man cease forever ... That it be possible for me to discover and to love man, wherever he may be. The Negro is not. Any more than the white man.'[102] Bill Ashcroft argues that Fanon's contention 'I am my own foundation' in this concluding passage is the proclamation of an 'almost Cartesian agency for the colonized subject.'[103] However, as much as Fanon is indebted to modern conceptions of the universal (European) individual, the subjectivity of this 'new man' is constituted in connection with others; Fanon concludes *Black Skin, White Masks* with the question: 'Was my freedom not given to me then in order to build the world of the *You*?'[104] The conciliatory tone and future-oriented recognition of the need for a new human bond among all peoples – that is not the fulfilment of European notions of humanism – contrasts starkly with

Fanon's description of revolutionary decolonization in *The Wretched of the Earth*. However, Fanon concludes this later work with similar assertions of the need for a 'new man'; his demand for reparations does not indicate a sense of blame, which he argues against in *Black Skin, White Masks*, but a development in his thought, which recognizes the material aspects of this 'new humanism'; Fanon's conceptualization of a new humanism is a call for material and cultural reconciliation.

Fanon's conciliatory rhetoric and construction of liberation as the fundamental transformation of human relationships is not recuperable within colonial discourse theory and is excised from treatments of his work that postulate resistance as necessarily oppositional. Further, the 'new humanism' of Fanon's *The Wretched of the Earth* functions as little more than an afterthought. After providing a detailed narrative of the development of revolutionary movements and the nature of nationalism, Fanon concludes with an abstract rhetoric of a revolutionary change in consciousness:

> Come, then, comrades, the European game has finally ended; we must find something different. We today can do everything ... so long as we are not obsessed by the desire to catch up with Europe ... When I search for Man in the technique and style of Europe, I see only a succession of negations of man, and an avalanche of murders ... Let us decide not to imitate Europe ... Let us try to create the whole man, whom Europe has been incapable of bringing to triumphant birth.[105]

In contrast to his description in *Black Skin, White Masks* of the way in which the colonized man desires to be a 'man among other men,'[106] where the implicit norm of those 'other men' is the European, this 'new man' Fanon imagines is based upon the rhetorical negation of modern European values and structures, including its 'states, institutions, and societies.'[107] However, this new humanism, like Gandhi's demand for citizenship rights in South Africa, nonetheless derives from the recognition of Europe's failure to perform its own ideals.

Fanon contends that the 'native laughs in mockery when Western values are mentioned in front of him';[108] yet, 'all the elements of a solution to the great problems of humanity have, at different times, existed in European thought. But the action of European men has not carried out the mission which fell to them.'[109] Fanon appropriates the rhetoric of European humanism, a humanism expressed as an idea but performed in such a way as to legitimize or rationalize the violence of the colonial project. Fanon takes this rhetoric and applies it to an argument for a form of post-colonial 'development' that seems to be as much social as economic, and which is not confined to European models or the desire to 'catch up' with Europe. This call for a revolution in consciousness as a negation of Europe in terms of its history of oppression seems to transcend the oppositional binary of the Manichean colonial relationship he describes: 'For Europe, for ourselves, and for humanity, comrades, we must turn over a new leaf, we must work out new concepts, and try to set afoot a new man.'[110] Fanon contends that 'the real *leap* consists in introducing invention into existence,'[111] a notion that, as I noted in the Introduction, Paul Gilroy has recently tried to recuperate. The sort of 'new humanism' Fanon imagines seems impossible within a climate of revolution based on the 'implacable enmity' of Manichean notions of identity – the desire and political mandate to destroy the colonizing Other.

Edward Said takes up Fanon's gestures towards an ideal of liberation that enacts the values of humanism in the form of economic and political relationships within post-colonial states and between post-colonial peoples and the colonial powers. Fanon's conception of liberation as a revolution in social consciousness provides the basis for Said's discussion of the way in which a 'rhetoric and politics of blame' constrains the vision of both public intellectuals and cultural historians. Said writes: 'If I have so often cited Fanon, it is because more dramatically and decisively than anyone, I believe, he expresses the immense cultural shift from the terrain of nationalist independence to the theoretical domain of liberation.'[112] Said posits his desire to formulate an alternative to both a politics of blame and a politics of confrontation and hostility as a central objective of his work. Arguing that the world is 'too small and interdependent' to allow the 'hostility between Western and non-Western cultures that leads to crises' to continue,[113] he seeks to apply Fanon's construction of liberation as a transformation of social consciousness to global conflicts in the post-colonial era.

Said praises Fanon's *Wretched of the Earth* for the way it represents colonialism and nationalism in their Manichean context, describes the anti-colonial independence movement that develops within this framework, and 'transfigures that movement into what is in effect a trans-personal and trans-national force.'[114] He argues that Fanon foresaw that unless 'national consciousness at its moment of success was *somehow changed* into a social consciousness, the future would hold not liberation but an extension of imperialism.'[115] I read Fanon's call for a 'new humanism' as confined by the theoretical domain within which it is constructed, and therefore outside, or in juxtaposition with, the quasi-historical description of an anti-colonial teleology of revolution described in *The Wretched of the Earth*. Similarly, I read in Said's recuperation of Fanon's appeal to a new humanism a tension between his project of illuminating and challenging the binary discourse of imperial relations of power and his interest in taking sides in an ongoing struggle for emancipation, whether in terms of the Palestinian struggle or a more global human liberation. To identify such a tension is not to claim a fundamental contradiction or flaw in Said's analysis but rather to identify a debilitating tension in the ideal of an anti-imperial humanism. Like Fanon and Césaire, Said posits liberation as a global human community, yet he depends upon an oppositional framework for imagining social transformation. As a result, like Fanon, Said seems ever only able to gesture towards an ideal of transnational understanding and connection.

Said interprets Fanon's concept of liberation as a 'process' or a way of being, rather than a goal or achievement: 'In the obscurity and difficulty of Fanon's prose, there are enough poetic and visionary suggestions to make the case for liberation as a *process* and not as a goal contained automatically by the newly independent nations ... Fanon wants to somehow bind the European as well as the native together in a new non-adversarial community of awareness and anti-imperialism.'[116] Said, here, identifies an ethical demand of emancipation: the demand to know, and relate to, the other, rather than the assertion of a national identity, which necessarily relies upon a politics of exclusion. Placing his engagement with Fanon's notion of a new humanism in the moment in which he wrote, Said argues for a more responsible way of engaging with the other:

> What is now before us nationally, and in the full imperial panorama, is the deep, the profoundly perturbed and perturbing question of our relationship to others – other cultures, other states, other histories, other experiences, traditions, peoples, destinies. The difficulty with the question is that there is no vantage *outside* the actuality of relationships between cultures, between unequal imperial and non-imperial powers, between different Others, a vantage that might allow one the epistemological privilege of somehow judging, evaluating, and interpreting free of the encumbering interests, emotions, and engagements of the ongoing relationships themselves.[117]

As Robert Young points out, however, Said's concern with 'how the other can be articulated as such' remains unfulfilled.[118]

For instance, in *Culture and Imperialism,* in which Said seeks to redress the way *Orientalism* not only failed to acknowledge resistance but to foreclose its possibility, he is much more concerned with identifying the relationship between imperial knowledge and power. While he is careful to define the concepts of 'culture,' 'colonialism,' and 'imperialism,' the concepts of 'resistance,' 'national liberation,' and 'liberation' are not specifically defined. He posits Fanon's 'new humanism' as (unfulfilled) liberation. Yet, he nonetheless refers to anti-colonial nationalist movements that lead to independent nation-states as 'successful Third World liberation movements.'[119] Similarly, despite his recognition of Fanon's articulation of liberation as a process, he uncritically reproduces Fanon's theory of decolonization as a series of stages. Said's characterization of the European and the native 'somehow' becoming bound together and national consciousness 'somehow' being transformed into a post-national social consciousness reveals the way in which the concept is limited by the 'theoretical domain' in which it is articulated. So, while he acknowledges Fanon's desire to imagine liberation as a transpersonal and transnational force, he does not work through Fanon's narrative to contend with just how the movement for national independence will, or can, be transfigured in this way.

There is a tension, then, between the essential antagonism of the anti-colonial nationalist movement and the production of a 'non-adversarial community' in the *process* of liberation. Though he critiques the binary construction of colonial knowledge elsewhere, his recuperation of Fanon's work on liberation retains the adversarial conflict between settler and native that, as I have argued above, Fanon seems to problematize. Such a discourse of resistance elides the complex problematic of power revealed in a text such as *Nervous Conditions*. Similarly, this tension is particularly evident when we read *Orientalism* or *Culture and Imperialism* against his analysis of the Palestinian struggle. Said's writings on the Israel-Palestine conflict have an immediacy of production (columns in weeklies such as *Al-Ahram, Al-Hayat, The Nation*) and a political investment or personal urgency that his analyses of the (historical) imperial project cannot. He is unable or unwilling to reconcile the demand for the dismantling of binary discourses of identity with the seeming necessity of such discourses within liberation struggles.

Sylvia Wynter argues that a new conception of freedom must move us beyond 'Man's "freedom-package," but also beyond those of Man's oppositional sub-versions, – that of Marxism's *proletariat*, that of feminism's *woman* (gender rights), and that of our multiple multiculturalisms and/or centric cultural nationalisms (minority rights), to that of gay liberation (homosexual rights), but also as a conception of freedom able to draw them all together in a new synthesis.'[120] She maintains that liberation will have to account not just for the way in which post-Enlightenment humanism constructs 'man' as superior to an 'other,' but for the production of gendered and sexualized subjectivities, as well as other forms of 'identity' that cannot be confined to the imperial/nationalist binary. Fanon's and Said's ideal of liberation implicitly seeks to overcome such binaries. Yet, as much as they gesture towards the redress of material inequality, they fail to account in any substantive way for subjectivities produced within other registers of power. The parties to liberation cannot be limited to the 'native' and the 'European.'

Further, Said's construction of resistance or decolonization as a narrative of stages fails to explore the implications of understanding liberation as a process, something I attempt to do in the second half of this book. As Anne McClintock argues, the term 'post-colonial' is 'haunted by the very figure of linear "development" that it sets out to dismantle.'[121] Significantly, while Ngugi characterizes imperialism as occurring in two stages, colonialism and neo-colonialism, he argues that national culture does not evolve in a mechanical process of steps and springs; rather, 'the processes are often evolving more or less simultaneously with one process generating several others at the same time.'[122] For Said, in contrast, at least in his more theoretical writings, this process is constructed as a linear progression towards an amorphous end. The nature of the relationship between political, material, and cultural forms of communal autonomy and identity is central to the sorts of problems postcolonialism seems to have in moving from deconstruction of imperial ideology to analysis of resistance and liberation.

The idea of liberation that Said constructs through Fanon's work is contingent upon the violence that precedes it. Noting that Fanon recognizes the nationalist phase of decolonization as crucial, yet insufficient, Said contends that 'out of this paradox comes the idea of liberation, a strong new post-nationalist theme that had been implicit in the works of ... Cabral, and Du Bois, for instance, but required the propulsive infusion of theory and even of armed, insurrectionary militancy to bring it forward clearly.'[123] Citing Fanon's assertion that 'the violence of the colonial regime and counter-violence of the native balance each other and respond to each other in an extraordinary reciprocal homogeneity,'[124] Said ambivalently argues that liberation will not be won through armed insurrection. Ignoring Fanon's own acknowledgment of the way in which violence and counter-violence create a permanent cycle, Said argues that violence is necessary to reveal the fact that 'the struggle must be lifted to a new level of contest, a synthesis represented by a war of liberation, for which an entirely new post-national theoretical culture is required.'[125] Said seeks to intervene in the 'rhetoric and politics of blame' that seems to constrain political thought and cultural critique by developing Fanon's vision of a non-antagonist relationship replacing colonialism and nationalism. In doing so, however, he seems to disregard the way in which Fanon constructs this 'new humanism' in relation to the necessity for material forms of compensation and cooperation; global harmony among humans and the eradication of hunger, ignorance, and poverty are reciprocal processes. While Said argues that the message of Fanon, Ngugi, or Achebe is that 'we must all write our histories and cultures rescriptively in a new way,'[126] he does not challenge the narrative Fanon constructs of colonial authority and anti-colonial resistance by interrogating the 'somehow' of liberation. Rather than expand the 'material proposed for attention and controversy by public intellectuals and cultural historians,'[127] Said problematically relies upon Fanon's narrative of revolution and call for liberation without interrogating the 'horizons that constrain and enable' Fanon's speech, horizons that Sekyi-Otu argues Fanon self-reflexively acknowledges in his work.[128]

In *Humanism and Democratic Criticism* (2004), Said acknowledges the way in which his language of freedom relies upon, but apparently undermines, invocations of freedom and democracy within the dominant American political discourse. Resigned to having no other language than the language of human rights and democracy that the Western powers use to justify the war in Afghanistan or Iraq, Said argues for the necessity of using that same language to 'recapture the subject, reclaim it, and reconnect it to the tremendously complicated realities these vastly overprivileged antagonists of mine have simplified, betrayed, and either diminished or dissolved.'[129] As I have been arguing, to reclaim this language in a way that connects it to these complicated realities requires its transformation; as Fanon argues, the narrative of 'good' vs. 'evil' and the rhetoric of humanism are simplistic and hence misrepresent the experience of power. Said contends that contemporary problems of domination, exploitation, inequalities between the North and South, environmental degradation, and fractious identity politics 'require new ways of thinking that can't be served and can't be advanced by the polemical and oppositional models of the past. That's what I was interested in very much ... In other words, modes of reconciliation where you can reconcile (without reducing) histories.'[130]

Yet, the notion of liberation Said identifies in the work of anti-colonial intellectuals is recognized as only a deferral or dream. He contends that Fanon's oeuvre is a *response* to theoretical elaborations produced by the culture of Western capitalism, and the aim of his work is to 'invent new souls.'[131] For the sort of liberation Fanon or Said imagine, however, must 'new souls' be invented? As I will argue in the next two chapters, there exists in the history of (neo)colonialism not just examples of subversions and interpolations of colonial culture but values and concepts of 'resistance' that reveal the way in which aspects of Fanon's 'new humanism' have been articulated as political praxis. Said was not unaware of such alternatives. For instance, as a lesson for the Palestinian struggle, he appeals to the anti-apartheid struggle not as a movement *against* a white Other or even the system of apartheid 'but as a means "for all of us to assert our common humanity."'[132] Such alternatives, however, were largely left undeveloped in his work and were confined to his political writing, rather than his critical and theoretical works. He contends that Fanon's failure to offer a 'prescription for making a transition after decolonization to a period when a new political order achieves moral hegemony is symptomatic of the difficulty that millions of people live with today.'[133] I would argue, in contrast, that the failure to imagine this transition is symptomatic of the impossibility of the oppositional paradigm and narratives of revolution to foster the sorts of relationships among humans Fanon, Said, or E. San Juan, Jr, among others, imagine as liberation.

3 Gandhism and Resistance: Transforming India

Gandhism and Postcolonial Studies

Mohandas Gandhi and the practical implementation of his ethic of non-violence had a profound role in unifying the peoples of India in the struggle for independence. As Partha Chatterjee contends, Gandhian ideology had a monumental historical impact on the evolution of Indian politics, indeed providing the 'ideological basis for including the whole people within the political nation.'[1] Similarly, Aijaz Ahmad notes that 'few political leaders anywhere in the modern world have commanded such hegemonic power over the social visions and even the spiritual life of so many people, as did Gandhi alone.'[2] Of course, Gandhi, the political leader, or this Gandhian ideology were by no means the sole inspiration for, or overriding foundation of, 'resistance' to British colonial rule. Indeed, the distinction between the struggle for 'independence' – and specifically the Gandhian influence on that struggle – and the form this independence ultimately took is an important one. In many ways, by the 1940s Gandhi was seen as a threat to the establishment of an independent Muslim state and as an obstacle to the achievement of the modern secular Indian nation envisioned by Nehru and others in the Congress Party. Gandhi refused to attend Indian independence celebrations on 15 August 1947 in protest not only of the partition creating India and Pakistan – and the horrific violence of partition – but also of the form of modern nationalism the Indian state sought to mimic. The fact that he was given a state funeral with military honours reveals the way in which Gandhi had become a cultural symbol for Indian nationalism rather than a moral and political 'leader' for the dominant political culture in the newly established state.

Despite the widespread acknowledgment of Gandhi's influential role in the Indian independence movement, and his status as one of the most significant social and political thinkers of the twentieth century, the significance of Gandhi and Gandhism have only recently begun to be more widely addressed, apart from the work of a few postcolonial theorists such as Chatterjee, and Ashis Nandy.[3] In this chapter, I seek to build upon the work of these few critics to argue for the way in which what Gandhi called his 'experiments with truth' – and particularly the concepts of *swaraj* ('self-government'), *sarvadoya* ('the welfare of all'), *ahimsa* (nonviolence), and *satyagraha* ('truth-force'), which guided and were the subject of those experiments – provide insight into ways in which resistance can be imagined and articulated alternatively to the dominant theories of resistance within postcolonial studies.

Partha Chatterjee's essay 'Gandhi and the Critique of Civil Society' was one of the first, and the few, attempts to contextualize and analyse Gandhi's critique of modernity and his theorization of *satyagraha* within a postcolonial framework. In the early work of the Subaltern Studies group, Gandhi figured in so far as he, as a figure of the independence movement, and his ideals were understood and used by the South Asian peasantry. For instance, drawing upon colonial documents that record, 'with astonishment,' the currency of the name 'Gandhi' in the most remote villages, Gyanendra Pandey describes the way in which Gandhi attained a mythical stature as a symbol of opposition to colonial rule for Indian peasants.[4] While rumours of Gandhi's supernatural powers circulated throughout rural South Asia, declarations of local leaders often appropriated the 'supreme status' of Gandhi's word. Rather than Gandhi's ideology of resistance – in the form of *ahimsa* and *satyagraha* – Pandey argues that British authority in rural areas was subverted more by Gandhi's stature as a symbol of resistance within peasant consciousness.[5] Analyses such as Pandey's reveal the way in which Gandhi, his ideology, and the political demands and expectations articulated by the Congress leader were subject to interpretation, transformation, and appropriation by local communities.[6]

Subaltern Studies contributors such as Chatterjee and Guha have focused more on the influence of Gandhi on Indian politics, specifically constructing his work as a tool of bourgeois nationalist aspirations. Chatterjee argues that Gandhian thought presented itself as 'a nationalism which stood upon a critique of the very idea of civil society, a movement supported by the bourgeoisie which rejected the idea of progress, [and] the ideology of a political organization fighting for the creation of a modern national state which accepted at the same time the ideal of an "enlightened anarchy."'[7] Gandhi reconciled these contradictions in his theory of *swaraj*, but most members of the leadership of Congress were neither willing nor able to seek to undo their privilege in this way; similarly, as Muhammad Iqbal would learn with the establishment of the state of Pakistan, the emergent framework of post-colonial global order would not allow for alternatives to the nation-state, as modes of post-colonial existence or community.[8] Chatterjee contends that the 'message of the Mahatma' superseded the demands of the 'people,' allowing for the movement to be appropriated by the Congress elite into the structural forms of a bourgeois and ultimately constitutional order. He characterizes the era of Gandhi's prominence in Congress – the 1920s and 1930s – as a 'moment of manoeuvre' that was appropriated and shaped by nationalist capitalist ideology, or the Nehruvian 'moment of arrival.' This is a significant critique of the historical development of the Indian nation-state, and Gandhi's role in it, in so far as it recognizes the limits of Gandhian thought and political praxis to overcome the ideological and structural dominance of a nationalist elite working against, but within, colonial structures of social and political power, as well as constructions of communal identities. While it is Gandhi who is often figured as the hero of Indian independence, the Indian nation and state, and the independence they appear to enact, bare little resemblance to the ideal of *swaraj* that Gandhi imagined.

As other Subaltern Studies contributors have shown, the 'Gandhi' of peasant consciousness primarily functioned through the cultural imaginary of the 'Mahatma.' The production of Gandhi as 'Mahatma' in both peasant and nationalist consciousness is revealed in much 'Gandhian literature,' in which Gandhi becomes primarily a figure through which resistance is articulated, rather than a 'leader' of that resistance or a visionary or guide. Raja Rao's *Kanthapura* (1938), for instance, provides a narrative of Gandhi as a mythologized figure, which complements the representation of Gandhi by contributors to *Subaltern Studies* but also provides a counter-narrative of the function of Gandhi and Gandhism in peasant communities. While Gandhi's ideals – from his challenge to the caste system, to his endeavours to empower women and transform gender roles, to his concern for the dignity of labour and the eradication of exploitative labour practices – are central to the novel's narrative, Gandhi, the Congress leader, is peripheral. Indeed, Rao frames the novel as a story 'from the contemporary annals of a village.'⁹ The stories the villagers tell of the 'Mahatma,' as Rao describes, 'mingle' with 'legendary history' and the present moment providing the context for a tale of social and cultural upheaval. *Kanthapura* is not so much a story about the struggle for an end to foreign rule and/ as the production of the Indian 'nation,' but the transformation of Indian communities; it reveals the way in which Gandhian-inspired constructive programs and non-cooperation campaigns troubled the social fabric of so-called Indian traditions as much as they did colonial power. Rao's representation of the performance of, and engagement with, Gandhism in a complex social, political, and cultural context provides a stark contrast to the way in which Gandhism has often been represented within postcolonial studies.

Though Gandhi and Gandhism have received intense critical analyses from scholars outside postcolonial studies, particularly in India, Gandhi's writings do not lend themselves to scholarly analysis as easily as does the work of other intellectuals of the period, such as Fanon, though as I noted in chapter 2, Ato Sekyi-Otu convincingly argues for the way in which contemporary postcolonial critics problematically produce a prescriptive theory for violent revolution in Fanon's work. The majority of Gandhi's writings – compiled in *The Collected Works of Mahatma Gandhi* (1958), which consists of one hundred volumes totalling more than fifty thousand pages – were produced for a mass audience in his weekly newspapers *Indian Opinion, Navajivan* (*Young India*), and *Harijan*. These essays, speech transcripts, accounts of events, and responses to readers are marked by their specific contexts and immediacy, and by the way in which journalism, philosophy, and spiritualism are intermixed. The production and reception of Gandhian thought – his writings on *ahimsa*, vegetarianism, *sarvadoya*, etc. – therefore, constitute a significant aspect of the dailyness of the Indian independence movement, and not just theories of social change. As David Hardiman argues, Gandhi's style of writing is dialogic rather than monologic;[10] his ideas are presented against, or in response to, the assertions of others. Because of this dialogic method, Gandhi's work does not formulate a coherent theory of power and resistance; his analyses and perspectives change throughout his life because he is willing to place them under scrutiny.

As I argue in chapter 2, Fanon's concern for issues of poverty and structures of material inequality has not been as recuperable for postcolonial theory as his analysis of colonial identities, his critique of nationalism, and his analysis of the violence of colonialism and anti-colonialism. Similarly, Gandhi and Gandhism has only been recuperable within the parameters of the colonial discourse postcolonialism purports to interrogate and deconstruct. For instance, Gandhi's critique of technology and capitalist labour relations, and the idiom of Indian history he draws upon to construct this critique, has been interpreted as reinforcing the colonial modern/tradition binary and characterized as an essentializing nativism.[11] As Leela Gandhi argues, however, 'postcolonialism fails to recognize ... that what counts as "marginal" in relation to the West has often been central and foundational in the non-West ... Postcolonialism continues to render non-Western knowledge and culture as "other" in relation to the normative "self" of Western epistemology and rationality.'[12] The Gandhism I trace in this chapter is inconsistent with some of the key assumptions of postcolonial studies as it has developed within the Euro-American academy. In particular, Gandhi's notion of Indian liberation required a broad social, cultural, and material transformation of South Asian society, which goes well beyond the rather narrow parameters of specifically colonial power, authority, and identity politics.

Anti-colonial nationalist thinkers such as Césaire and Senghor critiqued the hypocrisy of European humanism in the exercise of colonial authority; however, their critiques relied upon the affirmation of modern ideals, specifically those related to material progress. In his articulation of a revised *negritude*, for instance, Senghor argues that decolonization requires the elimination of the flaws of colonial rule 'while preserving its positive contributions, such as the economic and technical infrastructure and the teaching of the French language.'[13] In *Empire*, Hardt and Negri argue that it was only at the moment of national independence – the apparent emergence of the colonized state into modernity – that the libratory forces of the 'subordinated' countries 'recognized that *the primary task is not getting into but getting out of modernity.*'[14] Similarly, noting how the proponents of decolonization attacked imperialism rather than modernity (or Europeanization), Simon Gikandi suggests that in the post-colonial era, the task becomes the critique of modernity and its dominant categories.[15] In Gandhi's analysis, modernity was the focus of critique, rather than colonialism.

One of the few critics to study Gandhi from a postcolonial perspective in any substantive way, Chatterjee contends that Gandhi was 'unhampered by the formal theoretical requirements of scientific disciplines and philosophical schools';[16] his thought was shaped by his cultural upbringing, including Hindu traditions and teachings, but also

Western epistemologies – philosophical, political, and religious – acquired through his British education. Breaking with the assumptions of post-Enlightenment reason, Gandhi's political praxis cannot be separated from spirituality and morality. As Nandy argues, 'Gandhi's politics involved the defiance of not merely authorities but of authoritative myths; ... unlike the liberal and socialist thinkers, Gandhi sought to break down the norms and the shared assumptions of a culture assiduously built up by the Western society over the previous three centuries.'[17] As a result, Gandhi is a mediated figure, and a fraught one; despite his production as an iconic figure and national leader in Indian history, in his own lifetime his message was mediated by the religious idioms of local communities, and, as Chatterjee describes, his ability to cultivate a 'national' movement that brought together a wide array of actors across caste, religious, gender, and class boundaries was co-opted by the secular nationalist movement. Further, Gandhi's analysis of relations of inequality in India and his 'experiments' (both practical and philosophical) with approaches to challenging and transforming these structures prefigure the poststructural and postcolonial theoretical critique of modernity, and particularly the modern/European notions of power, nation, sovereignty, progress, and reason.

In chapter 1, I focused on Gandhi's actions – his performance of resistance in South Africa – and I argued for the way in which these actions disrupted colonial power yet also revealed the way in which Gandhi was, to borrow David Scott's term, a 'conscript of modernity.' During his time in South Africa, however, Gandhi's understanding of colonial power shifted quite dramatically, from an emphasis on the power and authority of the colonist and the desire for political rights within the colonial state to a critique of the ideological framework of colonialism as a manifestation of European post-Enlightenment reason. From concerns with race, rights, and vindication, as well as the laws, leaders, and figures of British colonialism, Gandhi turned his attention towards the ideological and structural experience of modernity. Of course, as the Gandhi-Irwin Pact of the 1931 Second Round Table Conference reveals, despite his altered analysis, he continued to privilege political negotiation, often making agreements that appear contrary to his ideals. In this chapter I focus on Gandhi's critique of power and his theories of nonviolence and social change in a way that seeks to contextualize his analysis in the political events in which these ideas developed, in part to disable or destabilize 'Gandhi' as epic revolutionary hero, while also engaging with, and utilizing, his analysis of power and subjectivity, and his ethic of resistance. By doing so, I seek to illuminate an alternative to the dominant approaches to power and resistance within postcolonial studies. Gandhi was, indeed, a political figure, and one who at times acted in ways that are inconsistent with his analysis of power and his vision of liberation. Gandhi's approach to the oppressive system of 'untouchability' and his notion of 'trusteeship,' for instance, reveal ways in which Gandhi had difficulty translating his analysis of power and his ethic of social change into political praxis.

However, I turn to the social and political thought of Gandhi because he argued many decades before the 'flag independence' of the former British colonies that true liberation constituted an alternative to the modern/Western nation-state and not its attainment; his critique was not limited to colonialism but included the dominant categories of modern European thought as well as indigenous modes of inequality and oppression. Gandhi's critique of Indian nationalism and his conceptualization of *swaraj*, or self-rule, and notion of *sarvadoya* provide valuable alternatives to the dominant materialist postcolonial analyses, which tend to narrowly equate modernity with capitalism, or to the discursive theories of postcolonialism, which tend to elide material relations of power altogether. While postcolonial theory has been preoccupied with the deconstruction of the Manichean relationship between the colonizer and the colonized, by focusing on 'modern civilization' as the system of domination to which the peoples of India are subject, and significantly, participate, rather than colonialism, Gandhi provides an anticipatory discourse of transformation.

Swaraj: From Decolonization to De-modernization

Gandhi became a prominent participant in the Indian independence movement in earnest with the publication of *Hind Swaraj* (or *Indian Home Rule*) in 1909/10. Banned in British India in March of 1910, *Hind Swaraj* critiques Indian aspirations for self-government through a polemical denunciation of modern Western civilization. Directed at 'moderates,' based largely in London, who seek the attainment of Indian self-government through constitutional means, and 'extremists,' who seek a violent overthrow of the British colonial regime, Gandhi critiques the ideological limitations of Indian nationalist consciousness. Specifically, he argues that *swaraj*, as it circulates within these anti-colonial discourses, defines what Indian nationalists are against, but not what they are for; *swaraj* is the common goal, but its meaning is ambiguous. As a result, Gandhi interprets the agenda of both the 'moderates' and 'extremists' as seeking merely 'English rule without the Englishman': 'You want the tiger's nature, but not the tiger; that is to say, you would make India English, and, when it becomes English, it will be called not Hindustan but Englistan. This is not the Swaraj that I want.'[18] Prefiguring Fanon's assertion that the colonized sought only to take the place of the colonizer, without altering the structure of the system, Gandhi argues that the dominant political notion of *swaraj*, or 'home rule,' implicitly assumed an Indian nation in distinctly modern social, economic, and political terms. *Hind Swaraj*, therefore, takes the form of an appeal to Gandhi's 'countrymen' to recognize that by concentrating their efforts on battling the English colonist rather than challenging the ideology upon which colonialism is based, they are following a 'suicidal policy.'[19] Gandhi argues that political independence will not end 'foreign' rule; while national independence may change the faces of power, the mentality of those with authority will not change, and it is this 'mentality,' India's 'mentality,' for which the struggle takes place.

The book appears to present a simplistic critique of colonial authority and European modernity through appeals to an idyllic, even Orientalist, pre-industrial past. Yet, as Anshuman Mondal argues, Gandhi deconstructs the binarisms of antiquity/modernity, tradition/innovation, and spiritualism/materialism upon which the book appears to depend.[20] *Hind Swaraj* takes the form of a dialogue between Gandhi and a composite Indian 'nationalist.' While the form echoes Western antecedents such as Plato's *Dialogues of Socrates*, Gandhi writes in the preface to the English edition that had he 'written for English readers in the first instance, the subject would have been handled in a different manner.'[21] Aimed specifically at an audience of the Indian elite, *Hind Swaraj* is a polemic against the ideological basis of the dominant Indian nationalist discourse of the time. Gandhi's critique of colonialism, modernity, and nationalism, however, was reconsidered and rearticulated throughout his life within a model of 'experimentation' that collapses the binary of scientific reason and spiritual faith.

In *Hind Swaraj*, Gandhi begins to articulate two interrelated ideas that I believe are crucial to an understanding of Gandhian resistance and that provide an alternative to both materialist and discursive postcolonial constructions of power. First, Gandhi reframes the debate over Indian independence from the presence/dominance of the colonist to the oppressive economic, political, and cultural structures of modern civilization. Second, premised on the idea that India can never be 'emancipated' simply through the eviction of the figures of colonial power, Gandhi imagines *swaraj* as a non-teleological expression of cultural, political, and economic transformation. Liberation is constructed as the transformation of the structures that shape social *relationships*. In Rao's *Kanthapura*, the story of the Indian independence struggle is articulated in the terms of a small community, the religious framework of the predominantly Hindu locale interwoven with a narrative of social transformation. The Gandhian Moorthy returns to his village to share Gandhi's teaching, and to do so, he translates them into the idiom of the community in a way that necessarily transforms both the idiom and the teachings: '"Siva is three-eyed," he says, "and Swaraj too is three-eyed: Self-purification, Hindu-Moslem unity, Khaddar."'[22] *Swaraj* constitutes not only political self-rule, but cultural and material transformation. For critics of postcolonialism's preoccupation with identity and discourse, colonialism can only be understood within the framework, and as a manifestation, of the globalization of capitalism. Aijaz Ahmad, for instance, suggests that 'we should speak not so much of colonialism or postcolonialism but of capitalist modernity which takes the colonial form in particular places and particular times.'[23] In many ways, Gandhi's critique of colonialism is consistent with such a perspective; yet, Gandhi is concerned with how social relationships are embedded within or legitimized through 'modern' values and cosmology. Further, Gandhi's critique of colonial authority and knowledge production emphasizes the exploitative political economy of imperialism (as the spread of a particular economic framework). His critique of modern civilization is, as Partha Chatterjee argues, a 'fundamental critique of the entire edifice of bourgeois society,' including its presumptions of continuous expansion, individual property, the 'free' market, and representative democracy.[24]

Gandhi seeks to persuade Indian nationalists, both 'moderates' and 'extremists' alike, that their opposition to British colonialism depends upon and reproduces the notion of civilization, which the British claim as the colonial project. In a letter to a friend that accompanies a draft of *Hind Swaraj*, Gandhi claims that he is concerned with arguing that the conflict manifested as Indian nationalism is not a conflict between East and West. Rather, Indian nationalism should be understood as providing an alternative to modern civilization, which oppresses Indians and the English alike.[25] Rather than British colonialism, Gandhi argues that Indians must resist Western notions of modernity and civilization. While he acknowledges that there are 'administrators' of colonialism, these administrators are not the 'enemy' and they are not responsible for the structure; indeed, the system produces these 'creatures of circumstances,' both European and Indian: 'It would be cowardly for three hundred million people to seek to destroy the three hundred authors or administrators of the system ... The purest man entering the system will be affected by it and will be instrumental in propagating the evil.'[26] Unlike the Manichean framework of Fanon's description of anti-colonial revolution, Gandhian thought does not conceive of liberation as possible through the destruction or displacement of an 'Other.' While such a framework appears to elide human responsibility for the violence of economic exploitation, poverty, and authoritarianism, as I will argue below, the Gandhian praxis of *ahimsa*, or nonviolence, depends upon an assumption of the responsibilities of both those who benefit from the colonial manifestation of modern civilization and those who are impoverished by it.

In *Hind Swaraj*, Gandhi provides an emotive critique of industrialization as a primary manifestation of modern civilization. His critique of the exploitative economic relations of colonialism shares much with that of Fanon, in terms of the way they each identify the contradiction between the colonial rhetoric of humanism and the distinctly unequal relations of power narrativized as progress. Gandhi's critique of Indian (bourgeois) nationalism, however, is distinct from Fanon's in its emphasis upon the critique of European modernity as a method of justifying the structural violence of colonialism and modern industrial social relations, whether they be capitalist or socialist. Gandhi's critique of modern civilization is articulated in both social and ethical terms, primarily in the way in which he argues that the ethic of materialism, which underwrites industrialization, not simply exploits and impoverishes but alienates; it is not simply colonialism that constructs identity but the modern social relations of which it is a part.

For Gandhi, modern technological progress and the ethic of material acquisition, and not simply colonialism, require the dehumanization of the subject. He writes: 'Formerly, men were made slaves under physical compulsion, now they are enslaved by temptation of money and of the luxuries that money can buy.'[27] In a 1916 speech to a college economics society, he argues that material affluence leads to moral degeneracy and characterizes materialism as a 'disease.'[28] Further, machinery in particular, Gandhi argues, had begun to 'desolate Europe.'[29] Gandhi describes machinery as the chief symbol of modern civilization; it has made the workers of Bombay's mills 'slaves': 'The conditions of the women working in the mills is shocking. When there were no mills, these women were not starving. If the machinery craze grows in our country, it will become an unhappy land.'[30] Modern machinery as it has been introduced to India, together with the ideal of technological progress, displaces labour and 'manufactures' deprivation.

Gandhi argues that industrialization and urbanization produce poverty by creating economies of dependence through, for instance, waged labour and the creation of employed and unemployed classes. Gandhi's Marxist contemporaries critiqued his representation of industrialism and progress in *Hind Swaraj* by arguing that 'sometimes he says things about industrialization which can more rightly be applied to capitalism and not to other forms of industrial organization.'[31] However, Gandhi is concerned not simply with capitalist organization but with the ecological consequences of centralized industrial labour, arguing that it misappropriates essential resources such as water and uses these resources inefficiently and in an ecologically unsustainable manner. The manner in which Gandhi presents his critique of modern machinery in *Hind Swaraj* and the seeming arbitrary condemnation of some products of technological progress, such as the steam locomotive, and the valorization of others, such as the Singer sewing machine, make his position ambivalent and problematic. My concern here, however, is to examine the notion of human dignity and subjectivity Gandhi constructs through his critique of materialism, and hence the way in which resistance requires both the affirmation of human connection (i.e., as the disruption of the binary framework of racial difference) and the alteration of structures of exploitation.

Gandhi critiques machinery as a way of explicating his larger concern that the people of colonial India are oppressed not by the British, the capitalist, or the landowner, per se, but by the ethic of materialism that is central to the 'spread' of European 'civilization.' Machines symbolize, because they facilitate, the dehumanizing effects of the ethic of material and technological progress:

> What I object to, is the *craze* for machinery, not machinery as such. The craze is for what they call labour-saving machinery. Men go on 'saving labour' till thousands are without work and thrown on the open streets to die of starvation ... I want the concentration of wealth, not in the hands of the few, but in the hands of all. Today machinery merely helps a few to ride on the backs of millions. The impetus behind it all is not the philan-

thropy to save labour, but greed ... It is an alteration in the condition of labour that I want. This mad rush for wealth must cease, and the labourer must be assured, not only of a living wage, but a daily task that is not a mere drudgery.[32]

Hence, Gandhi describes the object of resistance not as the usurping of the role of the oppressor, but as the transformation of political and economic relationships that produce poverty. Gandhi's critique of the structures of inequality of the colonial economy and the spread of apparently capitalist relations is by no means unique. In what now seems a prophetic, yet banal, assertion, Gandhi argues that 'it is possible to visualise a stage at which the machines invented by man may finally engulf civilisation.'[33] While Indian nationalist ideology envisions 'self-rule' as the control of the means of industrial production – indeed, for Nehru, Indian national identity was nearly synonymous with the modern narrative of economic progress, manifested in rapid industrialization and mega-projects – Gandhi identifies industrialization and materialism as an obstacle to *swaraj*, thereby redefining the terms of 'self-rule.' As Nandy argues, unlike Marx, Gandhi wanted to give up modernity rather than reform its social relationships.[34] For Gandhi, 'self-rule,' or liberation, signifies the transformation of the value system that is enabled by, and justifies, the inequality and alienation produced by 'modern civilization.'

Gandhi's critique of nationalist aspirations for independence, and their imbrication within the values and structures of modern civilization, provides the basis for his reconceptualization of *swaraj* through the concept of *sarvadoya*, or the 'welfare of all.' Gandhi's writings on *swaraj* and *sarvadoya* are at times prescriptive and at times abstract. In a way, my discussion of them requires the construction of a 'theory' that does not exist in his writing and that elides some of the paradoxes and limitations of the discourse, many of which Gandhi acknowledged. My concern, however, is not so much with the models of social order that Gandhi, at times, quite narrowly describes, but with what sort of transformation these notions of liberation require.

The *swaraj* that Gandhi begins to describe in *Hind Swaraj* entails a 'total emancipation' from all forms of social, cultural, political, and material structures of privilege and inequality, and not just those understood as colonialism. This, in itself, is by no means novel for anticolonial thought; Fanon's critique of colonialism is a critique of poverty and the global structures that produce material inequality. However, Gandhi's thought on this matter is significant, for while he recognizes a relationship between colonial discourse and colonial power, his critique was not limited by this discourse. Further, Gandhi was not primarily concerned with critiquing colonialism, per se, or even modernity and industrialization; rather, his analysis focuses on the 'power' of the Indian masses to maintain or transform the various forms of oppression and achieve individual and collective 'self-rule.' Gandhi's reformulation of *swaraj* does not produce liberation as the end product of a teleology of struggle or revolution but as a way of being:

> Complete independence through truth and non-violence means the independence of every unit, be it the humblest of the nation, without distinction of race, colour or creed. This independence is never exclusive. It is, therefore, wholly compatible with interdependence within or without. Practice will always fall short of the theory, even as the drawn line falls short of the theoretical line of Euclid. Therefore, complete independence will be complete only to the extent of our approach in practice to truth and non-violence.[35]

Swaraj is not just a political ideal but a practice of consciousness; the transformation of social and political structures requires the transformation of Indian (and ultimately human) values, ideals, and ways of understanding the world. *Swaraj*, therefore, is an individual and a social aim that is not so much a utopian ideal state but an ever-present practice.

In the models of anti-colonial opposition I examine in chapter 2, the national community appears to pre-exist struggle but is actually a product of the political struggle *against* a colonial adversary as Other. For Gandhi, the struggle for *swaraj* is a means of forming a national community, but because the struggle for *swaraj* is primarily a program of social and cultural transformation, and because it depends so much on the idea of individual empowerment, national identity is not produced negatively through the bond produced by shared antagonism against a foreign Other. As Leela Gandhi argues, 'Nationalist discourse may also be seen, through a Gandhian intervention, as releasing the "object" of Orientalist theory into a subject capable of theorizing him/herself, in terms of his/her particular and utopian future.'[36] The Indian national community of Gandhian thought, as opposed to that imagined by the Congress movement, is produced through political and social programs that are dependent upon an ethico-spiritual framework.

Nonetheless, in *Hind Swaraj* Gandhi appeals to India's 'Ancient Civilization,' which he calls the 'best civilization' or the 'Kingdom of God.' Typically, this appeal to tradition is characterized as an appeal to an essentialized pre-colonial past. Gandhi's use of such an idiom contradicts his own vision of *swaraj* and, as I will discuss below, impedes his stated concern for Hindu-Muslim unity or caste reform. Although he uses this language, however, Gandhi's reformulation of *swaraj* should not be understood as a 'retrieval' of past 'Indian' greatness. Gandhi's appeal to a pre-colonial 'Indian' community problematically draws upon a local, and in this case a specifically Hindu, idiom, but his vision of this national community is not based upon a shared identity in cultural terms (i.e., religion, ethnicity, language) but in terms of a particular 'way of life' that transcends religious difference and privileges the rural: 'The English have taught us that we were not one nation before ... This is without foundation. We were one nation before they came to India. One thought inspired us. Our mode of life was the same.'[37] Gandhi utilizes a rhetoric of India's 'changelessness' to challenge the acceptance of 'modern civilization' by nationalists, and the appeal to cultural tradition, as social practices, is at least in part a means of constructing a national community from the diverse and divided religious, ethnic, and caste communities of South Asia.

However, not only did Gandhi's notion of *swaraj* not accord with the ideal of the secular modern state, but it entailed the rejection of the political state: 'If national life becomes so perfect as to become self-regulated, no representation is necessary ... In the ideal state therefore there is no political power because there is no State. But the ideal is never fully realized in life.'[38] Gandhi's development of the idea of *swaraj* led to the conceptualization of *sarvadoya*, which overtly figures the 'aims' of Indian resistance as the achievement of an egalitarian community, rather than simply political independence and the end of British rule. As a result, Gandhian resistance is articulated as the transformation of 'traditional' systems of princely rule, the exploitation and degradation of the 'untouchable' caste within the social structure of Hinduism, or child marriage, as much as it is the colonial structure of domination.

Gandhi's thought on *sarvadoya* is influenced by the Western philosophies of socialism and anarchism, but it is very much derived from praxis, developed through 'experiments' in communal living, which he would theorize as 'the village republic.' Gandhi spent much of his time during the independence struggles living in *ashrams* – small subsistence-based communal villages – experimenting with diet, spiritual enlightenment, and communal politics. Based on these practical 'experiments' with alternative social, political, and economic relationships, he wrote extensively on alternatives to centralized industrial production, theorizing the ideals of such communities as full employment, shared (or 'bread') labour, equality, decentralization, self-sufficiency, and cooperation. For instance, based on the principle that all have the right to equal opportunity though all do not have the same capacity, Gandhi revised the notion of *swadeshi* – which had provided the framework for nationalist campaigns against the British in which Indians were urged, and often coerced, to only purchase goods manufactured in India – into a formulation of solidarity.[39] He wrote extensively on education, the development of 'cottage industries' such as the manufacture of *khadi* or home-spun cloth, and meticulously described models of participatory democracy and local governance.[40]

Many critics of Gandhi have cited these experiments with village life as indicative of Gandhi's 'romantic' and even 'reactionary' position within the Indian independence movement. Ahmad, for instance, argues that 'there is also in Gandhi a full-blown rhetoric of an idyllic Golden Age somewhere in the Hindu past which was casteless, classless, ungendered.'[41] Similarly, Gandhi's Marxist contemporaries argued that his rejection of Western civilization and technology and 'glorification' of cottage industries constituted a 'primitive philosophy which could never lead India towards progress and prosperity.'[42] Of course, this is precisely the point; Gandhi's conception of liberation does not construct prosperity in purely material terms. Partha Chatterjee argues that unlike philosophers such as Carpenter and Ruskin, who influenced Gandhi's critique of modern industrial civilization, Gandhi's 'idealization of a peaceful, non-competitive, just and happy Indian society of the past could not have been "a romantic longing for the lost harmony of the archaic world," because unlike romanticism Gandhi's problem is not conceived at all within the thematic bounds of post-enlightenment thought.'[43] Gandhi's philosophy of simplicity also cannot be understood in terms of 'nativism' or 'cultural essentialism,' as the early articulations of *negritude* have been. As Nandy argues, Gandhi 'reformulated the modern world in traditional terms to make it meaningful to his traditional society.'[44] While Gandhi's use of 'traditional' idioms, and particularly Hindu idioms, alienated non-Hindus, it is clear that while Gandhi used such a discourse, his theorization of the 'village republic' did not seek a 'return' to an idyllic and earlier age; rather, he rejected much that was 'traditional' in South Asian, and particularly Hindu, cultures, including what he called the 'tyranny' of Indian princes, gender oppression, and hierarchies based on caste.[45] Gandhi sought to transform India in a way that collapses the modern/traditional binary; he sought a novel notion of the state in which the welfare of all was pre-eminent.

While *sarvadoya* appears idyllic, and to some degree echoes modern liberal ideals of human equality, Gandhi articulates this 'equality' within an ethico-spiritual discourse that conceives of equality as a lived practice rather than an ideal that justifies the state:

> If we would see Panchayat Raj, i.e., democracy established, we would regard the humblest and the lowliest Indian as being equally the ruler of India with the tallest in the land. For this everyone should be pure. If they are not they should become so. He who is pure will also be wise. He will observe no distinctions between caste and caste, between touchable and untouchable, but will consider everyone equal with himself. He will bind others to himself with love.[46]

Swaraj or liberation does not entail simply a change in political leadership but a transformation of lifestyle and values. For instance, Gandhi's notion of *sarvadoya* is based on a discourse of 'necessary virtues' that include self-control, the rejection of material possessions, the respect for all religions, and anti-untouchability. It is particularly significant that Gandhi frames these ideals of national liberation not as citizen rights, or in terms of government structures or policies, but in terms of an ethical or even religious dedication: 'Actual taking over of the Government machinery is but a shadow, an emblem. And it could easily be a burden if it came as a gift from without, the people having made no effort to deserve it ... We have everywhere emphasized the necessity of carrying on the constructive activities as being the means of attaining *swaraj.*'[47] Hence, *sarvadoya* is conceived of as process or practice rather than end.

Remembering that much of Gandhi's writings were directed at participants in the independence struggle, or reflected on events and strategies of the movement, the 'virtues' Gandhi describes are embedded in the 'experiments' with small-scale communities, constructive programs, and more confrontational campaigns of non-cooperation. Hence, Gandhi's musings on village self-reliance, economic 'trusteeship,' *sarvadoya* democracy, Hindu-Muslim unity, the rights of minorities, and the radical transformation of the caste structure and gender roles both shape and are shaped by practical initiatives that sought to illuminate the injustice of political and economic structures or produce alternative structures. For instance, the 1930 *Satyagraha Namak* (immortalized as a metonym of 'Gandhi's' struggle against the 'British'), which began with a 240-mile march to the seaside town of Dandi and culminated in a mass campaign in which Indians produced their own salt, challenged the British colonial monopoly on the production and consumption of salt. In contrast, 'constructive programs,' which included the development of village industries – most notably *khadi* or homespun cloth – in which communities produced and distributed their own goods, developed an economy of trade outside the structures of the emerging capitalist model of British colonialism. Such practices emulate *sarvadoya* through the production of an alternative dailyness of social interaction, while confrontational and symbolic campaigns, such as the Dandi march, illuminated specific injustices and popularized alternatives. It is important to bear in mind that while *satyagraha* is popularly remembered as a tactic of opposition against British colonialism, it was primarily organized to illuminate and challenge injustices that were not specifically, or only, colonial in character; for instance, to secure increased wages for textile workers, disrupt the sale of alcohol, or open Hindu temples to members of all castes. Such programs were not conceived within the rubric of anti-colonial (and modern) nationalism, and hence their effect was, at times, to disrupt the production of an Indian national imaginary and divide the anti-colonialist or nationalist movement by challenging various registers of privilege based on caste, economic wealth, or gender.

Gandhi's position on untouchability was one such element of his notion of *swaraj* that fractured, rather than fostered, Indian 'nationalism.' In *Hind Swaraj*, Gandhi defends the *principle* of *varna*, but he rejects the *institution* of the Hindu caste system. The eradication of untouchability became a dominant theme in Gandhi's message to the Indian people throughout the Indian independence movement. Yet, Gandhi's position on untouchability was subject to sustained critique from both those privileged within the caste system and those advocating for the rights of untouchables. In particular, B.R. Ambedkar constructs the struggle of those deemed 'untouchable' as a nationalist struggle in itself; only through their own independence would they be free from both British colonial and Hindu oppression. On one level,

Ambedkar regards Gandhi's campaign to eradicate untouchablity as impeding 'progress,' and, specifically, the demands of 'untouchables' for greater political rights, which Ambedkar believes would dismantle the barrier between them and caste Hindus. He also asserts that Gandhi's position on untouchablity is 'marked by so many twists and turns, inconsistencies and contradictions, attacks and surrenders ... that the whole campaign has become a matter of mystery.'[48] The theory of resistance I am drawing out of Gandhi's work, like the postcolonial project more generally, privileges the analysis of anti-colonial or nationalist *critique* rather than analysis of historical practices and movements. Ambedkar contends that Gandhi failed to effectively translate his analysis of untouchability, as a form of oppression, into practical political initiatives.

Swaraj, for Gandhi, was the exercise of self-rule by the people of India, and not a political condition to be won by a vanguard elite, whether bourgeois or communist. *Swaraj* and *sarvadoya*, and the constructive programs and political activism that these principles activated, do not constitute a 'revolutionary' movement, in the sense described by Fanon, or a process solely of 'decolonization.' Surveying Marxist responses to Gandhian thought, Subrata Mukherjee argues that prominent Indian Marxists of the period criticized Gandhi for concentrating on 'relatively minor issues of social reform' rather than leading massive political movements.[49] Though Gandhi writes about, and experiments with, 'ideal' village communities, *swaraj* and *sarvadoya* are conceptualized not as the final victory of a narrative of emancipation. Indeed, Gandhi argues that constructive work should be undertaken 'for its own sake' and that Indians should be prepared to continue these programs endlessly.[50] Further, Gandhi argues: 'Real Swaraj will come not by the acquisition of authority by a few but by the acquisition of the capacity by all to resist authority when it is abused ... Swaraj is to be obtained by educating the masses to a sense of their capacity to regulate and control authority.'[51] Hence, Gandhi conceptualizes *swaraj* not as a state (both in terms of a political state or a state of being), but as a condition of existence.

Based in a critique of modern civilization, rather than foreign rule, Gandhi's conception of *swaraj* is inconsistent with anti-colonial discourse; *swaraj* is neither the inevitable end of decolonization, as liberation seems to be in Fanon's and Said's analyses, nor is it an ideal state to be achieved once and for all. *Swaraj* and *sarvadoya* are shaped by an analysis of the structures of oppression that function within a discourse of social transformation that does not adhere to History, in the Modern, or specifically Marxist sense. While Gandhi utilizes discourses of the Indian nation, his notion of liberation is not the modern state. The Gandhian dialectic provides a radical alternative to the dominant theories of colonial power, as articulated by such critics as Fanon, Guha, and Bhabha. Gandhi's efforts at articulating, and enacting, a process of demodernization constitute a discourse of possibility that requires a notion of resistance radically different from those dominant within postcolonial studies.

The Politics of Possibility: *Ahimsaic* Resistance

Partha Chatterjee contends that Gandhi's concept of *ahimsa* constitutes a 'science of resistance.' He argues that *ahimsa* is 'both ethical and epistemological because it was defined within a moral and epistemic practice that was wholly "experimental."'[52] Chatterjee also argues, however, and he quotes Gandhi to provide support, that Gandhi placed *ahimsa* before Congress as a 'political weapon,' recognizing that while *ahimsa* is his 'creed' he does not expect Congress to accept it as such. As a result, Chatterjee identifies a disjuncture within Gandhian ideology between morality and politics, private conscience and public responsibility, and, ultimately, between 'Noble Folly and *Realpolitik.*'[53] To argue such a disjuncture, and to characterize *ahimsa* as merely a useful tactic in the struggle to win Indian independence, disregards Gandhi's critique of nationalist conceptions of *swaraj* as simply the end of British/foreign rule.

Gandhi could not 'demand' that Congress adopt *ahimsa* – as an ideology of social conduct, rather than simply a political tactic – as a 'creed' or 'ethic' of struggle. Indeed, Gandhi's ideal of *ahimsa* challenged both the structure of political power within Congress and the function of the party itself. In many ways, the transformation of Congress – from a political party to a social movement – was as much a goal for Gandhi as the end of colonialism. While Congress adopted various forms of non-cooperation and civil disobedience as tactics in the struggle for national liberation, for Gandhi, *swaraj* and the struggle were one; within Gandhi's ideology of *ahimsa* and *satyagraha*, the political and the moral, personal conscience and public responsibility, are synonymous:

> Literally speaking, Ahimsa means 'non-killing' ... It really means that you may not offend anybody; you may not harbour an uncharitable

thought, even in connection with one who may consider himself to be your enemy ... Those who join the Ashram have literally to accept that meaning.

That does not mean that we practice the doctrine in its entirety. Far from it. It is an ideal which we have to reach.[54]

Recognizing that the majority of Congress members accepted nonviolence only as a matter of policy and not an article of faith, in 1930 Gandhi writes that he will renew the movement only with those who have committed to nonviolence as an ethic.[55]

Gandhi developed *ahimsa* within, and out of the necessity of, a struggle to end oppression, but *ahimsa* is not a tool of 'anti-colonialism'; it is not structured by the dichotomies of colonial knowledge and nationalist discourse. *Ahimsa*, as an ethic of conduct, and *satyagraha* – which connotes the practical principles of nonviolent non-cooperation – are based upon an understanding of power and the nature of oppression that is radically different from that which informs the anti-colonial critiques of Fanon, Ngugi, or Nehru, or from the postcolonial constructions of power of Guha or Bhabha. Gandhi's concept of *ahimsa* directs attention to the oppressed – rather than the oppressors – as actors or participants in a system of privilege and exploitation. English colonial authority, as one structure of dominance, depends upon the practical cooperation of the Indian people in its day-to-day functioning, from civil servants fulfilling their duties to peasants paying land taxes. Indians – and particularly the English-educated elite class – maintain colonial power through their complicity not just in the production of colonial difference as colonial knowledge but in the ideology of modern civilization. Gandhian resistance, therefore, radically reconfigures the role of the oppressed within the dynamic of oppression, collapses the distinction between the 'ends' of struggle and the 'means,' and deconstructs the oppressor/victim binary without eliding material and cultural 'difference.' *Ahimsa* provides a politics of conflict that escapes the 'rhetoric of blame' but does not dispense with responsibility.

Before turning to Gandhi's writings and a more developed treatment of the alternative constructions of power, agency, and the Other *ahimsa* provides, I wish first to discuss a few episodes from Raja Rao's *Kanthapura*, for I believe this novel provides a useful preface to an examination of Gandhi's concept of *ahimsa*. Set within the context of the larger 'anti-colonial' struggle, like many works of 'Gandhian literature,' the immediate story of *Kanthapura* is one of the tensions that surround initiatives to transform structures of domination within the social formation of a predominantly Hindu village, from the caste system to child marriage to prohibitions on marriage between members of different castes or religions.

Upon his return to the village to 'work with the masses,' Moorthy begins to work with the 'pariahs' and as a representative of Congress introduces the spinning wheel as a practical symbol of the ideal of self-sufficiency. Significantly, Moorthy's initial acts concentrate on challenging indigenous structures of privilege and subjugation within the community. While each of these endeavours may be understood within a Gandhian ideology of social transformation, *ahimsa* is introduced as an ethic of resistance in religious terms. The story of Gandhi, 'the Mahatma,' is presented to the village as the story of a saint: 'As he grew up ... he began to go out into the villages and assemble people and talk to them, and his voice was so pure ... that men followed him ... and so he goes from village to village to slay the serpent of the foreign rule. Fight, says he, but harm no soul. Love all, says he, Hindu, Mohammedan, Christian or Pariah, for all are equal before God.'[56] This ethic of resistance, which demands struggle without violence, however, is not easily translated into practice. When Moorthy attempts to enter the Skeffington Coffee Estate to visit the exploited and abused workers of the plantation, he is stopped by the police. The Muslim police officer, Badè Khan, is berated and abused by the gathered crowd, leading him to strike Moorthy with his *lathi*. The group then attacks Khan, viciously beating him, while Moorthy pleads: '"No beatings, sisters. No beatings, in the name of the Mahatma."'[57] *Ahimsa* is not simply a tactical choice, derived from a rational assessment of the utility of violence in a particular conflict, but a moral imperative.

As discussed above, Gandhi draws upon discourses of Indian spiritual and cultural superiority to contrast what he characterizes as British preoccupations with the material. The use of a Hindu idiom for his teachings, then, was derived from his critique of modernity but also served a utilitarian end; he was able to articulate his philosophy in an idiom that the Hindu peasant masses could comprehend and accept. The dependence upon such an idiom, however, impeded Gandhi's ability to foster the sort of ethic of *ahimsa* that he desired or the social transformation he sought. His reliance upon distinctly Hindu symbolism and imagery alienated 'untouchables' and Muslims. Further, as Rao's depiction of Gandhi suggests, the use of this idiom allowed Gandhi to be figured as a 'saint' and his work as somehow solely religious rather than political. While Gandhi imagined *ahimsa* and *sarvadoya* in a way that positioned them as a 'realist' necessity, for the majority of Congress, Gandhi's philosophy seemed naive and inappropriate for the realpolitik of the independence movement. Indeed, his conceptualization of *ahimsa* was divisive in another sense as well; Orthodox Hindu nationalists argued that his conception of *ahimsa* was not a tenet of Hinduism and that *ahimsa* weakened the Hindu 'nation.'[58]

In *Kanthapura*, *ahimsa* is not treated as an essentially Hindu concept, but it is very much represented as deriving from spiritual faith. Moorthy's commitment to introduce 'constructive programs' to his village and his willingness to suffer in confrontations with the administrators of state power derive from an experience in which the Mahatma appears to him in a vision and tells him: '"There is but one force in life and that is truth, and there is but one love in life and that is the love of mankind, and there is but one God in life and that is the God of all."'[59] Gandhi conceptualizes 'God' – which he sees as the only potential means of unifying India's diverse peoples – from various religious and ideological traditions and ultimately understands God as Truth or Love. While forms of resistance such as tax evasion or labour strikes have a political effect, Gandhi argues that unless the participants in such actions or campaigns are 'non-violent in thought, word and deed and ... living in perfect friendliness with all whether co-operators or non-co-operators' this effect will not be the establishment of *swaraj* but 'no-*raj*.'[60]

Rao's representation of Gandhian resistance in a small village is unquestionably celebratory of Gandhi and Gandhism. Unlike Richard Attenborough's film *Gandhi* (1982), however, which idealizes and simplifies the ease with which Gandhi, and many other Indians, suffered and sacrificed, Rao depicts the difficulty of translating *ahimsa* as a moral principle into social and political conduct. For instance, Moorthy's 'Pariah-mixing' is regarded as polluting his family and the community, and the participation of women in the picketing of toddy booths, among other contributions to the movement, disrupts gender-role expectations both inside and outside the domestic sphere as well as the functioning of that sphere. For instance, the participation of women in constructive activities and acts of civil disobedience disrupts the order of the household; their husbands' meals are not prepared and the women seem to 'vagabond about like soldiers.'[61] The novel's chaotic conclusion – in which a nonviolent march erupts into a riot, and attempts to maintain nonviolence, both in deed and spirit, are juxtaposed with images of the national flag and memories of 1857 – provides an ambivalent representation of *ahimsa*. *Kanthapura* depicts the difficulty of *ahimsa* as practice, and the way in which anti-colonial nationalist, local and traditional, and Gandhian discourses intersect and compete in the production of the national imaginary.

The initiatives towards *swaraj* depicted in *Kanthapura* disrupt the ideological bases of both colonial/modern and orthodox/traditional power/knowledge, and, I believe, undo the modern/traditional binary, and particularly the paradox of this binary as a framework for imagining the Indian nation. Gandhi's analysis of the role of women, for instance, was deeply problematic. While he challenged the patriarchal structure of, particularly, Hindu society by advocating for an end to child marriage and by demanding that women cook simple meals so that they are not a slave to the stove, he also put the onus for moral behaviour on women, idealizing women as naturally nonviolent and without sexual desire. Nonetheless, the role of women in the constructive programs and *satyagraha* and the aim of gender transformation, which was so much a part of Gandhi's ideal of liberation, provide an example of the way in which Gandhi's conceptualization of power dismantles the colonizer/colonized, modern/traditional binary.

Chatterjee argues that rapid changes took place in the lives of women during the colonial period, 'mostly outside the arena of political agitation, in a domain where the nation thought of itself as already free ... It was the home that became the principal site of the struggle through which the hegemonic construct of the new nationalist patriarchy had to be normalized.'[62] The points of emphasis in the spiritual/material, home/world, and feminine/masculine dichotomies upon which the orthodox-nationalist discourse produces itself are different from those of colonial discourse in that, for instance, 'India' is constructed as spiritually superior to Europe and spirituality is privileged over materialism. Hence, Chatterjee maintains that nationalist discourse is trapped within colonialism's 'framework of false essentialisms.'[63] Significantly, however, as Rao's depiction of, and indeed emphasis upon, the role of women as agents of social and political change in *Kanthapura* reveals, women's *ahimsaic* resistance transcends these dichotomies, at once challenging the colonial and capitalist structures of power in the 'arena of political agitation' and the domestic patriarchal structure of the 'domain where the nation thought of itself as already free.' As a result, *ahimsa*, as it is presented in *Kanthapura*, disrupts the dichotomies of home/world, India/Europe, and, significantly, feminine/masculine by figuring resistance as occurring simultaneously in each realm. Indeed, the master/slave dialectic is intimately related to the masculine/feminine. In the work of Fanon and Ngugi, among others, violence, as the sole means of achieving liberation and self-determination, is a distinctly male practice, and, hence, nonviolence is regarded as 'passive.' For instance, Ngugi's anti-colonial dialectic seeks to challenge the depiction of the 'good' African as the 'non-violent, spineless type, the type who turns the other cheek.'[64]

Drawing upon Gandhi's critique of male sexuality and his construction of an asexual gender ideal, critics such as Nandy and Leela Gandhi critique the masculinist preoccupations of nationalist discourse. However, I believe that *ahimsa* as an ethic of social and political conduct functions to transcend and collapse these hierarchical dichotomies. In South Africa, Gandhi's initial 'experiments' with nonviolence were called 'passive resistance.' He soon realized the inadequacy of the term for expressing the spiritual and political interdependence of the principles underlying Indian agitation for greater freedom: 'When in a meeting of Europeans I found that the term "passive resistance" was too narrowly construed, that it was supposed to be a weapon of the weak, that it could be characterized by hatred, and that it could finally manifest itself as violence, I had to demure to all these statements and explain the real nature of the Indian movement.'[65] In response, Gandhi coined the term *satyagraha*, often translated as truth-force, or love-force. While Spivak dismissively reduces *satyagraha* to 'hunger strike,' linking it to the practice of *sati*, Leela Gandhi contends that Gandhi's use of militaristic metaphors, such as his characterization of the Indian struggle as a 'nonviolent battle,' reveals the way in which he 'is not so much an inventor of insurgency as a discursive innovator of systems/meanings that are already in circulation.'[66] To this end she quotes Nirmal Bose's assertion that rather than a substitute for war, *satyagraha* '"is war itself shorn of many of its ugly features."'[67] Characterizations such as these reflect the way in which *satyagraha* has become synonymous with nonviolent *opposition*. However, according to Gandhi, *satyagraha* constitutes not just a tactic of opposing oppression and exploitation but a mode of social change requiring the transformation of its practitioners and, hence, the transformation of culture/politics; this aspect of Gandhian resistance was consistently marginalized within Congress's nationalist discourse of liberation.

Gandhi theorizes *ahimsa* and *satyagraha* as radically transforming, if not rejecting, the 'systems/meanings' of anti-colonial struggle. These concepts collapse the distinction between the domestic and the political, conscience and expedience. Gandhi recognizes *satyagraha* as part and parcel of the individual's ongoing struggle for self-purification and self-realization – or 'self-rule' – and that the social or political transformation signified by the idea of *swaraj* is inseparable from individual transformation; liberation requires a transformation not just of political and economic structures but of values, attitudes, and individual behaviours. Based on his various experiments with *satyagraha* both in South Africa and India, Gandhi writes that a *satyagrahi* must in daily life vow to continually seek truth, practise nonviolence, fearlessness, and self-control, as well as actively work towards religious harmony and an end to the oppression of those deemed 'untouchable.'[68] Hence, while *satyagraha* recognizes an 'adversary' or 'opponent,' this opponent is re-characterized as a 'wrong-doer.'[69] This is not simply a semantic alteration; the *satyagrahi* does not seek to defeat or destroy the adversary. *Satyagraha* requires that the *satyagrahi* harbour no anger, refuse to retaliate against assaults in word or deed, and willingly sacrifice his or her life but refuse to take the lives of others. As a theory of conflict, *satyagraha* cannot be considered a 'battle,' in the dominant or normal sense of the term. While Gandhi does, at times, characterize the British system as 'evil' and the Indian system as 'good,' as an ethic of resistance *ahimsa* constructs the parties involved in conflict in radically different ways than do the models of resistance that are dominant in postcolonial studies.

In Fanon's description of violent opposition, colonial domination 'can only be called in question by absolute violence,' and the 'intuition' of the 'colonized masses' tells them that 'their liberation must, and can only, be achieved by force.'[70] In practice, however, as Fanon also acknowledges, 'the atmosphere of violence, after having colored all the colonial phase, continues to dominate national life.'[71] Libratory violence has perpetuated a cycle of violence seemingly without end in Algeria, Sri Lanka, Kashmir, Congo, or Zimbabwe. Significantly, revolutionary violence is not simply a practical political tactic; the direct violence of civil war and authoritarian oppression reinforce both the structural violence of material inequality and exploitation and the cultural violence of colonial discourse. Fanon describes the way in which the structural and direct violence of colonialism and the violent resistance it produces leads to a cycle of violence, and he acknowledges that there must be coherence between the tactics of struggle and its desired 'victory.' Robert Young argues that (modern) radical politics require the future; such projects require a utopian goal, as a guiding desire, even though that utopia is impossible to realize. However, end-oriented or teleological discourses impede the achievement of the sorts of ends imagined through them: 'There is also a danger that such utopian moments, if projected uncritically, may in fact perpetuate the very structures of the systems that they seek to displace, that they may project the past back into the future, not changing history but repeating it.'[72]

Fanon imagines a 'new humanism' as an alternative to both the particularly local and self-interested desires of the peasant (i.e., to take back the settler's land) and the ideal of the nation-state, which replicates the structures of material exploitation of the colonial order. Similarly, Cabral argues that 'victory' must be translated into a 'cultural leap' for 'liberation' to occur. In both cases, liberation will come after the 'goal' of national independence is achieved; there is a clear distinction between the 'means' of resistance and its intended 'ends.' The ideological perspective of Nehru, the dominant figure in Indian nationalist politics by the late 1930s, was typical of the great many other bourgeois leaders of nationalist movements. Resistance, for Nehru, is particularly end-oriented; the 'real progression of history' is fulfilled through the establishment of the nation: '"The real thing is the attainment of the goal and every step that we take must be taken from the viewpoint of the very early attainment of this goal."'[73] The anti-colonial nationalist project was conceived within realpolitik and constructed within a teleological framework. Gandhi's *satyagraha* and his stature among the Indian 'masses,' therefore, provided Congress a useful tactic through which to gain independence. Nehru argues that social reform could only take place *after* power had been taken away from the colonizer and a nation-state had been established, constructing this within a narrative of the progress of the nation wherein the ends are not related to the means.[74]

Gandhi's discourse of *ahimsa* provides an alternative conception of the relationship between ends and means to both Nehru and Fanon/Cabral. Gandhi's construction of ends and means, in its most simple form, depends upon the idea that something 'good' (egalitarian, democratic, empowering) cannot be constructed through 'evil' (hierarchical, authoritarian, coercive) methods:

> Let us first take the argument that we are justified in gaining our end by using brute force, because the English gained theirs by using similar means. It is perfectly true that they used brute force, and that it is possible

for us to do likewise, but, by using similar means, we can get only the same thing that they got. You still admit that we do not want that. Your belief that there is no connection between the means and the end is a great mistake ... Your reasoning is the same as saying that we can get a rose through planting a noxious weed.[75]

Gandhi critiques the notion that liberation can be achieved through violence by arguing, first, that violent resistance replicates the tactics and structures of colonialism and material exploitation, and, second, that an egalitarian, democratic order cannot be achieved through coercion and based on an authoritarian structure of power. Gandhi's conception of ends and means, however, also differs from that of Nehru or Fanon in three other important ways.

First, Gandhi does not conceive of struggle within a teleological framework wherein the goal of struggle is imagined as a 'state' of liberation. In contrast to the nationalist Hindu project, which constructed a linear Hindu history of India along the lines of Western progress, Gandhi understands Indian history as 'a special case of an all-embracing permanent present, waiting to be interpreted and reinterpreted.'[76] Indeed, *ahimsa*, as an ethic of struggle, constitutes an alternative cosmology from the modern cosmology, which is structured by an understanding of time as progressive.[77] The second distinction is related to the first. On a social/political level, Gandhi did articulate the goals of *swaraj* and *sarvadoya*; yet even these concepts of liberation were articulated as necessarily ideals, and so goals-in-process. Hence, ends and means are convertible terms in Gandhi's discourse of *ahimsa*; the means of struggle constitute not simply a tactic to *bring about* change but an ethico/spiritual (or moral) imperative that constitutes that change.

Finally, as a much more complex concept than the precept of not doing physical harm to others, *ahimsa* also must be understood in terms of Gandhi's analysis of domination as a structure. By positing the structural and direct violence of colonialism, the caste system, and the economic systems of India as the problem, rather than the presence of the colonist, the Brahmin, or the landowner, Gandhi challenges the notion of struggle as opposition. For Gandhi, violence is the enemy: the violence of colonial repression, such as the Jallianwala Bagh massacre, the violence of economic exploitation, such as unfair taxation, and the violence of hierarchies of status and privilege, such as colonial discourse or the Hindu caste system. As a result, struggle must be primarily constructive. *Ahimsa* constitutes not simply an alternative to the physical 'battle' of war but the ideological and discursive assumptions that construct battle as a means of achieving liberation. As Ashis Nandy argues, in *ahimsa* Gandhi produces a 'model of dissent' that escapes the limitations of the 'victor's values' because it is constructed not as a form of oppositional resistance – a reaction – but as an ethic of social conduct.[78]

Understanding Power, Transcending Fear

To recognize oppression as a structure, rather than a practice, and Indian *swaraj*, or independence, as the economic, political, and cultural transformation of both the structures of domination of 'traditional' India and modern civilization, is to radically reconceptualize the nature of power within the colonial context. While Gandhi seems to assume a model of native agency more consistent with that espoused by anti-colonial intellectuals such as Fanon than postcolonial theorists such as Bhabha, he understands the functioning of power much differently. In order to explore Gandhi's construction of power and agency, it is useful first to return to the work of Ranajit Guha. In *Dominance without Hegemony*, Guha responds to the dominant British histories of India, which represent the colonial endeavour as a hegemonic project, wherein the British seemingly rely on persuasion rather than coercion to establish and maintain their authority. Guha writes:

> The presumption of hegemony makes for a seriously distorted view of the colonial state and its configuration of power ... In colonial India, where the role of capital was still marginal in the mode of production and the authority of the state structured as an autocracy that did not recognize any citizenship or rule of law, power simply stood for a series of inequalities between the rulers and the ruled as well as between classes, strata, and individuals.[79]

Guha acknowledges the British use of modes of persuasion, but he argues that democratic discourses of citizenship, legality, and civil rights were largely occluded from British rule in India, a system of governance that instituted and/or reinforced autocratic structures of power that produced order through coercion: 'Order, as an idiom of state violence, constituted a distinctive feature of colonialism ... it was allowed to intrude again and again into many such areas of the life of the people as would have been firmly kept out of bounds in Metropolitan Britain.'[80] The 1857 'mutiny' takes on a presence in the Indian historical consciousness, therefore, not just as a symbol of resistance but as a reminder of the real physical, but just as importantly, psychological, power of the British 'sword.' Guha contends that 'the exercise of authority in realms far from metropolitan Europe came to rely on fear rather than consent.'[81] Hence, British power in India constituted dominance without hegemony.

Unlike Guha, who focuses upon understanding how the colonizer exercises power, in Gandhi's writings on *ahimsa*, *satyagraha*, and *swaraj*, power is theorized at the level of the experience of oppression. Hence, Indians – the elite bureaucrats and officials as well as the 'masses' – are not 'victims' or 'oppressors' but subjects within a system of privilege and exploitation. Gandhi rejects the notion that British power is maintained by the sword. This is not to say, however, that he denies the importance of coercion as a tool of British colonial power; Gandhi does not argue that British authority was hegemonic in the sense that Guha critiques. Yet, in *Hind Swaraj* Gandhi contends that while 'some Englishmen state that they took, and they hold, India by the sword ... these statements are wrong. The sword is entirely useless for holding India. We alone keep them.'[82] His writings on *ahimsa* and *satyagraha* concentrate on understanding the function of the people of India as participants within, rather than as victims of, these structures of power.

On one level, the 'we who keep them' of Gandhi's discourse is (only) the 'English-knowing men, that have enslaved Indian,' upon whom the 'curse of the nation' will rest, not the English.[83] In a practical sense, Gandhi argues the British do not have forces sufficient to subdue India's enormous population; colonial authority is therefore maintained through Indian enthralment with modernity. Gandhi argues that the Indian nationalist lawyers, doctors, and other elite figures – the so-called mimic/middle-men – must cease fighting 'the imagined enemy without' and concentrate upon the 'enemy within' by renouncing and unlearning their privilege. Yet, in so far as authority is maintained through physical coercion – the use or threat of the sword – in Gandhi's theory of *ahimsa*, power still depends on cooperation. Where Guha concentrates on the practices of British authority, arguing that the British Raj maintained order not through acquiring the consent of the Indian population but by instilling fear through the threat, and exercise, of violence, Gandhi focuses on the Indian's experience of fear: 'I found, through my wanderings in India, that my country is seized with a paralyzing fear. We may not open our mouths in public; we may only talk about our opinions secretly ... if you want to follow the vow of Truth, then fearlessness is absolutely necessary. Before we can aspire to guide the destinies of India we shall have to adopt this habit of fearlessness.'[84] Echoing Leo Tolstoy's contention that England is only able to enslave Indians because Indians '"recognised, and still recognise, force as the fundamental principle of social order,"'[85] Gandhi recognizes force or coercion not merely as material or physical acts and structures but as a psychological or cultural condition.

It is not (just) the sword that establishes and maintains colonial authority but the culture of fear that violence produces and depends upon. Intervention, therefore, can take place at the level of the experience of oppression by those who suffer within it rather than (only) at the level of its exercise. If fear is the necessary condition of domination, as experienced by those who are subjugated, then to overcome the psychological and cultural condition of fear is to undo the control this fear produces and to undo the authority of those who depend upon violent coercion. For the *satyagrahi*, to take the vow of fearlessness was necessary for the endurance of the suffering *satyagraha* often included, but this idea of 'fearlessness' was just as significant in the broader cultural sense.

While dominance may not require consent, both hegemony and dominance require compliance and cooperation. Remembering that Gandhi characterizes modern civilization as essentially material and colonization as an enterprise motivated by commerce, if not in terms of the development of new markets, then the exploitation of resources, for the purposes of the argument of *Hind Swaraj* he simplistically argues that money is the 'god of the English': 'It follows that we keep the English in India for our base self-interest. We like their commerce, they please us by their subtle methods, and get what they want from us. To blame them for this is to perpetuate their power.'[86] To imagine oppression in terms of a Manichean framework or the Hegelian master-slave dialectic is to produce the illusion of that structure of power as reality. The theory of power that informs Gandhi's notions of *ahimsa* or *satyagraha*, therefore, not simply *deconstructs* this dialectic but opens a space to alter relationships.

Gandhi's emphasis upon *khadi*, or the production of home-spun cloth as a method of increasing rural self-sufficiency, is a response to oppression not in terms of agitation against the 'oppressor' but in terms of altering the system of oppression. In practice, however, the *swadeshi* movement was nonetheless often regarded by Indians as a mode of struggle *against* the English. Gandhi argues that the textile mills of

Manchester, and more importantly their workers, cannot be blamed for producing cloth for the Indian market.[87] *Swaraj*, as Gandhi imagines it, will not come from depriving the workers of Manchester from producing cloth so that it can be made in industrial mills in Bombay, but through the transformation of the economy so that Indians *and* the English are no longer exploited by wage labour and are able to achieve a level of self-sufficiency: 'The spectacle of three hundred million people being cowed down by living in the dread of three hundred men is demoralizing alike for the despots as for the victims. It is the duty of those who have realized the evil nature of the system, however attractive some of its features, torn from their context, may appear to be, to destroy it without delay.'[88] Resistance, then, is an act of cultural and structural transformation.

Gandhi's advocacy on behalf of 'untouchables,' and his response to Dalit activism, and particularly that advocated by Ambedkar, is informative here. Although the Gandhian tactic of *satyagraha* was used to challenge norms that denied 'untouchables' access to temples, Gandhi, while he often supported these actions to open roads outside temples or provide temple entry, did not initiate them. Unlike his more aggressive strategies against British rule (i.e., the non-cooperation movement), Gandhi sought to change the attitudes of high-caste Hindus by appealing to their conscience in more diplomatic ways. In part, this may have to do with his subject position as subjugated within a colonial structure of power but privileged within the caste system. Hence, colonial oppression was to be illuminated, and challenged, by overcoming fear of the sword and withdrawing cooperation from the colonial economy; resistance against colonial rule in Gandhi's thought emphasized the agency of the oppressed. On the other hand, Gandhi's strategy of fostering a change of attitude among caste Hindu, without, for instance, challenging *varna* itself, seemed to Ambedkar to disempower 'untouchables'; Gandhi's writing on untouchability focuses on the position of the privileged-caste Hindus, among whom he was a member, rather than the position of the oppressed, those deemed 'untouchable.' Ambedkar saw this strategy as preventing structural change in the nature of social, political, and economic relationships.[89] As David Hardiman argues, it was only as a result of Ambedkar's criticism of Gandhi's approach and his self-representation as the legitimate representative of the 'untouchables' that Gandhi's position became more radical, supporting the initiatives of the 'untouchables' themselves.[90] In many ways, it is just this sort of controversy that informed Gandhi's conception of power. His efforts on behalf of transforming the caste hierarchy met with tremendous resistance from Hindu nationalists. Similarly, his willingness to welcome 'untouchables' into his *ashrams* troubled many of the members of these communities and led to acts of violence against the *ashrams* and the withdrawal of financial support for the struggle, revealing the relationship between social and political structures and cultural values.[91]

Leela Gandhi contends that both Fanon and Gandhi reconceptualize the colonizer/colonized relationship so that the slave no longer regards 'itself *as*, or in the image of, the master' but is 'urged to see itself *beside* the master.'[92] While I agree with her first assertion, the second is much more problematic; indeed, it contradicts the first. In the example of Gandhi's letter to Smuts, which I discussed in chapter 1, Gandhi upsets Smuts by positioning Indians as *beside* whites; in doing so, however, he refused to recognize whites as masters or the self as slave. It may be true that Fanon worked to 'demystify' colonial knowledge, helping to figure the native/slave as the subject of their own history, but Gandhi's analysis extends beyond the colonial paradigm, and hence Hegel's master/slave dichotomy that Fanon translated into the colonial predicament.

Gandhi recognizes no homogeneous slave who is named and subjugated by a colonial master; rather, Gandhi's critique, as I have argued above, recognizes a myriad of subject positions within the Indian colonial moment, a moment shaped by the emergence of what Gandhi identifies as the structure of power of modern civilization, yet also informed by various extra-colonial structures. *Swaraj* marks not just the liberation of oppressed 'Indians' from foreign colonial rule but also the end of the structural violence of untouchability, the cultivation of Hindu-Muslim unity, and the transformation of the status, if not the role, of women. To argue that the slave should see itself beside the master is to recognize the colonizer/colonized relationship as dominating all other relationships of privilege and subjugation. As a young lawyer in South Africa, Gandhi was enamoured with the ideals and principles of the British constitution. While his feelings towards the English people, and more importantly, the ideals of the British Empire, were certainly altered by his experiences in South Africa, the 1919 Jallianwala Bagh massacre, the Rowlatt Act, and the Khilafat crisis, *ahimsa* and *satyagraha* were nonetheless shaped not as the ethics and 'rules' of antagonism, nor of opposition *against* the British, but as the ethics of struggle *for swaraj*.

The Duty of Resistance (as Transformation)

Gandhi's discourse of resistance, as it was articulated in South Africa, depended upon the modern conception of Rights. The Indian campaigns in South Africa sought to prevent legislation that limited what few rights they had as subjects within the British Empire with the ultimate aim of securing citizenship rights. After the Jallianwala Bagh massacre, Gandhi all but gave up this discourse in favour of a discourse of resistance that depends on individual transformation, particularly in terms of human duties, or *dharma*: 'In Swaraj based on Ahimsa people need not know their rights, but it is necessary for them to know their duties. There is no duty but creates a corresponding right, and those only are true rights which flow from a due performance of one's duties.'[93] Gandhi's linkage between rights and duties, however, is not simply a reaction to his disappointment with the failure of the British Empire to live up to its democratic discourse of rights, but a condition of his evolving understanding of power. In *Hind Swaraj* he writes: 'We, therefore, have before us in England the farce of everybody wanting and insisting on his rights, nobody thinking of his duty. And where everybody wants rights, who shall give them to whom?'[94] To demand or expect rights is to acknowledge the state as the pre-eminent legitimate authority, both in terms of investing one's well-being in the state's ability to provide protection and recognizing that such rights can only be granted and 'protected' by this authority.

Duty, in contrast, invests in the individual the regulation and control of structures of authority, like the state. The Hindu concept *dharma*, from which Gandhi derives his notion of 'duty,' denotes such ideas as morality, conduct, duty, and custom, and constructs relationships and roles within the caste hierarchy and local power structures. In *Dominance without Hegemony*, Guha argues that the nationalist elite drew upon the Hindu idiom of *dharma* to justify the nationalist agenda and to secure their authority: 'The notions of authority, obligation, right and wrong implied in [Dharmic Protest] referred to the traditions of a precolonial past which the rulers never managed fully to explore, and to those primordial aspects of community and religion which they neither understood nor sympathized with.'[95] Further, Guha contrasts this Hindu idiom of duty with the modern concept of Rights. In contrast to liberal democratic discourses of equality and rights, according to Guha, *dharma* reflects the fact that Hindu society is essentially unequal, and because people are not citizens but subjects of an elite authority, they have no rights but only duties.

While Rights and *dharma*, in this sense, are seemingly radically different discourses of social conduct, Guha's comparison reveals the similarity of the structures of power within which they function. In the democratic state, citizens have Rights, while in the *dharmic* state, subjects have duties towards the elite. However, *dharma* identifies not only the duties subjects have to their rulers, but the duties that rulers have towards their subjects, and members of upper castes have towards lower. In both discourses, then, the *dharmic* and the democratic, the citizen/subject depends upon the protection of the State/King and has the obligation of overthrowing this authority if it should fail to adhere to its democratic ideals/*dharma*.[96] For Guha, Congress's reliance upon a discourse of *dharma* reveals the way in which Hindu wisdom and tradition is appropriated to serve the needs of the bourgeois elite. He argues, for instance, that during the 1903–8 *swadeshi* movement, the idiom of *dharma* fused Hindu religiosity with patriotic duty. This religious idiom reinforces hierarchy and subordination, solidifying the authority and privilege of the Hindu middle classes within the nationalist movement, with the effect of dividing the nation, 'ranging the rural gentry against the peasantry, upper castes against Namasudras, and above all Hindus and Muslims against each other.'[97] Further, Guha argues that the liberal-Hindu or liberal-nationalist formula, which he associates with Gandhism, was ultimately undermined by this *dharmic* idiom, as it was unable to harness and control subaltern insurgency.

Gandhi's idiom of *dharma* or duty, like many of the other key concepts of his thought, derives from an indigenous antecedent but is not synonymous with that antecedent. In this case, Gandhi's emphasis upon duty derives from his unwillingness to separate political agitation from individual conscience. *Dharma* constitutes the 'moral' point of this 'square of Swaraj,' meaning 'religion in the highest sense of the term. It includes Hinduism, Islam, Christianity, etc., but is superior to them all.'[98] Gandhi's conception of duty, while drawing upon the Hindu idiom of *dharma*, transforms the concept, at least in theory, from a mode of personal responsibility that structures and maintains systems of inequality, to a mode of personal conduct that recognizes human interdependence:

> If instead of insisting on rights everyone does his duty, there will immediately be the rule of order established among mankind. If you apply this

simple and universal rule to employers and labourers, landlords and tenants, the princes and their subjects, or the Hindus and the Muslims, you will find that the happiest relations can be established in all walks of life without creating disturbance in and dislocation of life and business which you see in India as in other parts of the world ... What, for example, is the duty of the Hindu to his Muslim neighbour? His duty is to befriend him as a man, to share his joys and sorrows and help him in distress.[99]

While it is the duty of all persons to non-cooperate with institutions of oppression, it is also their duty to recognize that their well-being is invested in that of others.

As a result, the development of an egalitarian order requires the wealthy to recognize that 'everything belonged to God and was from God' and therefore 'when an individual had more than his proportionate portion he became a trustee of that portion for God's people.'[100] Based on the notion that no just and egalitarian society could develop out of the (violent) dispossession of the wealthy from their land and possessions, Gandhi conceived of trusteeship as a duty of the wealthy. For Guha, like Marxist nationalists of the period, Gandhi's theory of trusteeship reveals the way in which 'the bourgeoisie used the idiom of Dharma in order to promote class conciliation as well as to secure a place for its own interests.'[101] Guha considers trusteeship a tactic to avoid a 'class war' while providing the appearance of economic reform.

Gandhi's theory of trusteeship is a deeply problematic idea articulated in vastly different ways in different contexts, and constructed as an ethical imperative without a clear description of possible modes of practical implementation. While Gandhi writes that his 'objective is to reach your heart and convert you so that you may hold all your private property in trust for your tenants and use it primarily for their welfare,'[102] he also argues that where the Socialists want to defeat or 'do away with' the privileged classes, he wants 'them to outgrow their greed and *sense of possession*, and to come down in spite of their wealth to the level of those who earn their bread by labour.'[103] In effect, as Gandhi writes elsewhere, *zamindars* must reduce themselves to poverty. Paradoxically, the latter proposition allows the *zamindar* the maintenance of wealth, in name, but in practice requires the forfeiting of the material privilege this wealth affords, while acquiring a greater consciousness of human interdependence, through such practices as 'bread labour.' Like the issue of untouchability, Gandhi again focuses his attention primarily upon those privileged within relationship, and largely confines himself to promoting a change in attitude, regarding structural change as developing out of, or following, such a cultural change; ultimately, if landowners, for instance, give up the privilege of their holdings and share their land, then their 'ownership' of that land becomes meaningless. Gandhi's emphasis on the privileged in extra-colonial relationships of inequality and his conceiving of change in terms of a cause and effect relationship are inconsistent with the theory of power I have traced in his writings, and the resistance as transformation I seek to theorize.

Gandhi writes that it does not matter how many trustees can actually attain this ideal: 'But as we strive for it, we shall be able to go further in realizing a state of equality on earth than by any other method ... It is my firm conviction that if the State suppresses capitalism by violence, it will be caught in the coils of violence itself, and fail to develop non-violence at any time ... That possessors of wealth have not acted up to the theory does not prove its falsity; it proves the weakness of the wealthy.'[104] If colonialism – and other forms of domination, as well – is, indeed, a matter of consciousness, then resistance requires not only the transformation of material and political structures (i.e., capitalism and colonial governance) but also the transformation of the values, attitudes, and perceptions of those who act within those structures. In the examples of 'anti-untouchability' and trusteeship, Gandhi seems to unduly limit his attention to the transformation of values, rather than structures. However, like Gandhi's conception of 'fearlessness,' the notion of agency constructed within trusteeship reveals the intimate relationship between the dominant and the subjugated, similar in so far that the end of domination requires the participation and transformation of both. Unlike Bhabha's theory of 'spectacular resistance,' which seemingly elides the responsibility for colonial domination of either those who are privileged or those who suffer by constructing both the colonized and colonizer as products of colonial discourse, Gandhi's idiom of *dharma*, within the larger discourse of *ahimsa*, constructs oppression as a structure constituted by those who participate within it and, hence, foregrounds the responsibility, and agency, of the subject.

The relation between the Self and the Other assumed within such a notion of responsibility is particularly visible, and problematic, in the emphasis Gandhi places on individual suffering as an act of 'resistance.' The value Gandhi places upon suffering constructs the individuation of the subject as being produced through acts acknowledging interdependence with the Other. Speaking to fellow Indians in South

Africa in 1906 on the decision to perform *satyagraha* against the so-called 'Black Act,' Gandhi explains: 'We will only provoke ridicule in the beginning ... We might have to go to jail ... might be deported ... some of us might fall ill and even die ... It is not impossible that we might have to endure every hardship that we can imagine, and wisdom lies in pledging ourselves on the understanding that we shall have to suffer all that and worse.'[105] If the welfare of all, or *sarvadoya*, is the goal of struggle, as opposed to what Gandhi calls 'utilitarian goals,' the votaries of *ahimsa* must see themselves as expendable in so far as this may aid the struggle: 'He will strive for the greatest good of all and die in the attempt to realize this idea.'[106] While *ahimsa*, as an ethic of social conduct, relies upon such themes as simplicity and selflessness, which include conscious and purposeful self-sacrifice and suffering, significantly, Gandhi constructs the concept of absolute suffering, or suffering unto death, only within the discourse of *satyagraha*.

In her critique of the competing European and Orthodox Hindu discourses of *sati*, Spivak notes the way in which, within the principles of *tatvajnana*, suicide ceases to become a killing of the self when it is performed as the realization of enlightenment: 'The paradox of knowing the limits of knowledge is that the strongest assertion of agency, to negate the possibility of agency, cannot be an example of itself.'[107] While 'selflessness' was central to the individual practice of *ahimsa*, as an ideal, rather than a tangible goal – in terms of seeking to reduce one's possessions and individuality, in so far as it was constructed in competition with that of others – suffering and suffering unto death are necessary in a struggle that depends upon the recognition of one's duty to others: 'Non-violence in its dynamic condition means conscious suffering. It does not mean meek submission to the will of the evil-doer, but it means the pitting of one's whole soul against the will of the tyrant.'[108] Unlike the *sati* that Spivak describes, in which Orthodox Hinduism constructs the woman's self-immolation as an act of devotion to her husband, revealing 'the structure of domination within the rite,'[109] the suffering that Gandhi speaks of is either a limited personal suffering for the purposes of purification or a willingness to suffer in order to reveal or expose a structure of domination to 'melt the stoniest heart of the stoniest fanatic.'[110] The *satyagrahi* suffers not in obedience to a superior 'other,' or as a 'martyr.' The absolute suffering of *satyagraha* is related to, but distinct from, the suffering of the desire for selflessness, in that as a mode of confronting oppression it does not recognize the opponent or adversary as an antagonist.

While Gandhi invests the performance of resistance within both the Indian elite and those subjugated within the system, recognizing their responsibility in the maintenance of an oppressive structure of relations, he does not absolve the administrators and beneficiaries of colonial, capitalist, or patriarchal relations of power from their responsibility. In Fanon's narrative of decolonization, colonial discourse shapes the native's perception of the self as the mirror image of that of the colonizer; in response to the Manichean framework of colonial discourse – in which the settler constructs 'the absolute evil of the native' – the native constructs its own identity against 'the absolute evil of the settler.'[111] Within such a discourse, conflict can only be 'resolved' through the total defeat or destruction of one or the other of the antagonists. Native resistance within a Manichean struggle, as Fanon describes it, is constructed through the belief that 'life can only spring up again out of the rotting corpse of the settler.'[112] The *ahimsaic* struggle, in contrast, figures the 'adversaries' in radically different ways than the discourse of 'battle.' While the tactics of *satyagraha* can quite accurately be characterized as simply a nonviolent violence, in the sense that civil disobedience can function coercively within an ideology of conflict in the same way that the tactic of guerrilla warfare does, Gandhi's notion of *ahimsa* is not simply a tactic of struggle. 'True democracy or Swaraj of the masses,' Gandhi writes, 'can never come through untruthful and violent means, for the simple reason that the natural corollary to their use would be to remove all opposition through the suppression or extermination of the antagonists.'[113] When Moorthy, in *Kanthapura*, pleads with his followers to not beat the police officer, he is acting upon the *ahimsaic* precept to hate the 'sin' but not the 'sinner': 'It is quite proper to resist and attack a system, but to resist and attack its author is tantamount to resisting and attacking oneself.'[114] Nonviolence, then, derives from a respect for interrelationships, recognizing the subject's agency to cultivate change, but also the ideological and structural conditions that inform behaviour.

As much as *swaraj* requires the liberation of the people of India from material exploitation and the cultural violence of colonial discourse and the ideology of caste, it also requires the 'liberation' of the British from the cultural violence of colonial discourse. Leela Gandhi argues that the theoretical *satyagrahi*, by definition, must assume that he or she possesses truth: 'The *satyagrahi*'s specific acts of resistance against contesting or authoritarian discourses begin with the knowledge that the moral victory has already been resolved in his/her favour.'[115] However, as much as struggle shaped by the principles of *ahimsa* derives from the moral certitude of the *satyagrahi*, it is nonetheless humble. By recognizing the humanity of the Other, the path of *ahimsa* requires that the *satyagrahi* appeal to the conscience of the adversary or to illuminate injustice. Gandhi recognizes, for instance, the way in which the colonial system conditions the British or Indian administrator to act coercively and violently; hence, structural change requires the administrator to become cognizant of the violence of which he is a functionary. Recurring throughout Gandhi's writings is the principle of conversion: 'I embark on my campaign as much out of my love for the Englishman as for the Indian. By self-suffering I seek to convert him, never to destroy him.'[116] Nonetheless, Gandhi also argues that 'we must refuse to wait for the wrong to be righted till the wrong-doer has been roused to a sense of his iniquity ... we must combat the wrong by ceasing to assist the wrong-doer directly or indirectly.'[117]

As I argue in chapter 2, oppositional discourses of resistance are derived from, and rely upon, the notion of 'implacable enmity.' Fanon's conclusion to *The Wretched of the Earth* appears incongruous with the Manichean framework of colonial discourse/power he constructs throughout the book. He writes: 'For Europe, for ourselves, and for humanity, comrades, we must turn over a new leaf, we must work out new concepts, and try to set afoot a new man.'[118] Fanon's 'new humanism' has no basis in the ideology of resistance he describes. Said does not seem cognizant of this paradox in Fanon's work, and he contends that he seeks to formulate an alternative to the politics of blame and political reality of confrontation, hostility, and the cycle of violence, though he fails to acknowledge the contradiction between the essential antagonism of anti-colonial insurgency and nationalism and the possibility of producing a non-adversarial community.

Remembering his fascination with the British Empire as a youth, Gandhi recollects the jarring effect of becoming conscious of the figure of the 'enemy' in the British anthem: 'How could we assume that the so-called "enemies" were "knavish"? And because they were enemies, were they bound to be wrong?'[119] The material reality of privilege and deprivation, domination and subjugation, is not elided in Gandhi's *ahimsaic* discourse. However, *ahimsa*, as an ethic of social conduct, confronts and requires the transformation of not only the material and social domination of oppression but the ideology of oppression or colonial knowledge/discourse. As Nandy argues: 'Ultimately, modern oppression, as opposed to traditional oppression, is not an encounter between the self and the enemy, the rulers and the ruled, or the gods and the demons. It is a battle between dehumanized self and the objectified enemy, the technologized bureaucrat and his reified victim, pseudo-rulers and their fearsome other selves projected on to their "subjects."'[120] Resistance, therefore, as understood through the concept of *ahimsa*, does not signify the insurgency of the 'oppressed' against the 'oppressor,' but the transformation of the material and discursive structures that maintain oppression; a 'new humanism' *is* resistance rather than its after-effect or aim.

The Subaltern Studies' representation of the ideological framework of peasant insurgency constructs resistance as a politics of blame and antagonism: 'We know, for instance, that the identification of the enemy in peasant revolts, the separation of the "they" from the "we," occurs within a framework where the distinct communities are seen as being in antagonistic relations with each other.'[121] Just as Rao reveals in *Kanthapura* the way in which Gandhi and Gandhism are subject to interpretation by peasant communities and are understood in terms of the dominant discourses of those communities, he also reveals the way in which the Gandhian construction of the enemy/Other challenges dominant notions of the nature of conflict and resistance. Following his beating by the police officer, Badè Khan, Moorthy attempts to explain that Khan is not the enemy:

> 'The great enemy is in us Rangamma,' said Moorthy, slowly, 'hatred is in us. If only we could not hate, if only we could show fearlessness, calm affection toward our fellow men, we would be stronger, and not only would the enemy yield, but he would be converted. If I, I alone, could love Badè Khan, I am sure our cause would win. Maybe – I shall love him – with your blessings!' Rangamma did not understand this, neither, to tell you the truth, did any of us. We would do harm to no living creature. But to love Badè Khan – no that was another thing.[122]

Ahimsa does not accord with the normative understanding of the narrative of conflict, in which the Self is constructed as 'benign,' 'just,' and acting only in 'self-defence' while the enemy/Other is constructed as 'evil,' 'unjust,' and 'aggressive.'

Moorthy's desire to 'love' Khan, however, when read within Gandhi's theory of conflict, does not reflect a utopian hope that the conflict situation can be simply transcended through a recognition of the common humanity of the adversaries. Gandhi counsels the *satyagrahi*:

> I want you to feel like loving your opponents, and the way to do it is to give them the same credit for honesty of purpose which you would claim for yourself ... I confess that it was a difficult task for me yesterday whilst I was talking to those friends who insisted on their right to exclude the 'unapproachables' from the temple roads. I confess there was selfishness behind their talk. How then was I to credit them with honesty of purpose? ... I am considering their condition of mind from their point of view and not my own ... And immediately we begin to think of things as our opponents think of them, we shall be able to do them full justice. I know that this requires a detached state of mind, and it is a state very difficult to reach ... three-fourths of the miseries and misunderstandings in the world will disappear, if we step into the shoes of our adversaries and understand their standpoint.[123]

Gandhi's deconstruction of the Self/Other binary of colonial discourse, and the dominant discourses of resistance, therefore, reconceptualizes conflict without eliding the structures of inequality that produce the conflict or the competing interests and perspectives of the parties involved.

4 Reconciliation as Resistance: Transforming South Africa

Resistance and the Apartheid Imagination

South African cultural production, from song, to poetry, to the novel, provided a prominent mode of fostering communities of opposition to the apartheid government. As much as oppositional literature or song provided representations of power from the perspective of the oppressed, however, it also often reinscribed the discursive construction of power and identity of apartheid (colonial) rule.[1] During the apartheid era, literary production challenged colonial authority and participated in the production of counter-narratives of South African identity. Many writers and artists were imprisoned or forced into exile. Alongside the rise of the Black Consciousness movement in the 1970s, a genre of literature developed that conveyed narratives of protest. This literature of protest recorded a history of oppositional politics that was occluded from the official narrative of apartheid; further, it sought to build community and inspire resistance. For instance, Jane Watts argues that 'Soweto novels' such as Sipho Sepamla's *A Ride on the Whirlwind* (1981), Miriam Tlali's *Amandla* (1980), and Mongane Serote's *To Every Birth Its Blood* (1981) 'educate the political awareness of the readers, help them to understand the mechanisms of community action, and ... deepen their commitment to a common cause.'[2] So-called 'novels of liberation' such as these provide a narrative of oppression from the perspective of those who suffer under it and who seek to dismantle it; these novels engage with the experience of violence. In contrast, works by Nadine Gordimer and J.M. Coetzee, writers whose work has received a much more prominent place in postcolonial literary studies, often ground narratives of oppression and opposition not in particular historical moments of apartheid violence, but in the condition of apartheid violence.

Nadine Gordimer's *July's People* (1981), for instance, reflects the limitations of apartheid discourse for imagining the future; it represents the way in which the assumption that apartheid could only end in/through a bloody civil war excludes the possibility of alternative models of social transformation. Written in the wake of the Soweto uprising, *July's People* contributes to the cultural entrenchment of the spectre of the uprising – rather than the event itself – in the consciousness(es) of South Africans. The novel portrays the escape of a white Johannesburg family – Bam and Maureen Smales and their children – from a bloody war between 'whites' and 'blacks' to the rural homestead of their black worker, July. While the novels cited above reflect upon the social and cultural impact of the cycle of violence precipitated by the brutal repression of student demonstrations in Soweto, Gordimer depicts this cycle of violence as the inevitable condition of South African experience. Set in a 'hypothetical, but really inevitable black rebellion,' as Abdul JanMohamed describes it,[3] the novel provides insight into the nature of the 'apartheid imagination.' *July's People* depicts South Africa's future as irrevocably one of mass violence. This bloodbath is the unavoidable expression of a structure of power in which there is no possible relationship between blacks and whites that is not hierarchical, unequal, and antagonistic. The apartheid imagination shapes the way in which power and identity are constructed and the way in which 'resistance' may be imagined. Further, as a particular manifestation of colonial discourse, the apartheid imagination limits the possibility of reconciliation; yet it is the discourse that reconciliation seeks to transform.

Tracing the beginnings of revolution to the industrial strikes of 1980, Gordimer constructs a narrative of apartheid's collapse, marked by riots in which white neighbourhoods are razed and by a well-equipped and well-organized black military insurgency, supported by Russia and Cuba. Hidden in the rural village of their servant July, the Smales hear reports on the radio of attacks from guerrilla bases in Mozambique and missile strikes against South Africa's cities. The bloodshed of civil war, however, provides merely a backdrop to Gordimer's story of the hypocrisy of white liberalism in South Africa. Maureen is confused by July's 'hope that everything will come back all right,' as if apartheid was not only better than civil war but an acceptable state of affairs.[4] Similarly, Bam is awestruck by the village chief's desire for Bam to teach him how to shoot, so that the village can defend itself against black insurgents from Soweto and Mozambique, whom the chief fears will come to 'take this country of my nation.'[5] The Smales' discomfort with the seeming complicity of these blacks with apartheid, however, belies their own presumptions of 'equality' with blacks. Both Maureen and Bam are also deeply troubled by their vulnerable position, suddenly dependent upon July's goodwill.

The anxiety the Smales experience over the disappearance of the keys to the car – their only means of escape – and then their gun – their only means of 'protection' – signifies their loss of mastery over their own well-being and, significantly, over July/blacks. As critical as Maureen and Bam may be of apartheid, and intellectually supportive of the black struggle, the seeming reversal of their long-established master/servant relationship is deeply unsettling. As JanMohamed argues, 'as [Maureen] becomes increasingly aware of the radical character of her dependency, she attempts to manipulate July in a progressively mean and desperate manner in order to retain her mastery.'[6] The fact that blacks now have guns and have begun to exercise this new-found means of power by blowing up the Union Buildings or burning master bedrooms suggests an 'explosion of roles.'[7] However, the Manichean discourse of black/white relations is not challenged; only the certainty of who occupies the role of master and of servant has been disrupted. Indeed, the reversal of roles Gordimer constructs in this novel conforms both to Fanon's narrative of struggle in which the colonized seek to take the place of the colonizer as well as to the National government's justification of the security state as a *reaction to* African belligerence and barbarity and the threat of the ANC and 'communists.' The violence of the colonial project, as Mamdani argues, was rationalized by the settler's projection of the spectre of genocide upon the desires of the colonized.[8]

After Bam and Maureen's heated exchange with July over the whereabouts of the gun, Maureen contemplates the extent to which she and her family are now dependent upon their former black servant for water, soap, and protection, which allows her, for a moment, to recognize the extent to which July had been dependent upon them: 'She matched the remembered total dependency with this one. – Used to come to ask for everything. An aspirin. Can I use the telephone. Nothing in that house was his. – Well ... he wasn't kept short of anything. Anything we had to give. – I wonder what would have become of him.'[9] Momentarily, Maureen seems to realize her complicity in apartheid. Yet Bam rationalizes this dependence as benevolence, and Maureen returns to a paternalistic understanding of their relationship; within the apartheid imagination, blacks are either a threat to the (white) nation or 'children' who need (white) protection and guidance. Maureen is unable to imagine a relationship between herself and July that is not one of dependence; hence, her realization of her own dependence on July is deeply unsettling. Caught in the 'interregnum' of the revolutionary moment, Gordimer's narrative depicts the dismantling of both white security and identity; the novel concludes with Maureen described in language reserved for non-human animals, as she flees the village into the unknown.

JanMohamed argues that the apartheid system constructs whites as independent from blacks through policies of 'separate development,' masking the real dependence of whites on exploited black labour: 'While zealously fighting godless communist totalitarianism, he has in fact created the most ruthless, authoritarian, and systematically inhuman society in the contemporary world.'[10] As a result, JanMohamed argues that the work of writers such as Gordimer or Alex La Guma must be examined within this 'violent, antagonistic, and Manichean society.' JanMohamed's reading of a novel like *July's People*, therefore, concentrates upon – and I would argue reinforces – the Manichean relationship Gordimer constructs as irrevocable. Within such a discourse of apartheid power, the relatively peaceful transition from apartheid to liberal democracy in South Africa appeared impossible. Novels like *July's People*, or even the Soweto novels cited above, construct a cultural memory of violent conflict as power and resistance.

The role of violent opposition in the cultural memory of the 'New South Africa' is particularly evident in assessments of the Truth and Reconciliation Commission (TRC), which was set up by South Africa's government of National Unity through the 1995 Promotion of National Unity and Reconciliation Act. By and large, these assessments focus upon the extent to which the commission has succeeded or failed to facilitate liberation, or rather, in the place of liberation, 'justice.' For the most part, these analyses fail to examine the way in which the apartheid discourse I have identified in Gordimer's *July's People* and in JanMohamed's analysis of it shapes perceptions of the TRC and the apartheid era, and fail to acknowledge their own (particularly Western) assumptions of power and justice. Indeed, in most criticism of the TRC, both academic and popular, it is referred to as the 'Truth Commission,' the idea of reconciliation marginalized by an overriding interest with how the commission produces 'Truth' about South Africa's past, and how it does so seemingly at the expense of (retributive) justice.

The ANC's ambivalent relationship with the TRC illuminates the sorts of contradictions between justice, liberation, reconciliation, and the limits of the apartheid imagination I seek to examine. While some critics have suggested that the TRC's mapping of South African history has unduly emphasized the ANC, and particularly its armed wing, Umkhonto we Sizwe (MK), the ANC was also hesitant to allow members to seek 'amnesty' for human rights abuses committed during the struggle for liberation. However, the simplistic equation of the anti-apartheid struggle with the ANC – and armed insurgency specifically – privileges the mythology of violent insurgency over the multitude of other modes of struggle practised by the ANC and other organizations.[11] Echoing the contention expressed in the TRC's final report that armed struggle was easily contained by the government, former MK organizer and, later, ANC government minister Ronnie Kasrils acknowledges that ANC-supported military insurgency never developed beyond the symbolic. He acknowledges that because the MK was small and poorly equipped, its main aim was to 'create propaganda amongst the people to inspire the people.'[12] The struggle against apartheid, though it included violence – both in the form of so-called 'black-on-black' violence and in the form of attacks on the government – drew upon a variety of tactics, from campaigns of non-cooperation to the establishment of alternative social and political structures to international divestment campaigns.

Recognizing these modes of resistance that sought to transform relationships, rather than, for instance, invert them, helps create a cultural memory within which reconciliation can be sought. Rosemary Jolly argues that 'as critics, teachers, and students, we need to forge a language beyond apartheid that refuses to hypostatize South Africa as the model in which the colonized black and the settler white eternally confront each other in the "ultimate racism."'[13] While postcolonial critiques of colonial authority identify the ambivalence of the colonial will-to-power or deconstruct the Manichean framework of colonial knowledge, the binary framework of colonial constructions of identity shaped, and continues to shape, memory, consciousness, and action. The fact that there was much more 'diversity and division' within the homogeneous black and white 'blocks' created through apartheid does not alter the reality that such simplifications nonetheless shape political action.[14] As Kenneth Christie argues, despite the ANC's stated aims of creating a non-racial nation, the structure of ANC ideology is based on the antagonism between the oppressed and the colonist: 'There is no language of moral ambiguities or nuances. The struggle is a just one, and there was no alternative to it.'[15] Indeed, although the civic movements undermined white authority much more significantly than the armed struggle, the songs of struggle, as much as they revealed the resilience of those who suffered under apartheid, or helped to boost morale and build community, often drew upon a rhetoric of violent militancy and total victory.[16] For instance, in the novel *Mother to Mother* (1998), which I discuss later in this chapter, Sindiwe Magona has the youth who kill a white American student chanting 'one settler, one bullet,' a sentiment expressed in many of the songs of struggle.

When questioned on his commitment to violent revolution throughout the 1980s, Nelson Mandela states that while he would not renounce violence to gain his release from Robben Island, he recognized that 'violence could never be the ultimate solution to the situation in South Africa and that men and women by their very nature required some kind of negotiated understanding.'[17] Significantly, Mandela suggests that 'liberation' cannot come through violent revolution (alone) but through mutual *understanding*. I think it is important, here, to distinguish between the ideas of mutual understanding and negotiated settlement, the first conforming to a notion of conflict transformation, and the latter to a notion of conflict resolution. Within the narrative structure of the apartheid imagination, such negotiation can only come *after* the struggle has ended. South African President F.W. de Klerk, who brokered the end of the political institution of apartheid, stated in 1990: '"The season for violence is over. The time for reconstruction and reconciliation has arrived."'[18] Similarly, Thabo Mbeki, ANC leader and successor to Nelson Mandela as president, conceives of reconciliation as an 'end-product' of a period of struggle to end apartheid.[19] The historical narrative of the apartheid imagination constructs the cultivation of understanding, therefore, as a post-conflict endeavour – following the 'genuine' (violent) struggle – rather than a means of conflict transformation.[20]

Within such a narrative, reconciliation functions as that 'great leap' from resistance to liberation. Hence, it is recognized as a step or period in a teleological narrative, following the 'battle' or 'conflict' and, significantly, preceding the next moment in South African history, the 'new' non-racial and democratic nation. The TRC, as a particular institution charged with *fostering* reconciliation, does occur *after* a period of negotiations and the first inclusive democratic elections. However, the ideals of reconciliation helped to shape many aspects of the anti-apartheid movement; the process of reconciliation, therefore, cannot be contained within the TRC. Indeed, though the commission published a wide-ranging and comprehensive final report detailing the history, strategies, and structures of apartheid, as well as forms of resistance to it, the most prominent and public aspects of the TRC's work, the victims' and amnesty hearings, which were broadcast and discussed daily for nearly a year between 1996 and 1997, focused specifically on experiences of direct violence, such as torture, state summary executions, and anti-apartheid militant insurgency. While women had a prominent place in the victims' hearings, they seldom spoke of their own experiences of the dailyness of apartheid oppression, but instead spoke for their dead husbands and sons and were expected to provide forgiveness to those who had killed them. Just as the voice of July's wife is largely silenced in *July's People*, the mandate of the hearings marginalized stories of the experience of structural violence.

I am not concerned with evaluating the mandate or work of the commission itself, or the figures of Tutu or Mandela within this particular initiative; rather, I am concerned with analysing how the concept of reconciliation is constructed within the TRC, as well as in both the rhetoric and strategies of the anti-apartheid struggle. By discussing the idea of reconciliation in terms of the concerns of postcolonial theory, I seek to analyse the interdependence of discursive and material relations of power within the concept, as it is articulated in the South African context. As Magona's novel reveals, the direct violence of state repression and youth revolt were enmeshed in the daily deprivations of apartheid structures and policies, from inadequate education and lack of access to employment, to the history of forced removals and family separations. These forms of violence were understood, and perpetuated, by narratives of belonging and difference. Through my analysis of the TRC and Magona's novel, I argue that the model of individual apology and forgiveness of the TRC does not provide the framework for the sort of cultural and material transformation imagined in the idea of the 'new' South Africa. I return to Said's notion of the rhetoric and politics of blame, and propose as a corollary to this the rhetoric and politics of denial. Both blame and denial are embedded in the mythologies, narratives, and values of the apartheid imagination, and limit the possibilities for social change. The project of reconciliation resists the apartheid imagination not just by deconstructing colonial knowledge, but by producing an alternative discourse and demanding an alternative structure of relations that focuses on recognition, redistribution, and connection.

Reconciliation: Deconstructing Antagonism / Dismantling Apartheid

The TRC provides an institutional mode of coming to terms with the history of a nation 'soaked in the blood of her children of all races and of all political persuasions,' to use Desmond Tutu's description.[21] The main responsibilities of the TRC were to establish as complete a history as possible of gross violations of human rights – including, for instance, abduction, torture, and murder – committed between the Sharpeville massacre of 1960 and May 1994; grant amnesty to those who disclosed their participation in politically motivated violations; facilitate the restoration of human dignity of the victims of these violations by providing them a venue to share their stories, and for relatives by allowing them to learn of the fate of their relations; recommend a regime of reparations for victims; and recommend measures to prevent future violations.

The commission's mandate, as well as the time and resources it was provided to fulfil this mandate, was extremely limited. For instance, the commission's public hearings on human rights abuses and amnesty define the subjects of apartheid as either perpetrators or victims; hence, these hearings privilege direct interpersonal violence over other forms of control and exploitation, and gross violations of human rights over the daily experience of the structural violence of apartheid. Further, although all of the parties participating in the government of national unity took part in the negotiations that designed the mandate of the TRC, the commission seems to have satisfied none of these parties. For instance, the National Party portrayed the commission as a witch-hunt against whites, the ANC impeded the work of the commission, and more marginalized anti-apartheid leaders, such as Inkatha's Mangosuthu Buthelezi, argued that the commission's framework simplistically produced the struggle as one between black resistance and white oppression, marginalizing human rights violations perpetrated among blacks, particularly by the ANC against members of Inkatha.

While the TRC follows the anti-apartheid struggle and marks an anticipatory moment of transformation, the process of reconciliation is not limited to the activities of the TRC; indeed, to some degree, the antagonisms the commission reveals – and perhaps reinforces – and the ideological limits of its mandate in some ways provide an obstacle to reconciliation. My concern, therefore, is not with analysing the TRC alone, but with examining how the idea of reconciliation in South Africa serves as both an ideal of liberation and a praxis of resistance. Despite the dominant representation of the anti-apartheid movement as violent opposition to the oppression of apartheid, anti-apartheid resistance, including that of the ANC, is much more ambivalent, and power – in terms of the relationship between government authority and anti-apartheid opposition – is much more complex. I believe that reconciliation provides a significant alternative narrative of resistance to the dominant narrative of ANC opposition as armed struggle against the white government. Albie Sachs argues that despite a chorus of claims that the avoidance of civil war was a miracle, the negotiated end to apartheid was completely predictable, and 'certainly the most unmiraculous.'[22] The reconciliation project in South Africa is not simply a pragmatic post-conflict initiative or an 'attempt to turn over a new leaf,' to use Fanon's analogy of the nature of liberation.

By fostering reconciliation between individuals and beginning a process of reconciling the 'new' nation with its past, the TRC was meant to continue the process of reconciling communities and groups with one another, thereby fostering national unity. For instance, a commission such as the TRC may restore confidence in basic procedural justice, constructed within the responsibility of the state to protect the citizen.[23] However, national reconciliation, as it is defined in the TRC report and by its chair, Archbishop Desmond Tutu, has a much broader mandate than revealing 'truths' or instilling confidence in the institutions of the state; indeed, reconciliation may challenge the status of such institutions. According to the TRC report, reconciliation seeks to allow individuals to come to terms with their own pain and neighbourhoods and communities to engage in their own formal and informal processes towards reconciliation. Such processes construct reconciliation not simply as 'explanations' of local histories, but as an alternative politics of inclusion and participation.[24]

As an attempt to permanently end the cycle of violence of oppression/opposition, reconciliation constitutes an interrelated process of material and cultural transformation and not just interpersonal reconciliation between the perpetrators and victims of human rights abuses. While postcolonial theorists problematize the binaries of colonial discourse as ambivalent, reconciliation acknowledges the way in which colonial discourse constructs the colonizer and colonized, settler and

African, and therefore shapes 'knowledge' of the conflict. As a result, I am particularly concerned with identifying ways in which the ethic of reconciliation informed aspects of the anti-apartheid movement. Reconciliation requires the deconstruction of the binary framework of the apartheid experience; yet, as a politics of social change, reconciliation challenges the politics of identity of the apartheid imagination, in order to transform relationships. As a mode of resistance, the object of reconciliation is not the oppressor/oppression but the antagonistic material and discursive relationship of colonialism. Based in the notion of *ubuntu*, a notion of subjectivity that constructs the self as interdependent with the other, reconciliation resists, by seeking to transform, the antagonistic binary framework of apartheid.

Reconciliation, as it came to be articulated in the TRC, has its roots within the anti-apartheid movement. While the ANC is often conflated with all anti-apartheid resistance – or 'black resistance' – against white rule, and the role of the MK tends to be privileged over other aspects of the ANC's work or other anti-apartheid organizations and initiatives, from its origins the ANC was an organization that was committed to working towards a non-racial state, rather than the eviction of the white settler, and it attempted to perform this change in its own institutional structure, welcoming members of all of the racially identified groups of the apartheid state. The 'Freedom Charter,' which was drafted at the 1955 Congress of the People, was adopted by the ANC in that year and reaffirmed in 1989. The Freedom Charter claims that South Africa 'belongs to all who live in it, black and white' and that 'our country will never be prosperous and free until all our people live in brotherhood, enjoying equal rights and opportunities.'[25] Organized around the call for democracy, equal rights, the nationalization of land, resources, and industry, the Charter utilizes a rights-based discourse to identify liberation, rather than one that equates liberation with the overcoming of the oppressor. The Charter's deviation from the dominant pan-Africanist discourses of the period set the ANC at odds with other nationalist movements within South Africa and on the continent.[26]

In many ways, however, the ideology of inclusion and equality espoused in the Freedom Charter was marginalized in popular representations of apartheid opposition; for instance, in the construction of the figure of Nelson Mandela as revolutionary hero (condemned as a 'terrorist' and lauded as 'hero/leader'), while he was in prison, anyway. Yet, Mandela is careful to describe the invitation to his jailer to be a special guest at his inauguration as president of South Africa in terms of the ideology of the Freedom Charter: 'In prison my anger toward whites decreased, but my hatred for the system grew. I wanted South Africa to see that I loved even my enemies while I hated the system that turned us against one another.'[27] Upon his release from prison, Mandela repeated a statement he made at the time of his sentencing in 1964: 'I have fought against white domination, and I have fought against black domination. I have cherished the ideal of a democratic and free society in which all persons live together in harmony with equal opportunities.'[28] Apartheid, as a conflict, is not a Manichean struggle between whites and blacks.

Yet, as evident from the rallying cry of 'one settler, one bullet,' the rhetoric of apartheid opposition, in its popular articulations, was very often constructed within such a Manichean framework. Government repression rendered the ANC politically ineffectual by the late 1960s, forcing many of those members who were not imprisoned into either hiding or exile. The violent repression of the Soweto student demonstrations in 1976 initiated a decade and a half of intense violence, primarily within the townships, pitting supporters of the ANC and United Democratic Front (UDF), Inkatha, and other organizations against one another, as well as against government security forces. However, while the 1980s and early 1990s were particularly violent, this violence did not primarily take the form of organized guerrilla opposition, directed against the settler, as in Fanon's narrative of anti-colonial violence or Gordimer's dystopian *July's People*. Further, it was not the primary mode of opposition or dissent. Initiatives and acts understood within apartheid's oppositional discourse – i.e., the anti-government discourse of 'one settler, one bullet' – shared the same space with organizations and campaigns that did not simply pay lip-service to the ideal of a nonracial South African future but incorporated this ideal into the praxis of struggle.

While the dominant or official historical accounts of the anti-apartheid struggle continue to privilege the initiatives of the ANC, the most prominent organizing networks of the 1970s and 1980s, the emergence of labour organizing across racial divisions, civic associations, and the United Democratic Front (UDF), which were uneasily linked with one another, were organized through a discourse of resistance that imagined power not as something to be 'won' or 'taken' but 'exerted'; change was imagined not simply as the destruction of apartheid but as the creation of a new South Africa. The UDF drew together South Africans of all racialized groups and political ideologies in a loose political network, affiliated with grassroots and community-based civic associations, women's groups, and youth groups. Originally formed in 1983 to coordinate opposition to a proposed constitution that would permanently exclude blacks from the democratic process, the UDF facilitated a wide variety of initiatives and actions throughout the 1980s. The political leadership, and hence the organization's ideology, was informed by the resurgence of Charterism in the period, though it emphasized the Freedom Charter's discourse of rights and inclusive non-racialism, with less of a commitment to the Charter's socialist vision.[29] The UDF functioned in the interstices of apartheid power, providing links between diverse groups that shared the desire for an end to apartheid. As such, the movement fit neither within the political discourse of apartheid, which recognized parties and organizations and understood the conflict in terms of terrorism and security, nor within the racial hierarchy, which was the basis of that discourse.[30]

On the other hand, the township-based civic associations, which, in some cases, became explicitly linked to the UDF, drew upon the idea of 'people power' to seek redress for local experiences of the structural violence of apartheid, from overcrowded housing to rent and bus fare increases. Over the course of the 1980s, the focus of many civic associations turned to the larger problem of the struggle for a democratic alternative to apartheid: 'The civics' choices of strategies and tactics rested upon several crucial universal norms, values and practices: non-racialism, mass participatory democracy, a commitment to fight apartheid (including its fake reforms) until one-person one-vote in a unitary state was obtained.'[31] While the civics often focused their attention, at least initially, on seeking redress from the state for specific and local material grievances – rather than struggling against the State and apartheid – these associations often functioned as alternatives to the state-sponsored township councils, not only in terms of providing a shadow government but by organizing in more democratic, participatory, and inclusive ways; for instance, women who were otherwise excluded from political institutions in the apartheid state undertook prominent roles in the civics. Hence, the demand for the alleviation of specific forms of apartheid's structural violence required the development of social and political structures that performed the alternative that the communities were seeking, at least in a limited way.

The persistent call by religious leaders such as Desmond Tutu and Allan Boesak for resistance imagined not as *opposition to* apartheid but the *production of* a non-racial, democratic, participatory, and just South Africa provides another example of the way in which reconciliation constitutes not simply a politically pragmatic policy in the post-apartheid era but an objective and ideal that served as a praxis of the anti-apartheid struggle. The warning of mass violence and suffering that recurs throughout Tutu's sermons and letters from the early 1970s onwards is coupled with the cultivation of the idea of reconciliation as its alternative. In his eulogy for Steve Biko in 1977, Tutu assures the crowd of more than fifteen thousand that liberation is coming, 'where all of us, black and white together, will hold hands as we stride forth on the Freedom March to usher in the new South Africa where people will matter because they are human beings made in the image of God.'[32] Tutu imagines reconciliation as being a means of the struggle, rather than a project to follow liberation from apartheid. Similarly, in a 1984 speech, Boesak counselled: 'Let us not build our struggle upon hatred, bitterness and the desire for revenge. Let us even now seek to lay the foundation for reconciliation between white and black in this country by working together, praying together, struggling together for justice.'[33] Tutu and Boesak do not construct 'victory' as the *transfer* of power from 'whites' to 'blacks,' or merely the transition from minority rule to democracy, but the *transformation* of racialized identities and relationships.

It is important here, however, to remember the critique of Steve Biko. The Black Consciousness movement, with which Biko is so closely identified, defined the South African 'problem' not simply as apartheid, or the political and economic system of separation, but white racism.[34] Hence, Biko did not advocate a rights-based approach in which whites continued to hold disproportionate influence and privilege, for such an approach, Biko argued, would integrate blacks into a system defined by the values of white culture and European dominance or superiority, without challenging the basis of that system.[35] While the Black Consciousness movement has been perceived as reinforcing the Manichean dualism of the apartheid imagination, the notion of 'Blackness,' for which the movement depends, challenges the colonial construction of race at the core of the apartheid system, and Biko invokes a notion of humanism that echoes that of Fanon. By including all peoples racialized as 'other' within apartheid South Africa under the category 'black,' the basis of the analysis, or movement, works to 'decolonize the mind.' Significantly, Biko's criticism of South African liberal politics foregrounds the importance of reconciliation not as a post-conflict project but as an approach to the conflict itself. For instance, he urges whites to come to terms with the fact that 'the history of the country may have to be rewritten at some stage and that we may live in a country where colour will not serve to put a man in a box.'[36] Biko's writings focus on the importance of coming to an alternative understanding or consciousness; the focus of his analysis is not on the need to 'overcome' whites, but the need to empower blacks, materially, through business cooperatives, for instance, and culturally, by promoting the values of sharing and community, as the alternative to fragmentation and individualism.[37]

In a 1988 address to an interfaith service, Tutu repeats a message and tone expressed in many of his speeches, sermons, and letters: 'Freedom is coming, and we want it also for you, Mr Vlok. We want you to be able to sleep at night and not wonder what we are up to ... Freedom is coming even for you, Mr P.W. Botha ... We want you to be here with us.'[38] Similar to Gandhi's overtures to Smuts, Tutu's appeals to National Party leaders not only articulate a hope of liberation as reconciliation – a process of re-humanizing all parties to the conflict – but constitute a reconciliatory act in itself, resisting the discursive construction of the antagonistic relationship between 'blacks' and 'whites.' Tutu claims that true revolution in South Africa would entail the transformation of the nation from an exploitative state that is dependent upon racial hierarchy to one that is democratic and non-racial.[39] Resistance, as reconciliation, as Tutu articulates it, escapes the power/counter-power dynamic of oppositional discourses, which inform National Party claims to be acting in the interests of South African 'security,' as well as oppositional – i.e., anti-colonial/anti-apartheid – constructions of resistance. Reconciliation, therefore, provides a significant alternative both to oppositional discourses of resistance and postcolonial analyses of the ambivalence of colonial power.

The TRC's final report summarizes the development of apartheid legislation, including the Group Areas Act, the Prohibition of Mixed Marriages Act, and the Bantu Education Act of the early 1950s. These acts institutionalized the racial hierarchy of South African society through separation, and they preceded the body of security legislation of the 1960s that directly responded to the campaigns of defiance and other forms of opposition to, and subversion of, this apartheid legislation. As Mandela describes in his autobiography, the South African government and the ANC became locked in a relationship of escalating conflict wherein each reacted to the tactics of the other. When, for instance, the defiance campaign of the 1950s – a nonviolent campaign of non-cooperation aimed at illuminating and challenging forms of structural violence, such as the pass laws – produced violent state repression, Mandela and other members of the ANC advocated for, and to a limited degree began practising, armed resistance. Characterized as 'terrorism' by the South African government, this threat of guerrilla insurgency led to the banning of the ANC, the mass imprisonment of ANC activists, and a variety of other modes of violent repression.

In its final report, the TRC *describes* the body of legislation that institutionalized the structural forms of apartheid violence. Analysis of these forms of structural violence foregrounds the differing and intersecting experiences of apartheid based on racial, gender, or class constructed positions; for instance, the Bantu education system specifically constructed different roles, and hence curricula, for boys and girls, and the separation of men from their families as labourers in factories or mines constructed particularly gendered experiences of apartheid for men and women. While people are harmed by such forms of structural violence, identifying the 'perpetrator' of such violence is more difficult, as this suffering is the effect of state policies rather than acts. The majority of the TRC's work, and the work that received public attention, focuses on individual experiences of direct violence, or gross human rights abuses and, as a result, marginalizes women's experiences of apartheid; women were not as likely as men to suffer direct violence by security forces but suffered as a result of structural forms of violence. The mandate of the TRC's most public and publicized work, the hearings and amnesty committees to investigate gross human rights abuses, actually reinforces the dominant discourse of black/white antagonism, in the form of ANC opposition to government violence and repression.

The South African 'security state,' however, is as much a response to resistance (opposition/subversion) as the violent opposition of the ANC is a response to repression. The violence of the apartheid state does not occur outside of history as an eternal conflict between evil and good, white and black. The violence of South Africa's security forces was neither an initial structure nor simply a response to violent insurgency. Rather, it preceded the ANC's turn to violence and was a response, therefore, to initiatives to foster unity and openness against the policy of 'separateness'; the South African 'security state,' and its reliance on methods of violent coercion, was, in large measure, a response to the refusal of racialized groups in South Africa to fulfil their positions within the political structures and, significantly, the discursive framework of apartheid, through various acts of non-cooperation and disobedience. The apartheid imagination had to be secured through violent repression. Hence, while there are individual perpetrators and victims of particular abuses, the individual experiences of the direct violence of apartheid shared at the various hearings of the TRC cannot function as a metaphor for the structure of power within which they occurred.

In *Empire*, Hardt and Negri conceptualize contemporary global power relations as a 'new' paradigm in which previous notions of sovereignty and political space no longer provide a useful critical framework for understanding power and social change. As a result, 'the traditional idea of counter-power and the idea of resistance against modern sovereignty in general thus become less and less possible.'[40] Hardt and Negri argue that with the emergence of 'Empire,' a 'new type of resistance has to be invented.'[41] I believe, however, that many of the qualities Hardt and Negri attribute to Empire can be discerned within South African apartheid, a social system that JanMohamed and others characterize as the most extreme example of 'traditional' colonial power. Resistance occurs along with the development of apartheid repression, rather than simply as a response to power, or, as Hardt and Negri imagine Empire, preceding power. Power and counter-power are interdependent and reinforcing. The apartheid 'security' state is not independent from opposition to it.

Mandela rationalizes ANC violence as both just and necessary because the oppressor 'dictates the form of the struggle' against it;[42] yet, in the case of South Africa, state repression or the methods of maintaining white oppression are as much a product of (nonviolent) resistance as resistance is a reaction to repression. As Kenneth Christie notes, mass non-cooperation in the 1980s and increasing violence in the townships during this period made the black population of South Africa progressively more ungovernable: 'The architects of the system of apartheid started to see power slipping away from them during the 1980s; it appeared to them that the only way to keep power was to increase levels of repression.'[43] Along these lines, Mahmood Mamdani argues that beginning in 1976 apartheid policy was dominated by the need to prevent the confluence of organized popular resistance among rural migrants in the townships and organized labour.[44] Gandhi's 'ultimatum' to Smuts, the burning of passes by members of the PAC and ANC in 1952, or the use of guerrilla warfare tactics challenged the status of white minority authority. These acts – both discursive and material –

escalated the conflict to the point where authority became impossible; as Hannah Arendt describes, state violence diminishes, rather than asserts, the power of that state.[45] Nelson Mandela, who was once recognized as a 'terrorist' by the state governments of Europe and North America, has been appropriated by Western media and officialdom, as well as the liberal left too, as a Third World hero, 'leader' of, and consequently metonym for, the anti-apartheid movement. However, violence in the townships, mass boycotts of white commerce, the instability of labour, and growing unwillingness by foreign governments and multinational corporations to support, and profit from, South Africa forced the National Party to negotiate secretly with Mandela and the ANC an end to the political system of apartheid. While these various modes of 'resistance' contributed to the escalation of the conflict, Tutu contends that the conflict did not escalate into civil war because of the way in which the notion of reconciliation informed much of this resistance and the desire for liberation.

Mamdani argues that many representations of the apartheid era, such as Asmal et al.'s *Reconciliation through Truth* (1997), reduce apartheid to its 'terror machine ... its evil to its gross abuses – and resistance to the armed struggle.'[46] Mamdani shifts the focus from direct violence to the economic and political *structures* of apartheid, and from the relatively limited and ineffective armed struggle to unarmed popular struggle. For instance, he emphasizes the 1973 strikes of white labourers in Durban and the 1976 Soweto 'uprising' by black youth as a great 'sea-change' in the struggle, shifting the agents of resistance from political organizations, largely operating from exile and depending on (the threat of) armed force, to community-based, largely nonviolent popular struggle:

> From the point of view of establishing a trajectory of reconciliation, Durban 1973 is an important marker, since it signified the move of radical white youth to the mainstream of resistance, blurring the identity of race with oppression. Similarly Soweto 1976 and Black Consciousness signified an even more important breach in the apartheid-nurtured identities of ethnic particularism. (Here, I include 'Indian' and 'Coloured' as ethnic identities.)[47]

Both of these moments, and the campaigns that developed out of them, respond not just to violent government repression but to the economic and political structures of apartheid.

While much critical analysis of the TRC concentrates upon the idea of truth or the failure of (retributive) justice within the process of public hearings, the narrative the TRC constructs in its final report carefully links the direct violence of human rights abuses to the structural violence of economic exploitation, displacement, etc. For instance, in its initial recommendations regarding reparations in volume 5, the commission draws on testimony from the business sector hearing to identify how 'political supremacy and racial capitalism impoverished Africans and enriched whites'; among other forms of structural violence, Africans were deprived of land and the right to own property, paid exploitative wages, and deprived of the human capital of education.[48] South African 'liberation' has a significant political character, in terms of inclusive liberal democratic governance and political rights. The libratory ideals of non-racialism and equity, however, also require a radical transformation of the economic system. As Tutu argues: 'Unless houses replace the hovels and shacks in which most blacks live, unless blacks gain access to clean water, electricity, affordable health care, decent education, good jobs, and a safe environment – things which the vast majority of whites have taken for granted for so long – we can just as well kiss reconciliation good-bye.'[49] In its final report, the TRC asserts that reconciliation requires radical social and material transformation, and not simply individual and collective acts of apology and forgiveness. The TRC and specifically the notion of reconciliation, however, have been, in large part, reduced to the notion of apology and forgiveness among individuals – as I will discuss below – and the politics of the 'new' South African state have been antithetical to the sorts of structural change Tutu argues constitute reconciliation.

However, as much as they are necessary for reconciliation, initiatives to redress the economic and social imbalances of apartheid – in the form of TRC-recommended reparations or policies of affirmative action – can also impede the cultivation of a non-racial political and social space. While Mamdani points to the Durban strikes and the Black Consciousness movement as important moments that blurred the distinction between oppression and racism and disrupted the black/white dichotomy that was so crucial to apartheid, the impact of apartheid-era social and economic policies was to make 'blackness' and 'poverty' nearly synonymous.[50] A process of reconciliation that emphasizes the experience of individual victims and individual perpetrators accounts for a very visible, but not the most comprehensive, facet of apartheid oppression. Rather than constructing the apartheid conflict in terms of 'perpetrators' and 'victims,' Mamdani argues that we must contend with a structure comprised of 'beneficiaries' and those who suffer:

> Beneficiaries are a large group, and victims defined in relation to beneficiaries are the vast majority in society. To what extent is the shift of focus from beneficiaries to perpetrators, and from victims as the majority to victims as a minority, likely to generate growing resentment amongst the excluded majority who understandably expect to gain from reconciliation and forgiveness? To what extent does a process that ignores the aspirations of the vast majority of victims, risk turning disappointment into frustration and outrage, creating room for a demagogue to reap the harvest?[51]

Reconciliation, therefore, cannot simply be about apology and forgiveness – whether individual or collective – *or* economic redress. Reconciliation must engage with the discursive, or cultural, structures that legitimize socio-economic inequality and the resort to violence as a means of 'security' or 'resistance.'

Jacqueline Rose asks: 'What comes first? Which form of transformation – psychic and subjective, or material and redistributive – will provide the real, sure foundation for the other?'[52] Rose reverts to the idea of truth and history, drawing on the TRC's emphasis on the production of a common understanding of the past as a necessary *precondition* for redressing economic legacies of the apartheid system. As I will develop more fully in my reading of Magona's *Mother to Mother* below, in the context of reconciliation, the initiative of 'collecting' the truth – particularly in terms of material structures and personal experiences – is not so much about recording History, or, as a number of critics have suggested, reconciling disparate narratives of the apartheid experience, as it is about transforming the *conditions* of conflict.[53] Conflict transformation requires that all parties to the conflict articulate their narratives, or perspectives, of the conflict and seek to understand the narratives of the other parties. I believe that reconciliation does not just postulate the recognition of the narrative of the Other, or the harmonizing of the narratives of conflicting groups, but a transformation in the discursive construction of the relationship between those groups. While Rose distinguishes between psychic or social truths and material structures, I am interested in the way in which the material and discursive structures of apartheid enabled one another in a way that makes them inextricable.

The TRC's various hearings created spaces in which individuals could express their experiences of suffering and their reasons for committing abuses; on the one hand, these hearings promoted 'healing' between individuals, but they also served to construct a narrative history of the apartheid regime and opposition to it. The TRC sought to foster the nation's reconciliation with its past, or a national 'coming to terms with painful truth.' The commission weaves a history of apartheid that includes excerpts of personal narratives of the impact of human rights abuses and the conditions and motivation for the perpetration of those abuses, summaries of all of the legislation and policies implemented to institute and maintain white dominance, and statements by representatives of the country's religious institutions, political parties, and organized opposition movements. As I argue in my discussion of *Mother to Mother*, this endeavour to reconcile the nation with its past is not framed in terms of a passive acceptance of the past, but an active engagement with how that past shapes present social, cultural, and material relationships. Further, constructing a historical record that provides 'as complete a picture as possible' is not synonymous with constructing a unitary 'official' truth. Even if all a truth commission can accomplish is reducing 'the number of lies that can circulate unchallenged in public discourse,' as Michael Ignatieff contends, the creation of such a record makes it ever more difficult for those privileged within the system to deny that the gross abuses of human rights occurred or to deny knowledge of these abuses.[54]

Yet, the TRC is limited as a reconciliation project by the way in which Truth – or the transformation of historical memory – is privileged over, or placed prior to, material transformation. Indeed, ironically, while the TRC hearings were being held in community centres around the country, their proceedings broadcast and commented upon in the media on a daily basis throughout 1996 and 1997, the ANC government initiated the Growth Employment and Redistribution program (GEAR) – in place of the promised Reconstruction and Development Program (RDP) – which firmly entrenched South African economic policy in the assumptions of neo-liberalism (i.e., 'growth' took precedence over 'redistribution'). Hence, while the TRC focused attention on individual stories of apartheid abuse and healing, arguably, the stratification of access to material resources and opportunities was being further entrenched. In many ways, the struggle for 'liberation' of racialized peoples in South Africa continues today; the organizational structures and tactics, and community relationships of the 1980s anti-apartheid social movements, including the civics and labour, have re-emerged under the umbrella term of the 'new social movements,' including landless peoples movements, community struggles against the privatization of electricity and water, HIV/AIDS activism, and struggles against chronic and widespread unemployment.[55] Nonetheless, while the TRC provides only a partial and limited step towards reconciliation, it does provide insight into how reconciliation must comprise interrelated transformation of the material structures of inequality and the discourses that make oppression, and opposition to it, understandable or legitimate.

As ambivalent as the subject positions of colonizer and colonized, settler and native, may be, colonial discourse – or the apartheid imagination – made the material inequalities of apartheid, the political and social project of separation, and the elaborate 'security' apparatus understandable. For many critics of postcolonial theories of the hybrid (post)colonial subject, such theories may be useful for understanding and challenging notions of power and knowledge, but they have not provided a politically useful intervention in avoiding or transforming conflict. I believe, however, that the analysis of colonial discourse, and particularly interrogations of how colonial discourse functions as cultural violence, is critical to understanding resistance and liberation. Among others involved in the TRC project, Tutu has echoed the sentiment of anti-colonial theorists such as Fanon and contemporary postcolonial critics, arguing that as subjects of colonial discourse, all are 'dehumanized by injustice and oppression.'[56] Such a position, however, does not postulate this shared experience of dehumanization as the same experience; nor, I think, does it collapse the 'settler' and 'native' into a singular, ambivalent, or hybrid colonial subject. Reconciliation has as its object colonial discourse, or the relationship between colonizer and colonized, beneficiary and exploited, with the two not necessarily being parallel. While theorists of reconciliation have characterized it as both a process and a state, within the context of postcolonial theories of resistance, reconciliation provides both a political praxis and a critical perspective.

Sindiwe Magona's *Mother to Mother*: Ambiguity and Understanding

In a 1989 address to an ANC seminar on culture, Albie Sachs argues that the ANC must no longer construct cultural production as a weapon of struggle. By limiting art to 'just another kind of missile-firing apparatus,' he argues, the ANC limits the potential of art to reflect the complexity of the experience of oppression and resistance, and to imagine transformation. Echoing Njabulo Ndebele's call for an end to a mode of realist writing that focuses on the horrors of apartheid oppression,[57] Sachs contends that conceived of as a tool of struggle, art conforms to a particularly oppositional anti-apartheid ideology that is constrained by the discourse of apartheid, rather than tests, challenges, and shapes that ideology: 'Whether in poetry or painting or on the stage, we line up our good people on the one side and the bad ones on the other ... never acknowledging that there is bad in the good, and, even more difficult, that there can be elements of good in the bad.'[58] Sachs laments the evacuation of love, tenderness, or beauty from literature and the way literature reinforces the Manichean framework of apartheid discourse. He argues: 'The power of art lies precisely in its capacity to expose contradictions and reveal hidden tensions.'[59] Reconciliation, as I have argued above, works to transform conflict rather than resolve it; in other words, it seeks to dismantle the antagonistic relationship of the apartheid imagination and produce a story that fosters mutual responsibility.

In *Mother to Mother*, Sindiwe Magona writes of the 1993 murder of white American student Amy Biehl in the township of Guguletu, near Cape Town. She provides a story of the day on which Biehl was killed within the social, political, and cultural context of South Africa's history of apartheid in its moment of transition. The novel does not conform to the sort of oppositional framework both Ndebele and Sachs decry, though it very much reveals the horrors of apartheid. While it is still an example of resistance art, the story, or framework, of resistance, however, has changed. Through the voice of Mandisa, the mother of Mxolisi, a fictional participant in Amy Biehl's murder, Magona reveals the ambiguity of the victim/perpetrator binary constructed within the TRC's amnesty process and the apartheid imagination. Consequently, she exposes the contradictions and tensions within (anti)apartheid discourse and within the TRC's endeavour to construct a historical record. Magona problematizes the construction of good versus evil, oppressors versus oppressed, while engaging with the antagonistic narrative within which Biehl's murder occurred. A visiting student in Cape Town, Amy Biehl was neither an oppressor nor a direct beneficiary of apartheid, yet she was killed to a chanting chorus of '*Amabhulu, Azizinja*/Boers, they are dogs.' While the poet/journalist Antjie Krog muses that after the 244 days of TRC public hearings, 'maybe writers in South Africa should shut up for a while,'[60] as works such as Magona's *Mother to Mother* reveal, literature has a role in resisting the maintenance of the antagonistic binary framework of apartheid discourse – the simplistic construction of a history of perpetrators and victims – and producing narratives that acknowledge and foster connection and responsibility.

Mandisa directs her tale to Amy's mother. She reveals to this American woman, whom she addresses as her sister-mother, the way in which hatred for whites was a 'knowledge with which I was born – or which I acquired at such an early age it is as though it was there the moment I came to know myself.'[61] Her father would return home from work to the solace of a bottle, grumbling about the 'dogs' he worked for, while her grandfather told her tales of the origins of white rule and Xhosa culture that her schoolteachers dismissed as superstition. For instance, Mandisa remembers her grandfather's tale of the Xhosa Cattle Killing, in which, based upon a prophecy, the Xhosa killed their cattle and burned their crops in 1857 with the expectation that such a sacrifice would 'drive *abelungu* to the sea, where, so the seer had said, they would drown. All, to the very, very last one.'[62] The sacrifice, of course, did not lead to Xhosa liberation. Instead, with the loss of their means of sustenance, the Xhosa became dependent upon the white settlers. For instance, in order to support their families, Xhosa men had to labour for European farmers. As prophecy had foretold, the Xhosa became subservient to Europeans, and their sense of identity and place was shaped through modes of social control, like 'the Good Volume and the button without a hole.'[63] These stories of the past produce a cultural identity that is intertwined with the 'deep roots of hatred' for those who stole the land and kept the Xhosa people in subjugation.

This discourse of antagonism shapes each generation's – including that of Mxolisi and his classmates – understanding of power and their place within it. As Mandisa tells Amy's mother, by the age of two Mxolisi could recite anti-white slogans. The murder of Amy Biehl occurs within the context of this narrative in which existence is understood as violent confrontation with the settler. Rather than fulfilment of 'the promise of return to the way of before,' however, Magona represents this narrative as a self-fulfilling cycle of violence, emotional trauma, and social upheaval.[64] Mandisa begins her 'testimony' with the statement, 'My son killed your daughter,' but goes on to ask the mother of Amy Biehl, 'What was she doing, vagabonding all over Guguletu, of all places ... Was she blind not to see there were no white people in this place?'[65] Though Mandisa characterizes Mxolisi as, from the beginning, 'nothing but trouble,' the story of his life she provides troubles the classification of him as 'perpetrator.' Mandisa, Mxolisi, and Amy Biehl do not fit neatly within a historical framework constructed through a discourse of justice that focuses solely on the actions of individuals and that is averse to ambiguity; the history of apartheid is not one of perpetrators and victims, those who must apologize and those who should forgive. By questioning Amy's decision to enter the township, however, Mandisa does not blame her for her death, or deny the responsibility of her son. Instead, the question illuminates ignorance of the harsh realities of South Africa's politics of race.

While the historical past constructed by the TRC may reduce the number of lies that can circulate in the society, it certainly does not produce a single, monolithic Truth to be shared by the 'nation.' With its twenty thousand submissions and hundreds of public testimonies in which individuals spoke the truth 'as they see it,' the TRC compiles a multitude of stories of individual pain that provide an element of South Africa's history absent in records of policy, representations of significant political events, or the facts and figures of specific crimes or the impact of structural violence.[66] These 'personal and narrative truths' as the final report characterizes the testimony, supplement 'factual or forensic' truth, which together promote the development of 'social truth' – produced through dialogue to reflect the essential norms and relations between people – and finally 'healing and restorative truth' – wherein 'facts and what they mean' are placed 'within the context of human relationships.'[67] By providing a participatory process in which relatively large numbers of people could share their perspectives of their experiences of gross human rights abuses, and by promoting a venue wherein individuals could acknowledge their crimes and institutions identify their roles within apartheid, the TRC compiles a history (in progress) that includes a multitude of voices.

Prior to the TRC, Benita Parry 'advance[ed] the case for recollection, for the constant renewal of historical memory.'[68] Theory, Parry argues, has a responsibility to participate in the construction of the past by scrutinizing strategies that validate discrimination and oppression, and she contends that this sort of critical historical recollection resists injustice and repression.[69] Parry's proposal for a critical and ongoing production-cum-critique of South African history seems to promote a theoretical engagement that departs from the construction of cultural resistance as 'counter-narrative.' The commission positions the production of historical Truth(s) as a means of 'knowing the past in order to avoid repeating it,' and as the final report purposefully acknowledges, the commission harboured no illusions as to its ability to either compile a 'full' history of apartheid or effect reconciliation. Yet, characterizations of the TRC as only a 'Truth Commission' privilege recollection over reconciliation: future injustice and repression will not be avoided simply by knowing the past, remembering.

John Noyes argues that the 'Truth Commission' in South Africa shows 'how language can reveal events where there had only been "history."'[70] Hence, the testimonies of the TRC take part in the process of reconciliation, but they are not synonymous with it. The TRC commissioners acknowledge that the production of a history – even a history that concentrates on personal interaction – is not a sufficient response to the horrors of apartheid. As stated in the final draft, the process of reconciliation must continue between individuals, within communities, and at the national level. South Africans must create spaces in which to recollect and, more importantly, collectively make meaning of those recollections. In *Mother to Mother*, Magona does not simply provide a story of the Amy Biehl murder that answers the questions of what happened; the novel is not a documentary account providing the 'full story' in hopes of some sort of closure. Instead, Magona translates the mode of recollection utilized in the TRC into an initiative towards reconciliation. Departing from the TRC's discourse of apology and forgiveness, as the means of translating recollection into reconciliation, Mandisa's story is not an apology: 'Let me say out plain,' Mandisa declares, 'I was not surprised that my son killed your daughter. That is not to say I was pleased ... But, you have to understand my son. Then you'll understand why I am not surprised he killed your daughter.'[71] Magona does not provide simply the background to the event of Biehl's murder but the social context in which such abuses occur – understanding rather than history.

In order to understand Mxolisi, it is necessary not simply to learn of his life but to understand that Mxolisi's life can be told only in terms of his relationships with others, and within the larger social and cultural context of his experience. Mxolisi's birth is unplanned, separating Mandisa from her family. The immediate context of Mxolisi's childhood and adolescence includes a community in which theft, murder, and rape are commonplace. Magona's portrayal of Guguletu reveals the intersections and interdependence of the cultural, structural, and direct violence of apartheid. Says Mandisa: 'I came to Guguletu borne by a whirlwind ... perched on a precarious leaf balking a tornado ... a violent scattering of black people, a dispersal of the government's making. So great was the upheaval, more than three decades later, my people are still reeling from it.'[72] The trauma of Guguletu is expressed through the experience of people; displacement separated people from land, which they related to as sacred, and their reassembly in the township destroyed their self-reliance. Echoing the consequences of the Cattle Killing, the upheaval Mandisa describes reinforces the exploitative relationships of the apartheid economy. Mandisa must work in the white suburbs for a woman who cannot pronounce her name, in order to provide for the children she no longer has the time to nurture: 'We laugh to hide the gaping hole where our hearts used to be. Guguletu killed us ... killed the thing that held us together ... made us human.'[73] The structural violence of apartheid cannot be measured only in terms of material lack; this violence is interdependent with the production and reinforcement of cultural narratives of identity and inequality. After witnessing security forces murder two young boys after he innocently pointed out their hiding place, three-year-old Mxolisi became mute for over two years. Although he would regain his voice, he did not regain his compassion; the trauma of the experience permanently damaged his *ubuntu* – his humaneness.

Sharing with Mrs Biehl how all-consuming the Manichean framework of good and evil became, Mandisa describes the way in which adults were complicit with their children's vigilantism. The Young Lions, who roamed the streets of the township, would 'necklace' the *gogga* (insects). Tires would be placed around the necks of those considered reactionaries or informers and be set ablaze: 'Our children fast descended into barbarism. With impunity, they broke with old tradition and crossed the boundary between that which separates human beings from beasts. Humaneness, ubuntu, took flight. It had been sorely violated. It went and buried itself where none of us would easily find it again.'[74] Yet the very structure of the novel, a second-person narrative directly addressing the mother of Amy Biehl, beginning with back and forth vignettes of the experience of Mandisa and her family and that of Amy Biehl on the day of her murder, functions to begin to restore this violated relational understanding of humanity.

Further, the story Mandisa shares undermines the discourse that guides the actions of subjects within it. Having been led to her hiding son, Mandisa expresses her angst to Amy's mother about whether or not to help him hide or deliver him to the police:

> Shame and anger fill me day and night. Shame at what my son has done. Anger at what has been done to him. I am angry at all the grown-ups who

made my son believe he would be a hero, fighting for the nation, were he to do the things he heard them advocate, the deeds they praised. If anyone killed your daughter, some of the leaders who today speak words of consolation to you ... mark my words ... they, as surely as my son, are your daughter's murderers.[75]

Mxolisi's actions are placed within the system of apartheid, both as a political and an economic system of inequality and depravation, but also, significantly, a discursive system of good and evil, monsters and heroes. Mandisa's shame at the actions of her son, and anger at the life he has had, undermines the discourse of power that constructs the world through a Manichean binary. In *Country of My Skull* (1998), Krog recounts a brief conversation with Wilhelm Werwoerd, an employee of the TRC and grandson of the former prime minister, who shares with Krog the assertion that ambiguity is just as much a casualty of war as truth and suggests that peace requires the creation of space for ambiguity.[76] Mandisa characterizes her son and his friends as 'monsters,' but the narrative of his life she shares with Mrs Biehl reveals the ambiguity of the seemingly simple and concrete oppositions of the apartheid imagination.

Mandisa cannot provide a definitive answer to the question of why Amy Biehl was killed, she tells Mrs Biehl, but she can provide a representation of the context in which such violence could occur: 'My son was only an agent, executing the long simmering dark desires of his race. Burning hatred for the oppressor possessed his being ... The resentment of three hundred years plugged his ears; deaf to her pitiful entreaties.'[77] Mandisa provides no apology and no excuse, but she does provide an explanation. To characterize Mxolisi as a subject constructed within a particular social context is not to ignore his responsibility. Understanding the murder of Amy Biehl and the horrific violence of the townships requires an understanding of the cultural and social structures that produced and legitimized that violence, and the way in which people participated in those structures: 'Your daughter has paid for the sins of the fathers and mothers who did not do their share of seeing that my son had a life worth living.'[78] Such a narrative is inconsistent with notions of (retributive) justice that are invested in liberal democratic discourse or the individual-defined restorative justice of the TRC. Individual acts of apology and forgiveness do not confront the responsibility of all members of a social system.

Desmond Tutu notes the way in which the construction of the enemy as monster makes it impossible to engage in a process of forgiveness and reconciliation, for a monster, by definition, is not human; the monster is incapable of understanding, remorse, or redemption. In the poem from which Coetzee took the title *Waiting for the Barbarians*, C.P. Cavafy asks: 'Now what's going to happen to us without barbarians?'[79] Without barbarians, apartheid implodes. The TRC victim and amnesty hearings were performed on the stages of community centres throughout South Africa. The roles of the participants were confined to victims and perpetrators. In sharing truths, perpetrators could regain their humanity. Victims and perpetrators could become humans to the other. The story of apartheid could be retold without barbarians. While the commission's final report documents structural violence, the framework of the public hearings does not provide space for the experience of that daily violence and degradation to be shared and discussed. By providing a narrative of the experience of the structural and cultural violence of apartheid, Magona places 'barbarity' in a context of human relationships and collective narratives. *Mother to Mother* provides no solution or resolution to apartheid, but it gestures towards transformation.

Apology, Forgiveness, Reconciliation

While the concept of reconciliation, as it is defined in the TRC's final report, constitutes a complex process working on multiple, yet interdependent, levels, the TRC was most visible – and analysed – as a project that brought together victims and perpetrators of human rights abuses. While apology and forgiveness were not requirements for amnesty, much importance is placed on the apologies of perpetrators and the victim's forgiveness. Tangible moments that can symbolize reconciliation, quite understandably, are important markers of the success of the idea/process. These 'moments' of reconciliation include Mandela's invitation to a former prison warder to attend his presidential inauguration, or the image of Ivy Gcina, one of the thousands who were detained and tortured under apartheid, hugging her former jailer Irene Crouse, the moment captured for posterity in the form of a front-page photograph in the *Eastern Province Herald*.[80] Such moments of symbolic reconciliation as 'embrace,' however, belie the complexity of reconciliation among individuals and problematically construct such moments as metonyms for national reconciliation. Reducing reconciliation to such moments of embrace reproduces the inevitability of post-colonial disappointment. The historical *moment* of independence – symbolized by the unfurling of a new national flag, for instance – is not the social, political, and economic *process* of transformation/redress it implicitly figures. Similarly, moments of apology and forgiveness between individuals during the TRC are not the *process* of reconciliation for the new nation.

Although the commission received more than twenty thousand stories of suffering and human rights abuses, very few white perpetrators of abuses came forward, and most of those who did were those who had carried out orders and not those who held decision-making positions. Hence, embraces between (white) perpetrator and (black) victim are symbolically so significant for the TRC in part because of their rarity. As a result, the much more subdued and reserved characterization of reconciliation articulated by former Air Force Major Neville Clarence appears to be more typical, because it does not involve the 'embrace' of apology/ forgiveness, and because it deals with the violence of the anti-apartheid struggle rather than that of apartheid repression. Clarence describes his 'reconciliation' with former MK cadre Abu Bakr Ismail, the person who planted the bomb that blinded him, as an important 'step' in South Africa's transformation, but their reconciliation includes no embrace: 'I don't have any bitter thoughts towards the bomber. I believe that spending my whole life bitter and twisted because of my blindness will achieve nothing ... people should be realistic about what they think they can get out of reconciliation. Ismail and I are not really friends, but I can say that we mean a lot to each other. We have, by chance, become an inextricable part of each other's lives.'[81] Reconciliation, in this case, does not constitute transcendence of the violence/hatred/fear that first brought the men together to produce some sort of healing, but simply the recognition of the way in which their lives are inextricably related. For Clarence, reconciliation is about understanding, not the achievement of 'harmony.' If reconciliation is to provide genuine healing, it requires time and 'involves people being accountable for their actions and showing a commitment to right their wrongs.'[82]

Reconciliation constitutes neither the utopian ideal of racial harmony nor a simplistic reduction of conflicting groups to a homogeneous 'human' commonality. While the ideal of reconciliation articulated in the image of two individuals embracing elides the complex relationship between material and discursive transformation, such images are politically significant as symbols. The testimony of the many hundreds who shared their suffering or acknowledged their abuses during the hearings of the TRC ground power, resistance, and transformation in human experience. If all are dehumanized by apartheid, then a central function of the TRC, as an initiative towards reconciliation, is to begin the restoration of human dignity. In her testimony about the murder of her son, Cynthia Ngewu asked if 'these *boers* have any feelings at all.'[83] On the concept of reconciliation, Ngewu says: 'This thing called reconciliation ... if I am understanding it correctly ... if it means this perpetrator, this man who has killed Christopher Piet, if it means he becomes human again, this man, so that I, so that all of us, get our humanity back ... then I agree, then I support it all.'[84] In this way, reconciliation seeks to acknowledge humanity in a way that *resists/transforms* the Manichean and antagonistic discourses of apartheid and anti-apartheid opposition that construct difference hierarchically or as total – discourses that justify the separation, exploitation, and subjugation of blacks as a means of maintaining white 'security,' and that construct the oppressor as lacking human feeling.

As much as the TRC is the product of a negotiated settlement of a conflict that lacked a 'victor,' the ideal of reconciliation is not merely political pragmatism *in place of* the trials that *should* have happened, if they had been possible. Tutu, for instance, contends that 'confession, forgiveness and reconciliation in the lives of nations are not just airy-fairy religious and spiritual things, nebulous and unrealistic. They are the stuff of practical politics.'[85] The TRC and the larger project of reconciliation aim to break the cycle of violence and build communities. Within the framework of restorative justice, the commissioners define 'crime' not as the breaking of laws established by a state, but as violations against fellow human beings. Restorative justice 'restores' and 'heals' both victims/survivors and offenders, and requires all parties to be involved in a process of conflict transformation, rather than relying on 'resolution' provided by the state, as 'impartial' third-party. Further, it aims to transform that which is 'wrong' rather than punish the 'wrong-doer.'[86] Reconciliation, as it is constructed within the TRC, seeks to re-humanize all parties involved in apartheid and now the new South Africa.

As a form of restorative justice, reconciliation does not simply depart from dominant modes of international justice derived from a specifically Western history but conflicts with the discourse of modern and specifically secular retributive justice. Many critics of the TRC, both inside South Africa and out, argue that the provision of amnesty, rather than of trials and punishment, is a failure to provide justice. An editorial in the newspaper *The Sowetan*, for instance, warned that 'reconciliation not based on justice can never work.'[87] Indeed, this lack of 'justice' impedes reconciliation, for 'a society cannot forgive what it cannot punish.'[88] Such critiques construct justice as retributive. As Rosemary Jolly argues, however, critiques informed by the assumption of retributive justice are invested in the individual, bourgeois, liberal subject of Western democratic discourse.[89] Jolly further challenges these critiques by arguing that to assume that victims/survivors believe that the punishment of perpetrators would provide healing or restoration in a way that the TRC cannot, or that they are incapable of understanding their own personal trauma in the context of South Africa's dramatic social and political change, occludes their subjectivity. Unlike the Nuremberg Trials, the TRC is simply one tool in a process and does *not* depend for its effectiveness on the creation of a sense of closure; rather, the TRC includes a 'surplus of meaning beyond the mechanics of secular and legal concepts of violation, testimony, proof, confession, judgment, punishment, financial compensation, even the truths the commission itself seeks to verify.'[90] Justice, in the framework of South Africa's transition, cannot be confined to legal proceedings, but must account for the cultural and material transformation necessary for a 'new democracy.'

For Cynthia Ngewu, the TRC will be valuable if it allows the 'perpetrators' and 'victims' of apartheid to have their humanity 'restored.' Reconciliation, as it has been understood in South Africa, draws upon a discourse of the 'restoration' of 'lost' human connection that is invested in both a Christian ethic of restorative justice and the southern African notion of subjectivity, *ubuntu*.[91] In a 1991 homily, uttered against the backdrop of escalating violence in the townships between supporters of the ANC and the Inkatha Freedom Party (IFP), Desmond Tutu said: 'It seems to me that we in the black community have lost our sense of ubuntu – our humaneness, caring, hospitality, our sense of connectedness, our sense that my humanity is bound up in your humanity.'[92] As Mark Sanders argues, the appeal to *ubuntu* in the TRC is always the lamentation for a 'loss.' *Ubuntu* is not so much a presence as a lack, noticeable in moments of violence and degradation. Yet, reconciliation requires not just a remembering (through 'truth') towards restoring *ubuntu*, for the phrasing of the loss of *ubuntu* is in the future perfect: 'The time of ubuntu that is posited has never had an actual existence, but rather, it exists at the level of possibility.'[93] Reconciliation, therefore, is not so much about apology and forgiveness, as the Clarence-Ismail example attests, but the recognition of the humanity of the other through the active acknowledgment and understanding, first, of the perspective of the other and, second, that the existence of the 'victim' and the 'perpetrator' are inextricably linked. It is this recognition of human interdependence and responsibility that is not, I would say, 'lost' in the future Gordimer describes in *July's People*, but is denied as a possibility.

Reconciliation, as I am interpreting it here as a postcolonial politics, is not really 'restorative' at all, but a process of anticipation or creation. Resistance, as reconciliation, challenges the antagonistic framework of colonial ideology and performs an alternative to it; it resists apartheid – a politics of separation – because it provides an ethic and politics of connection. Significantly, *ubuntu* is not what is expected of a member of a narrowly defined community towards another member of that community, but a connection and responsibility between strangers.[94] Indeed, as Sanders argues, the formulation challenges assumptions about the constitution of the community or the nation.[95] Liberation, consequently, becomes not the end or absence of a particular oppressive structure (apartheid), but the presence (as process) of a profoundly different construction of identity, subjectivity, and human relations: 'When the identity of the nation as an entity existing in time is no longer a given, what it means to remember or forget is, in turn, altered ... When memory of the past guides what is to be done now, ubuntu stands as an example of how, when the past is understood as invented, it can yield a structure of ongoing responsibility rather than a remedy to work once and for all.'[96] Reconciliation's *deconstruction* of colonial antagonism requires the *production* of historical narrative (as accountability) as well as structural transformation (or the 'righting of wrongs').

While colonial discourse theory's deconstruction of colonial identity problematizes the historical function of power and authority within the colonial project, it does not provide a framework for dismantling these structures of identity or contending with their political effects. On the other hand, while anti-colonial theorists such as Fanon, Cabral, and Memmi imagine liberation as a 'new humanism' or a radical breach with the colonial past, their constructions of resistance against colonial oppression are confined by the structures of identity and relationships established through colonial discourse. Mamdani argues:

> If part of the legacy of apartheid is the identities enforced by it, then a healing process that transcends this legacy will have to take as its starting

point the identities generated by the process of resistance. If power sought to impose a racial/ethnic grid on society, to what extent was resistance able to break out of it? ... Reconciliation may be a moral imperative, but it will not happen unless it is also nurtured as a political possibility. This is why if truth is to be the basis of reconciliation, it will have to sum up not only the evil that was apartheid but the promise that was the resistance to it.[97]

Reconciliation requires the production of a historical account – a coming to terms with the past – which does not simply acknowledge the abuse, structures, and discourse of apartheid violence (as important as such an account is) but transforms the discourse that provides such a narrative meaning, not for the past, but for the present and future.

The TRC's final report states: 'The road to reconciliation ... means both material reconstruction and the restoration of dignity. It involves the redress of gross inequalities and the nurturing of respect for our common humanity ... It implies wide-ranging structural and institutional transformation and the healing of broken human relationships.'[98] 'Truth,' as produced by a commission such as the TRC, is not sufficient for reconciliation, but material change cannot occur without a transformation of perceptions and values. As a narrative framework that shapes people's perceptions of their place in the world and their understanding of power, colonial discourse – or specifically, the apartheid imagination – must be transformed. Neither the effort toward reconciliation reflected in the story of Neville Clarence and Abu Bakr Ismail nor that represented in Magona's *Mother to Mother* depends upon a bond of apology and forgiveness. Ismail does not seek Clarence's forgiveness and Clarence does not offer it. Clarence characterizes the TRC, on the whole, as successful, 'because until it took place, nobody knew what was going on in the minds of those who planned apartheid.'[99] Mandisa does not seek Mrs Biehl's forgiveness, and as the addressee of a second-person monologue, Amy's mother is not provided a space to express forgiveness within the text.[100] Mandisa provides a narrative that describes the conditions under which such violence could take place, and the perspective of those constructed as 'barbarian' within the discourse of apartheid. Significantly, however, by problematizing the narrative of apartheid, and the structures through which it is recollected – as a relationship between 'perpetrators' and 'victims' – Sindiwe Magona privileges the importance of understanding not only the 'personal truths' of apartheid's gross human rights abuses but the discursive structures that legitimized those acts and impede social and material transformation.

The TRC's Amnesty Committee did not require those seeking amnesty to express remorse, and the commission's mandate did not include *effecting* reconciliation between victims, the community, and perpetrators.[101] Those cases in which 'perpetrators' came forward to seek forgiveness were of great political significance, however, both for the legitimacy of the commission and for the creation of a national dialogue. After Colonel Horst Schobesberger's apology during hearings on the Bisho massacre, Tutu responded: 'It isn't easy, as we all know, to ask for forgiveness and it's also not easy to forgive, but we are people who know that when someone cannot be forgiven there is no future.'[102] The request of a white security force leader for understanding, to be forgiven, and accepted back into the community was a rare occurrence during the hearings of the TRC, and for that reason all the more significant. Referring to the apologies of white security forces personnel during the Bisho massacre hearings, however, Commissioner Mapule F. Ramashala notes: 'None of them has said: "As a demonstration, perhaps of how sorry I am, this is what I would like to do."'[103] As symbolically significant as the utterance of apology is, for many participants in the process, such an utterance must also involve action; it must be an acknowledgment of responsibility not just for the past but in the present.[104]

As too-easy as it may seem to simply utter an apology without any commitment to making reparations, genuine apology and forgiveness are deeply emotional endeavours. For instance, Margaret Madlana made the following statement in regard to the death of her son: 'The way they killed my son hitting him against a rock, and we found him with a swollen head. They killed him in a tragic manner, and I don't think I will ever forgive in this case ... If these two policemen, come and tell us why he killed these sons of the wars and also ask for forgiveness before the mothers of these children. It is then that I can forgive him.'[105] Many observers contend that commissioners exerted pressure upon victims to express forgiveness during their testimony, even in cases where the perpetrator was not present or had not sought forgiveness.[106] For influential architects of the reconciliation project in South Africa, such as Tutu, the Christian ethic of forgiveness is paramount and is regarded as the foundation for reconciliation, an act of agency on the part of those who have been wronged. He argues: 'If the victim could forgive only when the culprit confessed, then the victim would be locked into the culprit's whim, locked into victimhood ... In the act of forgiveness we are declaring our faith in the future of a relationship and in the capacity of the wrongdoer to make a new beginning.'[107]

The Christian framework of individual contrition and forgiveness, however, does not translate easily into a framework of collective transformation. The wrongdoer, too, must acknowledge the relationship, if there is to be such a new beginning. As deeply flawed and mismanaged as the commission was, Antjie Krog argues that it 'kept alive the idea of a common humanity' and 'chiseled a way beyond racism.'[108] Krog concludes her memoir of the hearings with a poem of apology that seems to link individual consciousness and conscience with collective healing:

> of my soul the retina learns to expand
> daily because by a thousand stories
> I was scorched
>
> a new skin.
>
> I am changed forever. I want to say:
>   forgive me
>   forgive me
>   forgive me
>
> You whom I have wronged, please
> take me
>
> with you.[109]

It is blanket apologies such as this that reveal the way in which the rhetoric of apology and forgiveness fails to function communally as it does between individual human beings. The moment of embrace between 'perpetrator' and 'victim' has a cathartic effect for the individuals involved, and this spectacle of reconciliation undoubtedly has an impact beyond these individuals. While apology/forgiveness may provide a measure of healing for the individuals involved – allowing them to regain their human dignity or providing some sense of closure – how can an apology or forgiveness for the 'systemic, all-pervading evil,' as the commission characterizes apartheid, be uttered and by whom?[110] Systemic racism and inequality is not an *act* performed by one agent upon another that can be identified, understood, and forgiven. The metaphor of individual reconciliation is not easily transferable onto the complex relations of power and privilege of apartheid. As a result, I conclude this chapter by turning away from the discourse of apology and forgiveness as the means of reconciliation to an approach that recognizes reconciliation as the transformation of the rhetoric and politics of blame and denial.

Resisting the Politics of Blame and Denial

In chapter 2, I discuss Said's critique of the rhetoric and politics of blame he identifies as a discursive impediment to the attainment of liberation. Blame is the source of the seemingly unending 'politics of confrontation and hostility' in the post-colonial world.[111] However, Said's critique of how the rhetoric of blame constrains the vision of public intellectuals and cultural historians, impeding the possibility of transforming the antagonistic, hierarchical binaries of colonial knowledge, does not develop beyond the 'somehow' of Fanon's theory of resistance and liberation. In Fanon's argument in *The Wretched of the Earth*, national consciousness – itself a product of colonial discourse – provides the counter-narrative that shapes opposition *against* the colonizer; according to Said, liberation requires that this national consciousness 'somehow' be transformed into a social consciousness that is particularly non-antagonistic, restoring the humanity to colonized and colonizer alike. Although Fanon 'could not make the complexity and anti-identitarian force of that counter-narrative explicit,' Said contends that he had committed himself to combat imperialism and nationalism 'by a counter-narrative of great deconstructive power.'[112] As I argue in chapter 3, however, people like Gandhi *were* able to articulate an ideal and mode of resistance in which the articulation of a 'new non-adversarial community,' to use Said's words, *was* the resistance to imperialism and nationalism. For Gandhi, liberation did not constitute a new order, to be created *after* colonialism had been defeated, but an alternative way of seeing and the performance of alternative social relations based on human connection and responsibility.

While Jolly argues that the TRC is found wanting by critics who can only understand 'justice' in terms of particularly Western and bourgeois models of subjectivity, criticism of the TRC is also constructed within a teleological narrative of liberation. Critiques of the TRC's failure to provide (retributive) justice place the commission as a *post*-conflict measure mandated to provide a *resolution* to the centuries-long conflict. In some respects, perceptions of the TRC's failures are shaped by the unrealistic expectations of the commission's ability to *resolve* the conflict and *achieve* reconciliation; the TRC had neither the mandate and the resources nor the commitment of political leaders to heal the social and psychological wounds of apartheid or redress the effects of decades of economic exploitation. Disappointment with the TRC echoes the disappointment that followed the achievement of national independence in states throughout Africa in the late 1950s and early 1960s. As I have repeated a number of times, in his critique of nationalist ideology, Fanon argues that Africans must not simply be liberated from foreign rule but from hunger, ignorance, and poverty. The newly independent, post-colonial state failed to fulfil the implicit promises of national liberation. While the TRC was most certainly limited and flawed, much of the criticism of it can be accounted for in the way in which participants and critics have expected the commission to perform that 'great leap' from opposition to liberation.

In my analyses of the TRC and Magona's *Mother to Mother*, I have attempted to illuminate the ambiguity of the terms 'perpetrator' and 'victim' and deconstruct the antagonistic discourse of apartheid power, arguing that this discourse and the material inequalities of apartheid (or colonialism) are interdependent; there can be no material change until the narratives that shape identity and power are transformed, and these narratives cannot be transformed without the transformation of social relations of inequality or domination. Though whites were as much a product of apartheid as blacks, and arguably therefore oppressed, diminished, or traumatized because of this, as the testimony of those who spoke at the TRC hearings makes clear, the disappearances, murders, and other gross human rights abuses of apartheid were primarily experienced by blacks and were not simply discursive. Yet, like Said's concern with blame, the TRC's framework for uncovering these abuses, naming them, and building understanding about their causes and conditions places the onus for reconciliation upon those who suffered most under apartheid: 'Forgiveness is not about forgetting. It is about seeking to forgo bitterness, renouncing resentment, moving past old hurt, and becoming a survivor rather than a passive victim.'[113] Many critics of the TRC have specifically pointed to the failure of 'justice' in the case of the murder in detention of Steve Biko. Because the case is so well known, there is great pressure on Biko's family to express forgiveness as a symbolic gesture that would further national catharsis. As Biko's mother said: '"Yes, I would forgive my son's killers ... But first I must know what to forgive, which means I must be told fully what happened and why.'"[114] How can people move past hurt and become survivors, if those who abused them not only do not seek forgiveness but are unwilling to even come forward and explain their actions?

Knowing 'fully what happened and why' requires not just the construction of the historical 'facts' of the event but analysis and understanding of the collective memories and world-views in which those events took place and are understood. In *Mother to Mother*, for instance, Magona portrays the role of 'deep hatred' and the memory of the Xhosa Cattle Killing as necessary elements of understanding why Amy Biehl was murdered. For many white perpetrators, on the other hand, their participation in abuses took place within the discursive framework of 'security.' From the perspective of most white South Africans, the police state was a product of the need for security against the 'threats' of communist revolution and black disorder. Placing individual abuses within a context of how the events were understood by the participants provides a starting point towards understanding, forgiveness, and reconciliation for those individuals. Yet, unlike the acts of abuse remembered through the victim and amnesty hearings, in which individuals could take ownership of, and responsibility for, their own actions and feelings, these collective narratives require acknowledging how structures of knowledge sanction ignorance. The narrative of white 'security' facilitates through its very structure white ignorance of the basis of their privilege, and hence the need for their security. Hence, 'security' in South Africa served as a rhetoric of denial.

The TRC's focus on individual events, as well as the relationship between apology and forgiveness among individuals, does not necessarily challenge the discursive framework within which these abuses occurred. As the commission acknowledges in the final report:

> The focus on the outrageous has drawn the nation's attention away from the more commonplace violations. The result is that ordinary South Africans do not see themselves as represented by those the Commission defines as perpetrators, failing to recognise the 'little perpetrator' in each one of us. To understand the source of evil is not to condone it. It is only by recognising the potential for evil in each one of us that we can take full responsibility for ensuring that such evil will never be repeated.[115]

By turning my attention to denial, I do not wish to disregard the nature of blame. The onus Tutu and the TRC place on the sufferer forgoing bitterness and resentment and Said's concern for the rhetoric and politics of blame are not misplaced. As this passage acknowledges, however, the oppression of apartheid was not *only* marked by gross human rights abuses perpetrated by individuals against individuals within the framework of apartheid discourse; resentment or blame derives as much from the effect of structural violence or the ever-present 'threat' of direct violence as it does gross abuses. Further, in this passage the commission once again grounds national reconciliation in individual acknowledgment and transformation. Here, though, reconciliation depends as much on 'forgiveness' (or forgoing blame) as on acknowledging complicity. Consequently, the 'politics of denial' are embedded in the 'politics of blame.' The antagonistic binary framework performed as a politics of blame cannot be deconstructed and dismantled without an acknowledgment of complicity.

The fact that just 5 per cent of amnesty applications were filed by whites reveals the extent to which white South Africans have been unwilling to account for the violence of apartheid.[116] Some whites who appeared before the TRC did express contrition. For instance, in his amnesty hearing for participation in the torture of detainees, Captain Jeffrey Benzien was asked how the commission of these abuses affected him as a human being; he replied: 'I, Jeff Benzien, have asked myself that question to such an extent that I voluntarily – and it is not easy for me to say this in a full court with a lot of people who do not know me ... approached psychiatrists to have myself evaluated, to find out what type of person am I.'[117] Benzien's testimony likely represents a largely unacknowledged, in public at least, high incidence of psychological trauma for South African soldiers and police officers. It also represents one of the few cases in which an 'honest' accounting of events occurred. The participation of many other white security personnel or government officials, however, as well as many anti-apartheid activists, only illuminates the complex rhetoric of denial at work in South Africa.

Members of the ANC were confounded by the idea that their 'resistance' should be characterized as gross human rights abuses; the MK acted in accordance with the Geneva Conventions, they argued, and theirs was a 'just war' against a brutal oppressor.[118] For many conservative whites, the amnesty process – despite the fact that amnesty provided 'perpetrators' a venue to avoid criminal prosecution – was a 'witch-hunt' against Afrikaners. Krog characterizes the contribution of the majority of SADF testimony as 'Operation Shut Up and Deny.'[119]

On one level, denial was overt. Members of the old South African government covered up the abuses of the system. As Tutu describes it, they 'lied as if it were going out of fashion.'[120] The rhetoric of denial used by others, however, took the form of refusal to acknowledge that their actions were abuses or criminal. Amnesty was refused the police officers who applied for their part in Steve Biko's death. They sought amnesty, but argued their innocence: 'They denied in effect that they had committed a crime, claiming they had assaulted him only in retaliation for his inexplicable conduct in attacking them.'[121] For others, atrocities committed in the name of South African security were described with little emotion and no remorse. For instance, commission members were stupefied by the way in which General Deon Mortimer described a 1983 operation in which the SADF attacked two ANC homes in Mozambique 'as if it's nothing' and no human beings were killed.[122]

While many government officials denied having knowledge of the abuses covered in the mandate of the TRC, blaming such actions on overzealous police officers, for instance, one of the aims of the commission was to make it impossible for any South African to claim ignorance as a justification for inaction. The 'little perpetrator' in whites allowed complicity with the system of apartheid, from justification for exploitative labour, to the benefits derived from unequal access to health care and education, to the myriad other unearned privileges of being white under the apartheid system. TRC hearings provided a venue for these various modes of the rhetoric of denial, from obstinacy to rationalization to exceptionalism, to be named and challenged. As Mandela argues, apartheid, as a politics of separation, divided people on the grounds of racialized categories in order to prevent cultural understanding.[123] Many of the overt abuses covered in the TRC would have taken place in the townships or outside South Africa, far away from the gaze of the white population. However, the body of apartheid laws and policies that restricted black agency compiled in the commission's final report or the mass displacement of whole communities could not have occurred without the knowledge, consent, and participation of the majority of the population. While few whites attended hearings in person, and the Afrikaans media in general did not provide the depth of coverage of English and African-language newspapers or radio, the public accounting for apartheid abuses did affect the consciousness of many white South Africans.[124] For instance, an eighty-one-year-old loyal member of the National Party responded to the disclosures made in the hearings by claiming that '"I did not know that my people could have done such terrible things."'[125] A culture of silence (as denial) allowed the policies and practices of the South African government to be translated into a narrative of innocence. 'Whereas before [the TRC], people denied that atrocities happened, now they deny that they *knew* they were happening,' Krog asserts.[126]

The rhetoric of denial utilized by the ANC can be explained by the anti-apartheid narrative of opposition within which their actions were undertaken. Similarly, the refusal of whites to acknowledge the abuses of the system may be explained not as malevolence but through the myth within which such acts took place. As discussed above, the white South African will to control both produced and was produced by black resistance. The ANC Freedom Charter, for instance, with its commitment to non-racialism, and equitable distribution of land and resources, was understood within Cold War ideology; the ANC's challenge to racialization, therefore, only reinforced the government's ideology of separation, in part as a means of controlling what was perceived, or at least presented to the general public, as a communist threat. As Tutu observes, 'White South Africans are not demons. They are ordinary people, mostly scared ... If I was white I would need a lot of grace to resist a system that provided me with such substantial privileges.'[127] Fear, then, was a manifestation of white complicity, a rhetoric of denial. Similarly, the collective historical narrative of Afrikaner victimization, developed through the memory of the conflicts with the British, further defined Afrikaners as a 'people' against an Other who is necessarily a threat. As Coetzee shows in *Waiting for the Barbarians*, the barbarian Other allows all misfortune that befalls the self to be blamed on that Other. Jolly argues that the TRC uncovered the myth of white ignorance as a lie: 'It has exposed the practice of (pro)claiming one's innocence, or ignorance, in the face of no verbal evidence to the contrary, for what it is: the coping strategy ... of a society pathologically involved in deceiving itself.'[128] The rhetoric and politics of denial, therefore, depend upon blame, and vice versa. As clinical psychologist Nomfundo Walaza tells Krog: 'Whites prefer to think they are being hated; then they don't need to change.'[129] If it is the discourses of blame and denial, as a form of cultural violence, that legitimize the violence of apartheid and its opposition, reconciliation is the process of illuminating and transforming these narratives or myths of identity.

The few, yet powerful, examples of apology and forgiveness facilitated by the TRC, therefore, must be translated into a process in which the majority of South Africans must recognize the 'little perpetrator' within them. Further, reconciliation, as resistance, must transform acknowledgment into responsibility, shame into redress: 'The emergence of a responsible society, committed to the affirmation of human rights (and, therefore, to addressing the consequences of past violations), presupposes the acceptance of individual responsibility by all those who supported the system of apartheid (or simply allowed it to continue to function) and those who did not oppose violations during the political conflicts of the past.'[130] This formulation of the problem of apathy continues to be limited by the mandate of the TRC to investigate gross human rights abuses and compile these stories in the context of apartheid policies and structures of inequality. Returning to Mamdani's emphasis on reframing the relationships within apartheid power to acknowledge the roles of all participants within the system rather than small minorities – that is, between beneficiaries and the disadvantaged, rather than perpetrators and victims – the politics of denial performed as inaction or apathy reinforces the way in which national reconciliation constitutes a radical reinterpretation of apartheid, by all of its subjects, in order to facilitate the transformation imagined as liberation.[131] While the parameters of the TRC's public hearings create the illusion of closure – by articulating their stories publicly, asking for forgiveness, or granting it, participants are able to 'move on' – as the commission states in its final report, the TRC is merely a starting point, and 'in this process of bridge building, those who have benefited and are still benefiting from a range of unearned privileges under apartheid have a crucial role to play.'[132] The political changes that constitute the 'new' South Africa, including the repeal of apartheid laws and the adoption of a new constitution that 'ensures' equality, have neither transformed the discursive structure through which South Africans understand their experiences nor drastically altered the demographic of who receives a quality education and who does not, who has access to clean water and who does not.

The Interim Constitution of South Africa included a brief postamble framing reconciliation as central to the nation-building project of a 'new' South Africa: 'The pursuit of national unity, the well-being of all South African citizens and peace require reconciliation between the people of South Africa and the reconstruction of society.'[133] Reconciliation is framed as a means of transcending the divisions and strife of South Africa's past and developing a nation 'on the basis that there is a need for understanding but not vengeance, a need for reparations but not for retaliation, a need for ubuntu but not victimisation.'[134] The TRC provides a significant intervention in the dominant narratives of apartheid power and its opposition. This form of critical reassessment is one way of 'undoing' the rhetoric of denial as well as resisting the narrative framework of blame. These narratives of collective memory, however, cannot be dismantled simply through legislation or the adoption of a new constitution. The political will to equality, in this case, precedes material and discursive transformation of the structure of power in South Africa.

Deconstructing and dismantling these structures will not be accomplished through institutions like the TRC alone and certainly not in such a limited time period. Indeed, the very notion of the 'accomplishment' of reconciliation needs to be re-evaluated. As Susan Dwyer argues: 'Reconciliation between blacks and whites in South Africa ... seems to involve the *dis*continuation of one story in favor of starting another ... Given that the very identity (self-conception) of blacks and whites in South Africa has been constructed in terms of oppressed and oppressors, the dissonance between these prior narratives and proposed post-apartheid stories of nonracialism and social equality may preclude the possibility of coherently continuing the prior narratives.'[135] The 'embrace' of reconciliation, therefore, should not be seen to symbolize the resolution of conflict – or the radical break from one story to another – but the continuation of a process of transforming both the narratives within which people understand their experiences and the material structures those narratives explain.

Conclusion:
Postcolonialism and Transformation

In 'Tragedy and Revolution,' Raymond Williams theorizes revolution as a politics of fostering human community. Specifically, he emphasizes that the recognition of the Other as human constitutes the 'impulse of any genuine revolution.'[1] Published in 1966, just after Fanon's *The Wretched of the Earth*, the essay takes part in the attempt by intellectuals of the period to make sense of the radical social and political movements, both in what would come to be known as the global south, and particularly Africa, as well as in Europe and the United States. However, the appeal to 'humanity' in both Williams and Fanon is stated without critical self-consciousness or meaningful elaboration. In the wake of the deconstruction of European universalist and essentialist concepts such as sovereign power, progress, the subject, and the human, such a notion of a human community appears simplistic and, indeed, indebted to the same European modernity that shaped, and was shaped by, the colonial project. Fanon's appeal to a universal humanism is at odds with the narrative of redemptive violence he describes and critiques. In *The Wretched of the Earth*, Fanon identifies the object of struggle, or the ideal of liberation, as the transformation of political and social structures and, hence, the values and narratives that legitimize relationships of exploitation and inequality.

Despite the dismissive criticism of postcolonial discourse theory by critics such as San Juan, Parry, and Dirlik, postcolonial theorists such as Gayatri Chakravoty Spivak – who has been so closely linked with postcolonialism's 'poststructural preoccupations' – can be seen as working within the radical tradition of critics like Fanon and Williams. Spivak's identification of the discursive limitations of the Subaltern Studies project, for instance, has been informed by a critical project that does not escape politics but seeks to think through the assumptions and implications of a libratory critical practice. For instance, in 'From Haverstock Hill Flat to U.S. Classroom,' she reflects on the teachings of Marx to identify a disjuncture between 'freedom from' – as the best critique can do – and the expectation of a post-revolutionary 'freedom to.'[2] Spivak identifies the problem of *how* people would be able to discard the modern ethic of materialism and individualism for an ethic of community and connection, thereby grounding material 'revolution' in cultural transformation. Further, by focusing attention upon this 'how,' she troubles the teleological narrative of revolution that, despite the influence of deconstruction on the field, continues to influence postcolonial constructions of resistance and liberation. In this book, I have provided examples of the way in which resistance can be conceptualized alternatively to critique and opposition; critique and opposition are unable to provide a politics as anything more than 'freedom from,' or the teleologically *post*-critique and seemingly unspeakable or utopian 'freedom to,' encapsulated in Fanon's notion of 'new souls.'

A number of theorists with whom I engage in this book are broadly interested in contending with such problems, or returning to, and hence redefining, postcolonialism's object. Postcolonial studies constitutes a critical practice that seeks to deconstruct the antagonistic discourse of colonial knowledge and, at the very least, gesture towards a libratory praxis. Formulations of resistance as conscious or organized opposition to the colonial presence or as subtle manipulations, appropriations, and subversions of colonial authority challenge colonial power and identify its limits and its complexity. However, these formulations of resistance do not seem able to acknowledge, or respond to, this complexity, in its experience; for instance, these ways of conceptualizing resistance have failed to account for the way in which other forms of domination and exploitation (patriarchy, capitalism, caste, etc.) are interrelated with colonial power. 'Liberation' is, in different moments and contexts: the formation of the post-colonial nation and its entrance into the international community of states; the dismantling of hierarchies of dominance and privilege, most particularly in terms of European exploitation of the land and peoples of their (neo)colonial holdings; the production of communal identities that counter those produced within modernity. If postcolonialism seeks to transform the antagonistic Manichean framework of colonial discourse or challenge the rhetoric and politics of blame and/or denial that impede such a transformation, the dominant conceptions of resistance within the field

Conclusion: Postcolonialism and Transformation 181

have failed to provide a framework for understanding such a transformation. Indeed, these notions of resistance have impeded the recognition of alternative models and conceptions of resistance. The subversion of the colonial Christian mission by reading the Bible in a way not intended, insurgency against settlers and colonists, the recognition of the hybridity of colonial identities, or 'unspoken' forms of social and cultural resistance as a 'saying no' to power all may problematize colonial discourses of power or even disrupt the operation of exploitative practices of colonial control. However, these notions of resistance do not provide the theoretical framework for the sort of transformation necessary if liberation is to be understood as a *freedom to*, rather than simply *freedom from*.

After a couple of decades in which deconstruction and poststructuralism had seemingly made any emancipatory critical praxis hard to defend, there has been a recent resurgence in the demand for a critical theory that moves beyond critique and deconstruction and articulates a politics of change. In Gilroy's recent work, this politics of change has been identified through the notion of a planetary humanism. Similarly, Spivak has evoked this term, and in *A Critique of Postcolonial Reason* (1999) she posits 'love' as a signifier for such a politics. Like Fanon, whose appeal to the idea 'that it be possible for me to discover and to love man, wherever he may be'[3] seems to function as an afterthought in *Black Skin, White Masks*, Spivak merely gestures towards a politics of love. I point to this idea of love or another 'new humanism' in the work of Spivak, Said, or Gilroy, framed as they are in terms of contemporary relations of power, rather than specifically historical, colonial relationships, for a few reasons. Love and humanism are articulated as permanently emergent – yet also debilitatingly residual (as nativist/utopian) – ideals within postcolonial studies, never moving beyond a rather cursory or abstract place within, first, anti-colonial and, now, postcolonial theories of social change. The idea of 'love' may be one approach to contending with that disjunctive, and seemingly indescribable, 'how' or 'somehow' that Spivak and Said identify, a caesura in postcolonial thought. If love can serve as a metaphor for the sort of transformation I have theorized through the examples of Gandhian *ahimsa* or the South African project of reconciliation, one that encompasses not only recognition and redistribution, but also connection, responsibility, and interdependence, it functions, in a sense, as the reconnect between the practice of resistance and the dream of liberation. It may be better, then, to understand this idea of love as a praxis of resistance/liberation, undoing the assumption of the emancipatory, and teleological, narrative in which liberation *follows* resistance (as opposition).

Spivak's formulation of love lends itself particularly well to the idea of resistance as transformation, as I have theorized it. She argues that love provides a conceptual notion for the kind of sharing and learning that 'we' – those who share this planet – require:

> What deserves the name of love is an effort – over which one has no control yet at which one must not strain – which is slow, attentive on both sides – how does one win the attention of the subaltern without coercion and crisis? – mindchanging on both sides, at the possibility of an unascertainable ethical singularity that is not ever a sustainable condition. The necessary collective efforts are to change laws, relations of production, systems of education, and health care. But without the mind-changing one-on-one responsible contact, nothing will stick.[4]

Significantly, Spivak draws together in this notion of love the material and the discursive, the need for structural change and the need for change in the values and ideologies that enable those structures. Yet, this is as far as she goes.

In a more developed or nuanced theorization of love, Chela Sandoval characterizes love as a 'political apparatus.' She contends 'that a diverse array of thinkers are agitating for similarly conceived and unprecedented forms of identity, politics, aesthetic production, and coalitional consciousness through their shared practice of a hermeneutics of love in the postmodern world.'[5] While Sandoval acknowledges anti-colonial theories of 'third world liberation,' which she argues 'shattered' the naturalized binaries of modern power,[6] with the exception of Fanon, Sandoval's 'thinkers' are limited to theorists aligned with the Western academy, and particularly deconstruction, including Derrida, Foucault, Barthes, Haraway, and Lorde. In part, such appeals to a hermeneutics of love respond to the idea, as Sandoval – indebted to Foucault – describes it, that 'citizen-subjects who are interested in generating effective modes of resistance capable of confronting neo-colonial postmodernism must first recognize the fact that much of our perceptual apparatuses and tactics for actions are based on past, outmoded yet residual conceptions of power and resistance.'[7] In my analysis of the construction of power within theories of reconciliation or Gandhism, however, I have challenged this contention – presently so in vogue – that 'our perceptual modes and tactics of actions' are outmoded because contemporary power is 'new.'

Hardt and Negri, who also appeal to the concept of love, calling rebellion a 'project of love,' posit Empire as a new form of global(izing) power, and hence challenge so-called outmoded notions of resistance.[8] They argue that

> the first question of political philosophy today is not if or even why there will be resistance and rebellion, but rather how to determine the enemy against which to rebel ... The identification of the enemy, however, is no small task given that exploitation tends no longer to have a specific place and that we are immersed in a system of power so deep and complex that we can no longer determine specific difference or measure. We suffer exploitation, alienation, and command as enemies, but we do not know where to locate the production of oppression. And yet we still resist and struggle.[9]

I do not disagree that assumptions of the Manichean nature of political relations or the equation of colonial power with colonial dominance are 'outmoded,' but the examples of *ahimsa/sarvadoya* and reconciliation suggest that they are outmoded not because the location of the production of oppression has changed (though current formulations of imperialism, as neo-liberalism, for instance, are certainly different from the sort of colonial structures of British India or apartheid South Africa). Rather, though *ahimsa/sarvadoya* and reconciliation were conceived in historical moments wherein the location of the production of oppression was *perceived* as certain, in both of these examples, resistance to oppression required the deconstruction of the binary and Manichean narrative frameworks for power and conflict, as well as a challenge to the idea that the 'enemy' was embodied by a necessarily infrahuman other, or locatable at all. Gandhi's analysis of power and his theorization of resistance and the notion of reconciliation both provide narratives of power and change that posit agency in terms of interdependence, and recognize the way in which discourses of belonging and identity enable material structures of inequality, or violence, and vice versa. While recognizing the heterogeneity of the operation of power across space and time, I think it is important to emphasize the distinction between new forms of power and control and outmoded conceptions of how power works.

Arundhati Roy, as a prominent spokesperson of a diverse collection of national and transnational social movements often labelled as a global justice movement, identifies a common predicament for marginalized peoples around the world as Empire, a structure of economic and political relations and a world-view. While her critique of neo-liberalism, for instance, positions power as a system, as opposed to a sovereign, she nonetheless relies upon a rhetoric of warfare that appears inconsistent with the sort of structural and cultural change that is implicit in her work: 'We need to look up and urgently discuss strategies of resistance, wage real battles, and inflict real damage.'[10] Paradoxically, to take up her call to 'lay siege' to Empire requires telling 'stories that are different from the ones we're being brainwashed to believe.'[11] While Roy provides a story of the struggle against the Narmada Dam Project that provides an alternative to dominant or official Indian stories of the project – both in form and content – her critique of the American response to the attacks of 11 September 2001, India's and Pakistan's nuclear weapons programs, or the BJP have been limited stories that identify what a global 'we' should be seeking 'freedom from.' Part of the resistance of *ahimsa/sarvadoya* or reconciliation is the way in which these approaches to social change necessarily deconstruct the dominant notions of power and control within their locales and the way in which their alternative conceptions of power, subjectivity, and agency inform them as praxes of resistance. Unlike Empire, the enemy/oppressor/other was clearly defined in British colonialism and in apartheid, but *ahimsa* and reconciliation are resistant precisely for the way they (seek to) dismantle (rather than critique or deconstruct) the binary framework of colonial knowledge and the dominant revolutionary or conflict narrative. Hence, these examples provide ways of understanding 'love' as a political praxis, in a way that Spivak's, Hardt and Negri's, or Sandoval's conceptualizations of love fail to do.

To argue that the examples of Gandhian *ahimsa* and *sarvadoya* or the South African reconciliation project provide ways of articulating this 'love' or 'mind-changing responsible contact' is not to position them as models, to be reproduced in other locales and under other conditions. Gandhi's particular theories of trusteeship and village kingdoms were imagined prior to the emergence of the Cold War and the establishment of the Bretton Woods model of global economic relations. Similarly, although the final report of the TRC emphasizes the need for structural redress and change, by focusing on 'perpetrators' and 'victims' within a narrow definition of violence, the TRC hearings failed to account for not only the daily experience of apartheid's violence but also the economic stratification reinforced by the ANC government's acceptance of neo-liberal economic policies. So, while both Gandhism and reconciliation must be understood in their historical conditions and acknowledged as limited in their particular relevance for contemporary struggles that seek to end 'institutionalized suffering' or enact a planetary ethics that 'implicates every human across nation-state boundaries,' they do articulate resistance in a way that is foreclosed by the dominant preoccupations of postcolonial thought.

Gandhism and reconciliation acknowledge the way in which Manichean or binary thought shapes colonial identities and politics. They seek to transform these discourses, and hence these identities, to produce a radically altered, rather than simply reversed, structure of material relations of power *and* identities; they reject the idea of the enemy as the location of the production of oppression and demand a recognition of the humanity of the Other. Reconciliation and *ahimsa/sarvadoya*, as theories of resistance, are both derived from praxis, wherein thought is intensified through action. The agent of resistance within Gandhism or reconciliation is not positioned outside of power, seeking to dismantle or destroy, but is positioned as a product of power, participating in the transformation of consciousness and structures from within. These examples provide an alternative framework for approaching the structures of power and the conflicting relationships of colonialism, and, indeed, contemporary experiences of exploitation, domination, and marginalization.

Notes

Introduction

1 Frederick Cooper, 'Conflict and Connection: Rethinking Colonial African History,' *American Historical Review* (December 1994), 1532.
2 For instance, Bill Ashcroft, Gareth Griffiths, and Helen Tiffin's *Post-Colonial Studies: The Key Concepts* (London: Routledge, 2000) does not include an entry for the concept 'resistance,' or, for that matter, 'opposition,' 'liberation,' or 'humanism,' all of which are concepts that are foundational for the field of postcolonial studies.
3 Ben Okri, *A Way of Being Free* (London: Phoenix, 1997), 112.
4 Sanjay Seth, 'A "Postcolonial World"?' in *Contending Images of World Politics*, ed. Greg Fry and Jacinta O'Hagen (London: Macmillan, 2000), 214; I distinguish between the hyphenated 'post-colonial' as a geographical and temporal marker and 'postcolonialism' as a field of study, which has as its object the 'post-colonial.'
5 Leela Gandhi, *Postcolonial Theory: A Critical Introduction* (New York: Columbia University Press, 1998), 140.
6 Simon Gikandi, 'Theory, Literature, and Moral Considerations,' *Research in African Literatures* 32:4 (Winter 2001), 4.
7 Ibid., 3.
8 Arif Dirlik, 'The Postcolonial Aura: Third World Criticism in the Age of Global Capitalism,' in *Contemporary Postcolonial Theory: A Reader*, ed. Padmini Mongia (London: Arnold, 1997), 295.
9 E. San Juan, Jr, *Beyond Postcolonial Theory* (New York: St Martin's, 1997), 253.
10 Dirlik, 'The Postcolonial Aura,' 305.
11 Ngugi wa Thiong'o, *Barrel of a Pen: Resistance to Repression in Neo-Colonial Kenya* (Trenton: Africa World Press, 1983), 75.

12 San Juan, *Beyond Postcolonial Theory*, 17; San Juan reacts against the influence of poststructural thought on the development of postcolonialism, at times conflating all criticism that goes under the name 'postcolonial' with a discourse theory that he claims 'mystifies the political ideological effects of Western postmodernist hegemony and prevents change,' 22.
13 Bill Ashcroft, *Post-Colonial Transformation* (London: Routledge, 2001), 20.
14 Raymond Williams, 'Tragedy and Revolution' (1966), in *The Raymond Williams Reader*, ed. John Higgins (Oxford: Blackwell, 2001), 102.
15 Ibid., 103.
16 Linda Tuhiwai Smith, *Decolonizing Methodologies: Research and Indigenous Peoples* (London: Zed, 1999), 26.
17 David Scott, *Conscripts of Modernity: The Tragedy of Colonial Enlightenment* (Durham: Duke University Press, 2005), 95.
18 Paul Gilroy, *Against Race: Imagining Political Culture beyond the Color Line* (Cambridge, MA: Belknap, 2000), 30. Outside of North America, *Against Race* was published as *Between Camps*.
19 Paul Gilroy, *Postcolonial Melancholia* (New York: Columbia University Press, 2005), 54, 56.
20 Ibid., 67.
21 Gilroy, *Against Race*, 351.
22 Crystal Bartolovich, 'The Eleventh of September of George Bush: Fortress U.S. and the Global Politics of Consumption,' *Interventions* 5:2 (June 2003), 194.
23 Arundhati Roy, *Public Power in the Age of Empire* (New York: Seven Stories, 2004), 55.
24 Frantz Fanon, *The Wretched of the Earth*, trans. Constance Farrington (New York: Grove, 1963), 35.
25 Yet, it continues to hold credence for many postcolonial theorists; Peter Hallward, in *Absolutely Postcolonial: Writing between the Singular and the Specific* (Manchester: Manchester University Press, 2001), for instance, agrees with Fanon that *every* 'emancipatory process, every emergence of a *new* figure of universality, must begin as no less divisive' than the exploitative, and specifically militaristic, colonial project, xv.
26 Fanon, *The Wretched of the Earth*, 35–6.
27 Ibid., 315.
28 Williams, 'Tragedy and Revolution,' 102, original emphasis.
29 Ibid., 36.
30 Ibid., 221–4.
31 Edward Said, *Culture and Imperialism* (New York: Vintage, 1994), xii.

32 Bill Ashcroft, Gareth Griffiths, and Helen Tiffin, *The Empire Writes Back: Theory and Practice in Post-Colonial Literatures* (London: Routledge, 1989), 27.
33 Ibid., 17.
34 Ibid., 24.
35 Ibid., 33.
36 Ibid.
37 Ashcroft, *Post-Colonial Transformation*, 32.
38 Arun P. Mukherjee, 'Whose Post-Colonialism and Whose Postmodernism?' *World Literature Written in English* 30:2 (1990), 6.
39 Stephen Slemon, 'Reading for Resistance in Post-Colonial Literature,' in *A Shaping of Connections,* ed. Hena Maes-Jelinik, Kristen Holst Petersen, and Anna Rutherford (Aarhus: Dangeroo, 1989), 104, original emphasis.
40 Ngugi wa Thiong'o, *Decolonizing the Mind: The Politics of Language in African Literature* (London: James Curry, 1986), 4.
41 Shari Stone-Mediatore, *Reading across Borders: Storytelling and Narratives of Resistance* (New York: Palgrave, 2003), 26.
42 Ibid., 3.
43 Johan Galtung, *Peace by Peaceful Means: Peace and Conflict, Development and Civilization* (London: Sage, 1996), 196–210.
44 Peter Childs and Patrick Williams, *An Introduction to Post-Colonial Theory* (London: Prentice Hall, 1997), 26.
45 Gilroy, *Postcolonial Melancholia*, 53.
46 See, for instance, Arundhati Roy, 'Ahimsa,' *War Talk* (Cambridge, MA: South End, 2003), and Edward Said, 'My Right of Return,' in *Power, Politics, and Culture: Interviews with Edward W. Said*, ed. Gauri Viswanathan (New York: Vintage, 2002).

Chapter 1

1 J.M. Coetzee, *Waiting for the Barbarians* (New York: Penguin, 1980), 72.
2 Ibid., 126.
3 Ibid., 51.
4 Ibid., 145.
5 Edward Said, *Orientalism* (New York: Vintage, 1979), 3.
6 Gayatri Chakravorty Spivak, 'Subaltern Studies: Deconstructing Historiography,' in *In Other Worlds: Essays in Cultural Politics* (New York: Methuen, 1987), 199.
7 Gayatri Chakravorty Spivak, quoted in Colin McCabe, Foreword to *In Other Worlds* (New York: Methuen, 1987), xvi.
8 Sumit Sarkar, 'The Decline of the Subaltern in *Subaltern Studies*,' in *Mapping*

Subaltern Studies and the Postcolonial, ed. Vinayak Chaturvedi (London: Verso, 2000), 315, 316.
9 Dipesh Chakrabarty, *Provincializing Europe: Postcolonial Thought and Historical Difference* (Princeton: Princeton University Press), 14.
10 Michael Hardt and Antonio Negri, *Empire* (Cambridge, MA: Harvard University Press, 2000), 144.
11 Homi K. Bhabha, *The Location of Culture* (London: Routledge, 1994), 6.
12 Homi K. Bhabha, 'Translator Translated: Conversation with Homi Bhabha,' interview with W.J.T. Mitchell, *Artforum* 33:7 (March 1995), 82.
13 Bhabha, *The Location of Culture,* 72.
14 Michel Foucault, *The History of Sexuality: An Introduction,* vol. 1 (1976), trans. Robert Hurley (New York: Vintage, 1990), 92.
15 Bhabha, *The Location of Culture,* 179.
16 Ibid., 111.
17 Bart Moore-Gilbert, *Postcolonial Theory: Contexts, Practices, Politics* (London: Verso, 1997), 131.
18 Bhabha, *The Location of Culture,* 23.
19 Ibid., 112.
20 Robert Young, *White Mythologies: Writing History and the West* (London: Routledge, 1990), 128; Jenny Sharpe, 'Figures of Colonial Resistance,' *Modern Fiction Studies* 35:1 (Spring 1989), 147.
21 Bhabha, *The Location of Culture,* 145.
22 Chakrabarty, *Provincializing Europe,* 10.
23 Aijaz Ahmad, 'The Politics of Literary Postcoloniality,' in *Contemporary Postcolonial Theory: A Reader,* ed. Padmini Mongia (London: Arnold, 1997), 290.
24 Rey Chow, 'Where Have All the Natives Gone?' in ibid., 128.
25 Hardt and Negri, *Empire,* 138.
26 Abdul R. JanMohamed, *Manichean Aesthetics: The Politics of Literature in Colonial Africa* (Amherst: University of Massachusetts Press, 1983), 59; Moore-Gilbert, *Postcolonial Theory,* 147.
27 Bhabha, *The Location of Culture,* 76.
28 Frantz Fanon, *Black Skin, White Masks* (1952), trans. Haakon Chevalier (New York: Monthly Review Press, 1967), 112.
29 Ibid., 146.
30 Bhabha, *The Location of Culture,* 76.
31 Ibid., 108.
32 Benita Parry, 'Signs of Our Times: Discussion of Homi Bhabha's *The Location of Culture,*' *Third Text* 28/9 (Autumn/Winter 1994), 13.
33 Ibid.

34 Bhabha, 'Translator Translated,' 118.
35 Bill Ashcroft, *Post-Colonial Transformation* (London: Routledge, 2001), 19–20.
36 Gyan Prakash and Douglas Haynes, 'Introduction: The Entanglement of Power and Resistance,' in *Contesting Power: Resistance and Everyday Social Relations in South Asia* (Berkeley: University of California Press, 1991), 3–4.
37 James C. Scott, *Domination and the Arts of Resistance: Hidden Transcripts* (New Haven: Yale University Press, 1990), 14.
38 Prakash and Haynes, 'Introduction,' 11.
39 Ross Chambers, *Room for Maneuver: Reading (the) Oppositional (in) Narrative* (Chicago: University of Chicago Press, 1991), 1, emphasis added.
40 Frederick Cooper, 'Conflict and Connection: Rethinking Colonial African History,' *American Historical Review* 99:5 (December 1994), 1533.
41 Bhabha, *The Location of Culture*, 116.
42 Ibid., 118.
43 Ibid., 112.
44 Ibid., 110–11.
45 Homi K. Bhabha, 'In a Spirit of Calm Violence,' in *After Colonialism: Imperial Histories and Postcolonial Displacements*, ed. Gyan Prakash (Princeton: Princeton University Press, 1995), 330.
46 Young, *White Mythologies*, 210.
47 Moore-Gilbert, *Postcolonial Theory*, 133.
48 Bhabha, *The Location of Culture*, 117.
49 For instance, in *A History of Negro Revolt*, *Fact* 18 (September 1938), C.L.R. James characterizes the 1915 native revolt in the British protectorate of Nyasaland, which has come to be known as the 'Chilembwe Uprising,' as one of the first examples of an educated African who turns his European and Christian education against colonial power, 47.
50 Ibid., 122.
51 Ibid., 121.
52 Sharpe, 'Figures of Colonial Resistance,' 141–2.
53 Thomas Macaulay, 'Minute on Indian Education,' in *The Post-Colonial Studies Reader*, ed. Bill Ashcroft, Gareth Griffiths, and Helen Tiffin (London: Routledge, 1995), 430.
54 Bhabha, *The Location of Culture*, 85.
55 Ibid., 121.
56 Ibid., 100.
57 Moore-Gilbert, *Postcolonial Theory*, 133.
58 Benita Parry, 'Problems in Current Theories of Colonial Discourse,' in *Postcolonialism: Critical Concepts in Literary and Cultural Studies*, vol. 2, ed. Diana Brydon (London: Routledge, 2000), 728.

59 Fanon, *Black Skin, White Masks*, 148.
60 Ranajit Guha, *Dominance without Hegemony: History and Power in Colonial India* (Cambridge, MA: Harvard University Press, 1997), 46, emphasis added.
61 Bhabha, *The Location of Culture*, 47.
62 Ibid., 46.
63 Mohandas K. Gandhi, *Satyagraha in South Africa* (1928), trans. Valji Govindji Desai (Ahmedabad: Navajivan, 1954), 66–7. Throughout his writings, Gandhi fails to recognize the way in which the presence of Indian 'British' subjects in South Africa furthers the colonial exploitation of the indigenous peoples of the region and its resources (see *Satyagraha in South Africa*, 92). In his writings from this period, there are numerous examples of his belief in a racial hierarchy; for instance, see Mohandas K. Gandhi, *The Collected Works of Mahatma Gandhi* (Ahmedabad: Ministry of Information and Broadcasting, Government of India, 1962), 3: 234, 8: 105, 135, and Balasubramanyam Chandramohan, '"Hamlet with the Prince of Denmark left out?" The South African War, Empire and India,' in *The South African War Reappraised*, ed. Donald Lowry (Manchester: Manchester University Press, 2000), 162, 164. As well, while he advocated for Indian equality with Europeans, Gandhi did not ally this campaign with similar endeavours to recognize African equality; see, for instance, Les Switzer, 'Gandhi in South Africa: The Ambiguities of Satyagraha,' *Journal of Ethnic Studies* 14:1 (1986), 125, 126, and Chandramohan, '"Hamlet with the Prince of Denmark left out?"' 158. However, while critics such as Guha fail to allow the possibility of the recognition of error, change, or redemption in their criticism of Gandhi's actions in South Africa, Gandhi's writings reveal a transformation in his thought. In his rewritings of his experiences in South Africa in *An Autobiography: Or, The Story of My Experiments with Truth* (1927), trans. Mahadev Desai (London: Penguin, 1982), he is careful to qualify his admiration for the British constitution and values as a position he held 'at the time,' and in his account of the Zulu Rebellion in his autobiography he challenges the European construction of Zulus as 'uncivilized,' 289.
64 Gandhi, *Satyagraha in South Africa*, 73.
65 Ashis Nandy, 'Towards a Third World Utopia,' in *Postcolonialism: Critical Concepts in Literary and Cultural Studies*, vol. 4, ed. Diana Brydon (London: Routledge, 2000), 1757.
66 Gandhi, *An Autobiography*, 166.
67 Quoted in Chandramohan, '"Hamlet with the Prince of Denmark left out?"' 157.
68 Ibid., 157; see also J.N. Uppal, *Gandhi: Ordained in South Africa* (New Delhi:

Ministry of Information and Broadcasting, Government of India, 1995), 152, and D.G. Tendulkar, *Mahatma: Life of Mohandas Karmchand Gandhi*, vol. 1, *1869–1920* (Delhi: Ministry of Education and Broadcasting, Government of India, 1960–3), 87.
69 Guha, *Dominance without Hegemony*, 4.
70 Bhabha, *The Location of Culture*, 95, 83.
71 David Scott, *Conscripts of Modernity: The Tragedy of Colonial Enlightenment* (Durham: Duke University Press, 2005), 115.
72 Fanon, *Black Skin, White Masks*, 229.
73 Gandhi, *Satyagraha in South Africa*, 69, emphasis added.
74 See Chandramohan, '"Hamlet with the Prince of Denmark left out?"' 159; L.S. Amery, ed., *The Times History of the War in South Africa, 1899–1902*, vol. 3 (London: Samson Low, Marston and Company, 1905), 100; Shula Marks, *Reluctant Rebellion: The 1906–8 Disturbances in Natal* (Oxford: Clarendon, 1970), 214; Thomas Pakenham, *The Boer War* (London: Weidenfeld and Nicolson, 1979), 341; and Uppal, *Gandhi: Ordained in South Africa*, 135.
75 Tendulkar, *Mahatma: Life of Mohandas Karmchand Gandhi*, 53.
76 Uppal, *Gandhi: Ordained in South Africa*, 159.
77 Gandhi, *Satyagraha in South Africa*, 92.
78 Ibid., 93–4.
79 Quoted in Uppal, *Gandhi: Ordained in South Africa*, 241.
80 See Gandhi, *Collected Works*, 8: 101, 230, 277; Uppal, *Gandhi: Ordained in South Africa*, 333.
81 Gandhi, *Satyagraha in South Africa*, 183.
82 Ibid., 182.
83 Ibid., 183–4.
84 Ranajit Guha, 'The Small Voice of History,' in *Subaltern Studies: Writings on South Asian History and Society*, vol. 9, ed. Shahid Amin and Dipesh Chakrabarty (Delhi: Oxford University Press, 1996), 3.
85 Chakrabarty, *Provincializing Europe*, 32.
86 Kenneth Ingham, *Jan Christian Smuts: The Conscience of South Africa* (London: Weidenfeld and Nicolson, 1986), 55.
87 Gandhi, *The Collected Works*, 8: 509.
88 Bhabha, *The Location of Culture*, 99.
89 Robert A. Huttenback, *Gandhi in South Africa: British Imperialism and the Indian Question, 1860–1914* (Ithaca: Cornell University Press, 1971), 177; see also W.K. Hancock, *Smuts: The Sanguine Years, 1870–1919* (Cambridge: Cambridge University Press, 1962), 321; and Gandhi, *Satyagraha in South Africa*, 189.
90 Jan Smuts, *Selections from the Smuts Papers*, vol. 7, *August 1945–October 1950*,

ed. Jean Van Der Poel (Cambridge, MA: Harvard University Press, 1973), 180.
91 See Gandhi, *Satyagraha in South Africa*, 144–5, 181, 186; and Gandhi, *Collected Works*, 7: 102, 8: 20.
92 Jan Smuts, *Selections from the Smuts Papers*, vol. 3, *June 1910–November 1918*, ed. W.K. Hancock and Jean Van Der Poel (Cambridge: Cambridge University Press, 1966), 151.

Chapter 2

1 The essays compiled in the section on 'Marxist, Liberation and Resistance Theory' in volume 1 of Diana Brydon's *Postcolonialism: Critical Concepts in Literary and Cultural Studies* (London: Routledge, 2000), provide critiques of colonialism and capitalism but, I would argue, not theories of liberation.
2 Laura Chrisman, 'Inventing Post-Colonial Theory: Polemical Observations,' *Pretexts* 5 (1995), 210.
3 Abdul R. JanMohamed, *Manichean Aesthetics: The Politics of Literature in Colonial Africa* (Amherst: University of Massachusetts Press, 1983), 8, 3.
4 Anthony Kwame Appiah, *In My Father's House: Africa in the Philosophy of Culture* (London: Methuen, 1992), 11.
5 Benita Parry, 'Problems in Current Theories of Colonial Discourse,' in *Postcolonialism: Critical Concepts in Literary and Cultural Studies*, vol. 2, ed. Diana Brydon (London: Routledge, 2000), 718, emphasis added.
6 E. San Juan, Jr, *Beyond Postcolonial Theory* (New York: St Martin's, 1997), 17, emphasis added.
7 Ibid., 30.
8 Ibid., 210.
9 Appiah, *In My Father's House*, 115.
10 Ibid., 251.
11 Bill Ashcroft, *Post-Colonial Transformation* (London: Routledge, 2001), 19–20.
12 Ibid., 21.
13 Edward Said, *Culture and Imperialism* (New York: Vintage, 1994), 207.
14 Ibid., 307.
15 Ibid., 276.
16 Ibid., 18.
17 Deepika Bahri, 'Disembodying the Corpus: Postcolonial Pathology in Tsitsi Dangarembga's "Nervous Conditions,"' *Postmodern Culture* 5:1 (September 1994) <http://muse.jhu.edu/journals/postmodern_culture/v005/5.1bahri.html>, par. 5–6.
18 Tsisti Dangarembga, *Nervous Conditions* (Seattle: Seal, 1989), 1.

19 See Aegerter, Bahri, Basu, Hill, McWilliams, Nair, Plasa, and Saliba.
20 Bahri, 'Disembodying the Corpus,' par. 1.
21 Ibid., par. 9 and par. 4, emphasis added.
22 Biman Basu, 'Trapped and Troping: Allegories of the Transnational Intellectual in Tsitsi Dangarembga's *Nervous Conditions*,' *Ariel* 28:3 (July 1997), 21.
23 Janice E. Hill, 'Purging a Plate Full of Colonial History: The *Nervous Conditions* of Silent Girls,' *College Literature* 22:1 (February 1995).
24 Frantz Fanon, *The Wretched of the Earth*, trans. Constance Farrington (New York: Grove, 1963), 53.
25 Ibid., 89, 84.
26 Dangarembga, *Nervous Conditions*, 1.
27 Therese Saliba, 'On the Bodies of Third World Women: Cultural Impurity, Prostitution, and Other Nervous Conditions,' *College Literature* 22:1 (February 1995), 142.
28 Sue Thomas, 'Killing the Hysteric in the Colonized's House: Tsistsi Dangarembga's *Nervous Conditions*,' *Journal of Commonwealth Literature* 27:1 (1992), 31.
29 Supriya Nair, 'Melancholic Women: The Intellectual Hysteric(s) in *Nervous Conditions*,' *Research in African Literatures* 26:2 (Summer 1995), 132.
30 Bahri, 'Disembodying the Corpus,' par. 14.
31 Basu, 'Trapped and Troping,' 13.
32 Dangarembga, *Nervous Conditions*, 135, 197.
33 San Juan, *Beyond Postcolonial Theory*, 70.
34 Saliba, 'On the Bodies of Third World Women,' 138.
35 Ibid., 133.
36 Dangarembga, *Nervous Conditions*, 196.
37 Ibid., 200.
38 Bahri, 'Disembodying the Corpus,' par. 17.
39 Pauline Ada Uwakweh, 'Debunking Patriarchy: The Liberational Quality of Voicing in Tsitsi Dangarembga's *Nervous Conditions*,' *Research in African Literatures* 26:1 (1995), 82; and Saliba, 'On the Bodies of Third World Women,' 142.
40 Saliba, 'On the Bodies of Third World Women,' 141–2.
41 Bahri, 'Disembodying the Corpus,' par. 25.
42 Nyasha's self-destructive violence is reminiscent of Okonkwo's suicide in Achebe's *Things Fall Apart* (1958), which I have taken up elsewhere: 'Violence, Culture and Politics: A Reading of Chinua Achebe's *Things Fall Apart*,' *Peace Review* 13:2 (June 2001), 195–200. Rather than a means of individual or communal self-determination or 'catharsis,' Okonkwo's violent response to colonial authority leads to his literal self-destruction and is as

much a contributing factor to, as a consequence of, the image of the community or culture as 'falling apart.'
43 Dangarembga, *Nervous Conditions*, 58–9.
44 Nair, 'Melancholic Women,' 133.
45 Ibid., 134. While Uwakweh, in 'Debunking Patriarchy,' acknowledges that Tambu's acceptance into the predominantly white Sacred Heart School affirms her mother's fear of the destructive force of acquiring the English language, she argues that Tambu 'finds liberation in the act of voicing "my own story, the story of four women whom I loved, and our men"' (83). Similarly, Miki Flockemann, in '"Not Quite Insiders and Not-Quite Outsiders": The "Process of Womanhood" in *Beka Lamb, Nervous Conditions*, and *Daughters of the Twilight*,' *Journal of Commonwealth Literature* 27:1 (1992), recognizes education as a means of escape from poverty into a racially determined class hierarchy, which, though it constrains Tambu in different ways, allows her to recognize and expose patriarchy (42). See also Gillian Gorle, 'Fighting the Good Fight: What Tsitsi Dangarembga's *Nervous Conditions* Says about Language and Power,' *Yearbook of English Studies* 27 (1997), 192.
46 Basu, 'Trapped and Troping,' 21.
47 Dangarembga, *Nervous Conditions*, 92–3.
48 Ibid., 152.
49 Ibid., 163.
50 Ibid., 120.
51 Ibid., 183.
52 Albert Memmi, *The Colonizer and the Colonized*, trans. Howard Greenfield (Boston: Beacon, 1967), 39.
53 Léopold Sédar Senghor, 'Negritude: A Humanism of the Twentieth Century,' in *Colonial Discourse and Post-Colonial Theory: A Reader*, ed. Patrick Williams and Laura Chrisman (New York: Columbia University Press, 1994), 28, 21.
54 Fanon, *The Wretched of the Earth*, 41.
55 Parry, 'Problems in Current Theories of Colonial Discourse,' 27.
56 Said, *Culture and Imperialism*, 271.
57 Ato Sekyi-Otu, *Fanon's Dialectic of Experience* (Cambridge, MA: Harvard University Press, 1996), 5.
58 Ibid., 25.
59 Ibid., 53.
60 Ibid., 34.
61 Fanon, *The Wretched of the Earth*, 93, 115–16.
62 Ibid., 67, 63.
63 Ibid., 95.

64 Ibid., 251.
65 Ibid., 41.
66 Ibid., 89.
67 Sekyi-Otu, *Fanon's Dialectic of Experience*, 140.
68 Fanon, *The Wretched of the Earth*, 76.
69 Ibid., 68.
70 Ibid., 144–5.
71 Ibid., 152.
72 Ibid., 94, 203.
73 Ibid., 163.
74 Frantz Fanon, *Black Skin, White Masks* (1952), trans. Haakon Chevalier (New York: Monthly Review Press, 1967), 224.
75 Fanon, *The Wretched of the Earth*, 37.
76 Ibid., 57–8.
77 Ngugi wa Thiong'o, *Barrel of a Pen: Resistance to Repression in Neo-Colonial Kenya* (Trenton: Africa World Press, 1983), 80.
78 Amilcar Cabral, 'National Liberation and Culture,' in *Colonial Discourse and Post-Colonial Theory: A Reader*, ed. Patrick Williams and Laura Chrisman (New York: Columbia University Press, 1994), 64, original emphasis.
79 Ibid., 65, emphasis added.
80 Benedict Anderson, *Imagined Communities: Reflections on the Origin and Spread of Nationalism*, rev. ed. (London: Verso, 1991), 7.
81 Memmi, *The Colonizer and the Colonized*, 129.
82 Ibid., 128.
83 Ibid., xiv.
84 Ibid., 129.
85 Aijaz Ahmad, *In Theory: Classes, Nations, Literatures* (London: Verso, 1992), 8.
86 Ashis Nandy, 'Towards a Third World Utopia,' in *Postcolonialism: Critical Concepts in Literary and Cultural Studies*, vol. 4, ed. Diana Brydon (London: Routledge, 2000), 1760.
87 Memmi, *The Colonizer and the Colonized*, 152.
88 Fanon, *The Wretched of the Earth*, 203.
89 Jawaharlal Nehru, 'A Tryst with Destiny: A Speech Delivered at the Constituent Assembly, New Delhi, August 14, 1947,' in *Postcolonialism: Critical Concepts in Literary and Cultural Studies*, vol. 1, ed. Diana Brydon (London: Routledge, 2000), 340.
90 Benita Parry, 'Liberation Movements: Memories of the Future,' *Interventions* 1:1 (1998), 45.
91 Ibid., 46.
92 Cabral, 'National Liberation and Culture,' 62.

93 Aimé Césaire, *Discourse on Colonialism* (1955), trans. Joan Pinkham (New York: Monthly Review Press, 1972), 25.
94 Ibid., 24.
95 Michael Hardt and Antonio Negri, *Empire* (Cambridge, MA: Harvard University Press, 2000), 133.
96 Frantz Fanon, *Toward the African Revolution (Political Essays)*, trans. Haakon Chevalier (New York: Monthly Review Press, 1967), 105.
97 Fanon, *Black Skin, White Masks*, 100.
98 Fanon, *The Wretched of the Earth*, 98.
99 Ibid., 102.
100 Ibid., 103, original emphasis.
101 Ibid., 106.
102 Fanon, *Black Skin, White Masks*, 231–2.
103 Ashcroft, *Post-Colonial Transformation*, 40.
104 Fanon, *Black Skin, White Masks*, 231–2, original emphasis.
105 Fanon, *The Wretched of the Earth*, 312–13.
106 Fanon, *Black Skin, White Masks*, 112.
107 Fanon, *The Wretched of the Earth*, 315.
108 Ibid., 43.
109 Ibid., 314.
110 Ibid., 316.
111 Fanon, *Black Skin, White Masks*, 229, emphasis added.
112 Said, *Culture and Imperialism*, 268.
113 Ibid., 18–19.
114 Fanon, *The Wretched of the Earth*, 269.
115 Ibid., 267, emphasis added.
116 Said, *Culture and Imperialism*, 274, original emphasis.
117 Edward Said, 'Representing the Colonized: Anthropology's Interlocutors,' in *Reflections on Exile and Other Essays* (Cambridge, MA: Harvard University Press, 2003), 306, original emphasis.
118 Robert Young, *White Mythologies: Writing History and the West* (London: Routledge, 1990), 11.
119 Said, *Culture and Imperialism*, 242.
120 Sylvia Wynter, 'Africa, the West and the Analogy of Culture,' in *Symbolic Narratives / African Cinema: Audiences, Theory and the Moving Image*, ed. June Givanni (London: British Film Institute, 2000), 41–2.
121 Anne McClintock, 'The Angel of Progress: Pitfalls of the Term "Post-Colonial,"' in *Colonial Discourse and Post-Colonial Theory: A Reader*, ed. Patrick Williams and Laura Chrisman (New York: Columbia University Press, 1994), 292.

122 Ngugi, *Barrel of a Pen*, 89–90.
123 Said, *Culture and Imperialism*, 224.
124 Fanon, *The Wretched of the Earth*, 88.
125 Said, *Culture and Imperialism*, 268.
126 Ibid., 274.
127 Ibid., 39.
128 Sekyi-Otu, *Fanon's Dialectic of Experience*, 51.
129 Edward Said, *Humanism and Democratic Criticism* (New York: Columbia University Press, 2004), 132.
130 Edward Said, 'Culture and Imperialism,' interview with Joseph A. Buttigeg and Paul A. Bové, in *Power, Politics, and Culture: Interviews with Edward W. Said*, ed. Gauri Viswanathan (New York: Vintage, 2002), 204.
131 Said, *Culture and Imperialism*, 268.
132 Edward Said, 'The Only Alternative,' *Al-Ahram Weekly On-Line* 523 (1–7 March 2001), par. 3.
133 Said, *Culture and Imperialism*, 236.

Chapter 3

1 Partha Chatterjee, *Nationalist Thought and the Colonial World: A Derivative Discourse?* (London: Zed for the United Nations University, 1986), 110; and 'Gandhi and the Critique of Civil Society,' *Subaltern Studies: Writings on South Asian History and Society*, vol. 3, ed. Ranajit Guha (Delhi: Oxford University Press, 1984), 189.
2 Aijaz Ahmad, *Lineages of the Present: Ideology and Politics in Contemporary South Asia* (London: Verso, 2000), 180.
3 For instance, in their introductions to the field, Leela Gandhi and Robert Young both foreground Gandhi as a political actor, an iconic figure of resistance, and an influential thinker. See Leela Gandhi, *Postcolonial Theory: A Critical Introduction* (New York: Columbia University Press, 1998), and Robert Young, *Postcolonialism: A Very Short Introduction* (London: Oxford University Press, 2003).
4 Gyanendra Pandey, 'Peasant Revolt and Indian Nationalism: The Peasant Movement in Awadh, 1919–1922,' *Subaltern Studies: Writings on South Asian History and Society*, vol. 1, ed. Ranajit Guha (Delhi: Oxford University Press, 1982), 164.
5 Ibid., 163.
6 See also Shahid Amin, 'Gandhi as Mahatma: Gorakhpur District, Eastern University Press, 1921–2,' in Guha, *Subaltern Studies*, vol. 3, and Ashok Sen, 'Subaltern Studies: Capital, Class and Community,' *Subaltern Studies:*

Writings on South Asian History and Society, vol. 5, ed. Ranajit Guha (Delhi: Oxford University Press, 1987).

7 Chatterjee, 'Gandhi and the Critique of Civil Society,' 178.
8 According to Mahmood Mamdani, Iqbal 'envisioned Muslim political identity not in terms of a nation-state, but as a borderless cultural community, the *umma* ... Instead of being the profound critique of territorial nationalism and the nation-state that Muhammed Iqbal had intended it to be, Pakistan was a territorial nation as banal as any other nation preoccupied with building its own state'; *Good Muslim, Bad Muslim: America, the Cold War, and the Roots of Terror* (New York: Three Leaves Press, 2004), 53–4.
9 Raja Rao, *Kanthapura* (1938) (New York: New Directions, 1967), vii.
10 David Hardiman, *Gandhi in His Time and Ours: The Global Legacy of His Ideas* (New York: Columbia University Press, 2003), 7–9.
11 See Anuradha Dingwaney Needham, *Using the Master's Tools: Resistance and the Literature of the African and South Asian Diasporas* (New York: St Martin's, 2000), 59.
12 L. Gandhi, *Postcolonial Theory,* ix–x.
13 Léopold Sédar Senghor, 'Negritude and African Socialism,' in *Postcolonialism: Critical Concepts in Literary and Cultural Studies,* vol. 3, ed. Diana Brydon (London: Routledge, 2000), 1007.
14 Michael Hardt and Antonio Negri, *Empire* (Cambridge, MA: Harvard University Press, 2000), 251, original emphasis.
15 Simon Gikandi, *Maps of Englishness: Writing Identity in the Culture of Colonialism* (New York: Columbia University Press, 1996), 18.
16 Chatterjee, *Nationalist Thought and the Colonial World*, 98.
17 Ashis Nandy, 'From Outside the Imperium: Gandhi's Cultural Critique of the "West,"' *Alternatives* 7 (1981), 181.
18 Mohandas K. Gandhi, *Hind Swaraj and Other Writings,* ed. Anthony J. Parel (Cambridge: Cambridge University Press, 1997), 26, 28.
19 Ibid., 7.
20 Anshuman Mondal, 'Gandhi, Utopianism and the Construction of Colonial Difference,' *Interventions* 3:3 (2001), 432.
21 Gandhi, *Hind Swaraj,* 6.
22 Rao, *Kanthapura,* 10.
23 Aijaz Ahmad, 'The Politics of Literary Postcoloniality,' in *Contemporary Postcolonial Theory: A Reader,* ed. Padmini Mongia (London: Arnold, 1997), 281.
24 Chatterjee, 'Gandhi and the Critique of Civil Society,' 162.
25 Mohandas K. Gandhi, *The Collected Works of Mahatma Gandhi* (Ahmedabad: Ministry of Information and Broadcasting, Government of India, 1962), 9: 479.

26 Gandhi, *Collected Works*, 43: 133.
27 Gandhi, *Hind Swaraj*, 36.
28 Gandhi, *Collected Works*, 13: 316.
29 Gandhi, *Hind Swaraj*, 107.
30 Ibid., 107–8.
31 Bose, quoted in Subrata Mukherjee, *Gandhian Thought: Marxist Interpretations* (New Delhi: Deep and Deep, 1991), 42.
32 Gandhi, *Collected Works*, 25: 251–2.
33 Gandhi, *Collected Works*, 48: 353.
34 Nandy, 'From Outside the Imperium,' 189.
35 Gandhi, *Collected Works*, 75: 146–7.
36 Leela Gandhi, 'Concerning Violence: The Limits and Circulations of Gandhian *Ahimsa* or Passive Resistance,' *Cultural Critique* (Winter 1996–7), 133.
37 Gandhi, *Hind Swaraj*, 48.
38 Gandhi, *Collected Works*, 47: 91.
39 Mohandas K. Gandhi, *Village Swaraj*, compiled by H.M. Vyas (Ahmedabad: Navajivan, 1962), 49.
40 See, for instance, Gandhi, *Village Swaraj*, and *Sarvadoya (The Welfare of All)*, ed. Bharatan Kumarappa (Ahmedabad: Navajivan, 1954), both of which are compilations of Gandhi's writings on these subjects.
41 Ahmad, *Lineages of the Present*, 10.
42 Mukherjee, *Gandhian Thought*, 121.
43 Chatterjee, 'Gandhi and the Critique of Civil Society,' 175.
44 Nandy, 'From Outside the Imperium,' 191.
45 See Gandhi, *Collected Works*, 13: 210–16.
46 Gandhi, *Collected Works*, 90: 420.
47 Gandhi, *Collected Works*, 47: 92.
48 B.R. Ambedkar, *Annihilation of Caste with a Reply to Mahatma Gandhi*, 2nd ed. (Punjab: Bheem Patrika Publications, 1971), 65; Ambedkar's critique of Gandhism is at times rather contentious, if not fallacious (i.e., he claims that Gandhi was a staunch opponent of Christianity, eliminated morality from politics, and introduced commercialism into Indian nationalism). Paradoxically, he criticizes Gandhi's status in Indian cultural consciousness as a 'saint,' yet finds fault in him for failing to be accountable for the interpretation and practice of his word by the masses.
49 Mukherjee, *Gandhian Thought*, 140.
50 Gandhi, *Collected Works*, 69: 275–6.
51 Gandhi, *Collected Works*, 24: 52.
52 Chatterjee, *Nationalist Thought and the Colonial World*, 107.
53 Chatterjee, 'Gandhi and the Critique of Civil Society,' 187.

54 Mohandas K. Gandhi, 'The Satyagraha Ashram,' in *The Gandhi Reader: A Sourcebook of His Life and Writings*, ed. Homer A. Jack (New York: Grove, 1956), 138–9.
55 Gandhi, *Collected Works*, 42: 497.
56 Rao, *Kanthapura*, 11–12.
57 Ibid., 59.
58 Brahm Datt Bharti, *Gandhi and Gandhism Unmasked (Was Gandhi a Traitor?)* (New Delhi: Erabooks, 1992), 19, and L. Gandhi, 'Concerning Violence,' 134.
59 Rao, *Kanthapura*, 33.
60 Gandhi, *Collected Works*, 22: 225.
61 Rao, *Kanthapura*, 105.
62 Partha Chatterjee, *The Nation and Its Fragments: Colonial and Postcolonial Histories* (Princeton: Princeton University Press, 1993), 133.
63 Ibid., 134.
64 Ngugi wa Thiong'o, *Barrel of a Pen: Resistance to Repression in Neo-Colonial Kenya* (Trenton: Africa World Press, 1983), 95.
65 Mohandas K. Gandhi, *An Autobiography: Or, The Story of My Experiments with Truth* (1927), trans. Mahadev Desai (London: Penguin, 1982), 291.
66 Gayatri C. Spivak, *A Critique of Postcolonial Reason: Toward a History of the Vanishing Present* (Cambridge, MA: Harvard University Press, 1999), 298; L. Gandhi, 'Concerning Violence,' 133.
67 L. Gandhi, 'Concerning Violence,' 133.
68 Gandhi, 'The Satyagraha Ashram.'
69 Gandhi, *Collected Works*, 17: 490.
70 Frantz Fanon, *The Wretched of the Earth*, trans. Constance Farrington (New York: Grove, 1963), 37, 73.
71 Ibid., 76.
72 Robert Young, *White Mythologies: Writing History and the West* (London: Routledge, 1990), 112.
73 Quoted in Chatterjee, *Nationalist Thought and the Colonial World*, 156.
74 Ibid., 132.
75 Gandhi, *Hind Swaraj*, 80–1.
76 Ashis Nandy, *The Intimate Enemy: Loss and Recovery of Self under Colonialism* (Delhi: Oxford University Press, 1983), 57.
77 See also Hardiman, *Gandhi in His Time and Ours*, 33.
78 Nandy, *The Intimate Enemy*, 111.
79 Ranajit Guha, *Dominance without Hegemony: History and Power in Colonial India* (Cambridge, MA: Harvard University Press, 1997), 20.
80 Ibid., 28.

81 Ibid., 65.
82 Gandhi, *Hind Swaraj*, 41.
83 Ibid., 104.
84 Gandhi, 'The Satyagraha Ashram,' 142.
85 Quoted in Anthony J. Parel, 'Editor's Introduction,' in *Hind Swaraj and Other Writings*, ed. Anthony J. Parel (Cambridge: Cambridge University Press, 1997), xxix.
86 Gandhi, *Hind Swaraj*, 41.
87 Ibid., 10.
88 Gandhi, *Collected Works*, 49: 133.
89 Ambedkar, *Annihilation of Caste with a Reply to Mahatma Gandhi*, 130.
90 Hardiman, *Gandhi in His Time and Ours*, 127.
91 See Bal Ram Nanda, *Gandhi and His Critics* (Delhi: Oxford University Press, 1985), 18, 24.
92 L. Gandhi, *Postcolonial Theory*, 21.
93 Gandhi, *Collected Works*, 69: 52.
94 Gandhi, *Hind Swaraj*, 82.
95 Guha, *Dominance without Hegemony*, 59.
96 Ibid., 58; see, for instance, the U.S. Declaration of Independence.
97 Ibid., 36.
98 Gandhi, *Collected Works*, 64: 191.
99 Gandhi, *Sarvadoya*, 6–7.
100 Ibid., 48.
101 Guha, *Dominance without Hegemony*, 38.
102 Gandhi, *Collected Works*, 58: 247.
103 Gandhi, *Village Swaraj*, 51, emphasis added.
104 Ibid., 52–3. Appeals to landowners to voluntarily give up their land to peasants, however, did find some success. After Gandhi's death, Vinoba Bhave initiated the 'Bhoodan' movement, which succeeded in persuading landowners to relinquish their land to the peasants who lived on it.
105 Mohandas K. Gandhi, *Satyagraha in South Africa* (1928), trans. Valji Govindji Desai (Ahmedabad: Navajivan, 1954), 99.
106 Gandhi, *Collected Works*, 32: 402.
107 Spivak, *A Critique of Postcolonial Reason*, 292.
108 Gandhi, *Collected Works*, 18: 133.
109 Spivak, *A Critique of Postcolonial Reason*, 293.
110 Gandhi, *Collected Works*, 27: 189.
111 Fanon, *The Wretched of the Earth*, 93.
112 Ibid.
113 Gandhi, *Collected Works*, 69: 50.

114 Gandhi, *An Autobiography*, 254.
115 L. Gandhi, 'Concerning Violence,' 124.
116 Gandhi, *Collected Works*, 42: 484.
117 Gandhi, *Collected Works*, 17: 490.
118 Fanon, *The Wretched of the Earth*, 316.
119 Gandhi, *An Autobiography*, 167.
120 Nandy, *The Intimate Enemy*, xvi.
121 Partha Chatterjee, 'For an Indian History of the Peasant Struggle,' *Social Scientist* 16:11 (1988), 12.
122 Rao, *Kanthapura*, 65.
123 Gandhi, *Collected Works*, 26: 271.

Chapter 4

1 While some critics argue that apartheid constitutes a special case of colonialism and cannot be understood through a postcolonial framework, Mahmood Mamdani argues that apartheid should be understood as the generic form of the colonial state in Africa; 'When Does Reconciliation Turn into a Denial of Justice?' (Pretoria: HSRC Publishers, 1998), 4. I make the distinction between apartheid discourse (or the apartheid imagination) and colonial discourse throughout this chapter to recognize the unique features of the apartheid system, as a form of colonial power, in South Africa, so as to avoid the implication that the resistance, as transformation, I describe in this case is, or should be, the paradigm for all (post)colonial spaces.
2 Jane Watts, *Black Writers from South Africa: Towards a Discourse of Liberation* (New York: St Martin's, 1989), 221.
3 Abdul R. JanMohamed, *Manichean Aesthetics: The Politics of Literature in Colonial Africa* (Amherst: University of Massachusetts Press, 1983), 139.
4 Nadine Gordimer, *July's People* (Middlesex: Penguin, 1982), 95.
5 Ibid., 119.
6 JanMohamed, *Manichean Aesthetics*, 140.
7 Gordimer, *July's People*, 117.
8 Mahmood Mamdani, *Good Muslim, Bad Muslim: America, the Cold War, and the Roots of Terror* (New York: Three Leaves Press, 2004), 10.
9 Gordimer, *July's People*, 155.
10 JanMohamed, *Manichean Aesthetics*, 84.
11 Kenneth Christie argues that 'the ANC's version of history is couched in terms of an armed struggle, a massive period of heroic resistance against a criminal apartheid'; *The South African Truth Commission* (New York: Palgrave, 2000), 28. For examples of the way in which postcolonial critics

collapse anti-apartheid resistance with the ANC, see Vijay Mishra and Bob Hodge, 'What Is Post(-)colonialism?' in *Colonial Discourse and Post-Colonial Theory: A Reader*, ed. Patrick Williams and Laura Chrisman (New York: Columbia University Press, 1994), 278, and Neil Lazarus, *Nationalism and Cultural Practice in the Postcolonial World* (New York: Cambridge University Press, 1999), 207.

12 Lucie Pagé, prod., *South African Freedom Songs: Inspiration for Liberation*, audio documentary, CD, Mayibuye Centre, 2000.
13 Rosemary Jolly, 'Rehearsals of Liberation: Contemporary Postcolonial Discourse and the New South Africa,' *PMLA* 100:1 (1995), 22.
14 Tinyiko Sam Maluleke, 'Can Lions and Rabbits Reconcile? The South African TRC as an Instrument for Peace-Building,' *Ecumenical Review* 53 (2001), 193.
15 Christie, *The South African Truth Commission*, 29.
16 See Pagé, *South African Freedom Songs*.
17 Nelson Mandela, *Long Walk to Freedom: The Autobiography of Nelson Mandela* (Boston: Little, Brown, 1994), 528.
18 Quoted in Nahem Yousaf, 'Apartheid Narratives,' in *Apartheid Narratives*, ed. Nahem Yousaf (Amsterdam: Rodopi, 2001), vii.
19 Antjie Krog, *Country of My Skull: Guilt, Sorrow, and the Limits of Forgiveness in the New South Africa* (New York: Three Rivers, 2000), 144.
20 David Attwell and Barbara Harlow contend that the 'remaking of South Africa' was 'heralded by a period of ... secret exchanges and public negotiation' *following* 'a generation of *armed struggle* against a system of state violence'; 'Introduction: South African Fiction after Apartheid,' *Modern Fiction Studies* 46:1 (Spring 2000), 1, emphasis added.
21 *Truth and Reconciliation Commission of South Africa Report*, vol. 1 (Cape Town: The Commission, 1998), 1.
22 Quoted in Jonathan Schell, *The Unconquerable World: Power, Nonviolence, and the Will of the People* (New York: Metropolitan, 2003), 255.
23 Rajeev Bhargava, 'Restoring Decency to Barbaric Societies,' in *Truth v. Justice: The Morality of Truth Commissions*, ed. Robert I. Rotberg and Dennis Thompson (Princeton: Princeton University Press), 45, 56.
24 *Truth and Reconciliation Commission*, 1: 107. National initiatives, community relations, and individual experiences were linked in unpredictable but at times significant ways. For example, Nicholas Links's acknowledgment of murdering Matan Jonga facilitated the initial step towards personal reconciliation between Links and the Jonga family and initiated a process of reconciliation within their community more broadly; *Truth and Reconciliation Commission*, 5: 399.

25 *The Freedom Charter* (1955), African National Congress <http://www.anc.org.za/ancdocs/history/charter.html> (accessed 3 April 2003).
26 Mandela notes that the governments of newly independent countries throughout Africa tended to support the Pan-Africanist Congress (PAC) rather than the ANC because the ANC policies and character did not conform to a 'pan-African' ideology; *Long Walk to Freedom*, 300.
27 Ibid., 568.
28 Quoted in Alton B. Pollard III, 'Rhythms of Resistance: The Role of the Freedom Song in South Africa,' in *This Is How We Flow: Rhythm and Sensibility in Black Cultures*, ed. Angela M.S. Nelson (Columbia: South Carolina University Press, 1999), 123.
29 Jeremy Seekings, *The UDF: A History of the United Democratic Front in South Africa, 1983–1991* (Cape Town: David Hill, 2000), 29, 288, 298.
30 While the UDF, and many of its key advocates, professed a commitment to non-racialism, the functioning of the organization revealed the tensions between the ideal of non-racialism, and the politics of multi-racialism, or the political reality described and perpetuated through the state's discourse of race. For instance, most of the groups affiliated with the Front organized in racially segregated constituencies; to contend with this problem, the Front's inaugural meeting at Phoenix included participants from all of the racialized groups within the South African state, but participants represented regions of the country rather than racial groups, such as 'black,' 'white,' 'coloured,' or 'Indian'; see Seekings, *The UDF*, 72, 91. AZAPO and Inkatha, for instance, were highly critical of the Front's constitution and ideals. Seekings contends that the UDF was committed to non-racial leadership, but relied on a strategy that, by necessity, was multi-racial in character, in which alliances were built between the various racialized and regionally based constituencies in the state; *The UDF*, 321.
31 Patrick Bond, 'South Africa's Resurgent Urban Social Movements: The Case of Johannesburg, 1984, 1994, 2004,' *Centre for Civil Society Research Report No. 22* (Durban: Centre for Civil Society, October 2004), 15.
32 Desmond Tutu, *The Rainbow People of God: The Making of a Peaceful Revolution*, ed. John Allen (New York: Image Doubleday, 1994), 21.
33 Quoted in Seekings, *The UDF*, 60.
34 Steve Biko, 'Black Consciousness and the Quest for a True Humanity,' in *I Write What I Like: Selected Writings* (Chicago: University of Chicago Press, 2002), 90.
35 Steve Biko, 'Black Souls in White Skins?' in ibid., 24.
36 Ibid., 25.
37 Biko, 'Black Consciousness and the Quest for a True Humanity,' 96–7.

38 Tutu, *The Rainbow People of God*, 143.
39 Ibid., 142.
40 Michael Hardt and Antonio Negri, *Empire* (Cambridge, MA: Harvard University Press, 2000), 308.
41 Ibid., 308.
42 Ibid., 537.
43 Christie, *The South African Truth Commission*, 16.
44 Mahmood Mamdani, 'Reconciliation without Justice,' in *Southern African Review of Books* 46 (November/December 1996) <http://www.uniulm.de/~rturrell/antho3html/Mamdani.html> (accessed 11 March 2003).
45 Hannah Arendt, *On Violence* (New York: Harvest, 1970), 53.
46 Mamdani, 'Reconciliation without Justice.'
47 Ibid.
48 *Truth and Reconciliation Commission*, 5: 409–10.
49 Desmond Tutu, *No Future without Forgiveness* (New York: Image Doubleday, 1999), 274.
50 Heather Deegan, *The Politics of the New South Africa: Apartheid and After* (Harlow, UK: Pearson Education, 2001), 116–17.
51 Mamdani, 'Reconciliation without Justice.'
52 Jacqueline Rose, 'Apathy and Accountability: South Africa's Truth and Reconciliation Commission,' *Raritan* 21:4 (Spring 2002), 186.
53 Susan Dwyer, 'Reconciliation for Realists,' *Ethics and International Affairs* 13 (1999), 92; Kader Asmal, Louise Asmal, and Ronald Suresh Roberts, *Reconciliation through Truth: A Reckoning of Apartheid's Criminal Governance*, 2nd ed. (Cape Town: David Philip, 1997), 46.
54 Michael Ignatieff, 'Articles of Faith,' *Index on Censorship* 5 (1996), 113; Maluleke argues that many critics of the TRC miss the commission's 'human factor'; he quotes Albie Sachs: '"I loved [the TRC report] because it was so uneven, it was rough, it had seams ... It contained the passion, the variety, and even the contradictions of the process itself,"' 197.
55 More than ten years after the end of apartheid, nearly 50 per cent of South Africans live in poverty, and both the wealth gap between rich and poor and the unemployment rate have increased, rather than decreased; Dominique Herman, 'Fifty Per Cent of SA Citizens Live in Poverty,' *Pretoria News* (13 June 2006), 4; see also, for instance, the Institute for Justice and Reconciliation <http://www.ijr.org.za/> or the research reports, publications, and other resources of the University of KwaZulu-Natal's Centre for Civil Society <http://www.ukzn.ac.za/ccs>.
56 Tutu, *The Rainbow People of God*, 124.
57 Yousaf, 'Apartheid Narratives,' vii.

58 Albie Sachs, 'Preparing Ourselves for Freedom,' in *Writing South Africa: Literature, Apartheid, and Democracy, 1970–1995*, ed. Derek Attridge and Rosemary Jolly (Cambridge: Cambridge University Press, 1998), 240.
59 Ibid.
60 Krog, *Country of My Skull*, 312.
61 Sindiwe Magona, *Mother to Mother* (Boston: Beacon, 1998), 173.
62 Ibid., 178.
63 Ibid., 182.
64 Ibid., 180.
65 Ibid., 1–2.
66 *Truth and Reconciliation Commission*, 5: 441.
67 *Truth and Reconciliation Commission*, 1: 111–14.
68 Benita Parry, 'Reconciliation and Remembrance,' *Pretexts* 5:1–2 (1995), 91.
69 Ibid., 90–1.
70 John K. Noyes, 'Nature, History, and the Failure of Language: The Problem of the Human in Post-Apartheid South Africa,' in *Relocating Postcolonialism*, ed. David Theo Goldberg and Ato Quayson (Oxford: Blackwell, 2002), 279.
71 Magona, *Mother to Mother*, 1.
72 Ibid., 48.
73 Ibid., 33.
74 Ibid., 76.
75 Ibid., 199.
76 Krog, *Country of My Skull*, 126.
77 Magona, *Mother to Mother*, 210.
78 Ibid., 3.
79 Quoted in Jolly, 'Rehearsals of Liberation,' 26.
80 *Truth and Reconciliation Commission*, 5: 393.
81 Quoted in Khadija Magardie, 'Blinded by Apartheid,' *Orbit* 78 (Autumn 2000), 9.
82 Chikane, quoted in Mamdani, 'Reconciliation without Justice.'
83 Quoted in Krog, *Country of My Skull*, 252.
84 Quoted in ibid., 142.
85 Desmond Tutu, quoted in *Truth and Reconciliation Commission*, 5: 353.
86 *Truth and Reconciliation Commission*, 1: 126.
87 Ann Gutmann and Dennis Thompson, 'The Moral Foundations of Truth Commissions,' in *Truth v. Justice: The Morality of Truth Commissions*, ed. Robert I. Rotberg and Dennis Thompson (Princeton: Princeton University Press, 2000), 22.
88 Robert I. Rotberg, 'Truth Commissions and the Provision of Truth, Justice and Reconciliation,' in ibid., 7; see also Attwell and Harlow, 'Introduction:

South African Fiction after Apartheid,' 2; David Little, 'A Different Kind of Justice: Dealing with Human Rights Violations in Transitional Societies,' *Ethics and International Affairs* 13 (1999), 65; and James L. Gibson, 'Truth, Justice and Reconciliation: Judging the Fairness of Amnesty in South Africa,' *American Journal of Political Science* 46:3 (July 2002), 546.

89 Rosemary Jolly, 'Desiring Good(s) in the Face of Marginalized Subjects: South Africa's Truth and Reconciliation Commission in a Global Context,' *South Atlantic Quarterly* 100:3 (Summer 2001), 694.
90 Ibid., 710.
91 For a discussion of the intersection of Christianity and the Southern African philosophy of *ubuntu*, as a basis for Tutu's conception of reconciliation, see Tutu, *No Future without Forgiveness* and *The Rainbow People of God*, as well as Michael Battle, *Reconciliation: The Ubuntu Theology of Desmond Tutu* (Cleveland: Pilgrim, 1997).
92 Tutu, *The Rainbow People of God*, 229.
93 Mark Sanders, *Complicities: The Intellectual and Apartheid* (Durham: Duke University Press, 2002), 120.
94 Ibid., 125.
95 Ibid., 126.
96 Ibid., 127.
97 Mamdani, 'Reconciliation without Justice.'
98 *Truth and Reconciliation Commission*, 1: 110.
99 Magardie, 'Blinded by Apartheid,' 9.
100 In the novel, Mandisa asks God to forgive her son 'this terrible, terrible sin,' but she does not ask for her sister-mother's forgiveness. Amy Biehl's parents did not oppose the amnesty applications of those who had killed their daughter; indeed, they attended the hearings and have set up a foundation for youth in Guguletu.
101 *Truth and Reconciliation Commission*, 5: 392.
102 Tutu, *No Future without Forgiveness*, 151.
103 *Truth and Reconciliation Commission*, 5: 403.
104 There are examples in the final report of such acts of responsibility. For instance, Captain Brian Mitchell confessed to and requested forgiveness for his participation in the Trust Feed massacre of 1988. After a long process of trust-building, the community and Mitchell agreed to a plan in which he would participate in the community's reconstruction as an overt act of repentance; see *Truth and Reconciliation Commission*, 5: 395.
105 Ibid., 380–1.
106 Rosemary Nagy, 'Reconciliation in Post-Commission South Africa: Thick

and Thin Accounts of Solidarity,' *Canadian Journal of Political Science* 35:2 (2002): 332.
107 Tutu, *No Future without Forgiveness*, 272–3.
108 Krog, *Country of My Skull*, 364.
109 Ibid., 364–5.
110 *Truth and Reconciliation Commission*, 1: 29.
111 Edward Said, *Culture and Imperialism* (New York: Vintage, 1994), 18.
112 Ibid., 274.
113 *Truth and Reconciliation Commission*, 1: 116.
114 Quoted in Aletta J. Norval, 'Reconstructing National Identity and Renegotiating Memory: The Work of the TRC,' in *States of Imagination: Ethnographic Explorations of the Postcolonial State*, ed. Thomas Blom Hansen and Finn Stepputat (Durham: Duke University Press, 2001), 191.
115 *Truth and Reconciliation Commission*, 1: 133.
116 Pieter Meiring, 'Truth and Reconciliation: The South African Experience,' in *Race and Reconciliation in South Africa: A Multicultural Dialogue in Comparative Perspective*, ed. William E. Van Vugt and G. Daan Cloete (Lanham: Lexington, 2000), 195.
117 *Truth and Reconciliation Commission*, 5: 370.
118 When the ANC threatened to prevent its members from seeking amnesty because they had been involved in a 'just war,' Tutu, as chair, threatened to resign; see *Truth and Reconciliation Commission*, 1: 10.
119 Krog, *Country of My Skull*, 76.
120 Tutu, *No Future without Forgiveness*, 24.
121 Ibid., 54.
122 Krog, *Country of My Skull*, 76.
123 Mandela, *Long Walk to Freedom*, 249.
124 Krog notes that for many white journalists, covering the TRC was a means of exploring their own guilt for their complicity in apartheid; *Country of My Skull*, 224.
125 Charles Villa-Vicencio, 'Restorative Justice in Social Context: The South African Truth and Reconciliation Commission,' in *Burying the Past: Making Peace and Doing Justice after Civil Conflict*, ed. Nigel Biggar (Washington: Georgetown University Press, 2001), 215.
126 Krog, *Country of My Skull*, 115.
127 Tutu, *The Rainbow People of God*, 102.
128 Jolly, 'Desiring Good(s) in the Face of Marginalized Subjects,' 700.
129 Krog, *Country of My Skull*, 212.
130 *Truth and Reconciliation Commission*, 1: 131.
131 Ironically, the two cases that I have come across in which South Africans

have come forward to seek amnesty for their apathy involve an Indian woman (Rose, 'Apathy and Accountability,' 175) and a group of black youths (Krog, *Country of My Skull*, 159).
132 *Truth and Reconciliation Commission*, 1: 134.
133 Ibid., 103.
134 Ibid.
135 Dwyer, 'Reconciliation for Realists,' 88–9.

Conclusion

1 Raymond Williams, 'Tragedy and Revolution' (1966), in *The Raymond Williams Reader*, ed. John Higgins (Oxford: Blackwell, 2001), 105.
2 Gayatri Chakravorty Spivak, 'From Haverstock Hill Flat to U.S. Classroom: What's Left of Theory?' in *What's Left of Theory?* ed. Judith Butler, John Guillory, and Kendell Thomas (New York: Routledge, 2000), 8.
3 Frantz Fanon, *Black Skin, White Masks* (1952), trans. Haakon Chevalier (New York: Monthly Review Press, 1967), 231.
4 Gayatri C. Spivak, *A Critique of Postcolonial Reason: Toward a History of the Vanishing Present* (Cambridge, MA: Harvard University Press, 1999), 383.
5 Chela Sandoval, *Methodology of the Oppressed* (Minneapolis: University of Minnesota Press, 2000), 4.
6 Ibid., 151.
7 Ibid., 162.
8 Michael Hardt and Antonio Negri, *Empire* (Cambridge, MA: Harvard University Press, 2000), 413.
9 Ibid., 211.
10 Arundhati Roy, 'How Deep Shall We Dig?' in *An Ordinary Person's Guide to Empire* (Cambridge, MA: South End, 2004), 117.
11 Arundhati Roy, 'Confronting Empire,' in *War Talk* (Cambridge, MA: South End, 2003), 112.

Bibliography

Aegerter, Lindsay Pentholve. 'A Dialectic of Autonomy and Community: Tsitsi Dangarembga's *Nervous Conditions*,' *Tulsa Studies in Women's Literature* 15:2 (Fall 1996): 231–40.

Ahmad, Aijaz. *In Theory: Classes, Nations, Literatures.* London: Verso, 1992.

– *Lineages of the Present: Ideology and Politics in Contemporary South Asia.* London: Verso, 2000.

– 'The Politics of Literary Postcoloniality.' *Contemporary Postcolonial Theory: A Reader.* Ed. Padmini Mongia, 276–93. London: Arnold, 1997.

Ambedkar, B.R. *Annihilation of Caste with a Reply to Mahatma Gandhi.* 2nd ed. Punjab: Bheem Patrika Publications, 1971.

Amery, L.S., ed. *The Times History of the War in South Africa, 1899–1902.* Vol. 3. London: Samson Low, Marston and Company, 1905.

Amin, Shahid. 'Gandhi as Mahatma: Gorakhpur District, Eastern UP, 1921–2.' *Subaltern Studies: Writings on South Asian History and Society.* Vol. 3. Ed. Ranajit Guha, 1–61. Delhi: Oxford University Press, 1984.

Anderson, Benedict. *Imagined Communities: Reflections on the Origin and Spread of Nationalism.* 1983. Rev. ed. London: Verso, 1991.

Appiah, Kwame Anthony. *In My Father's House: Africa in the Philosophy of Culture.* London: Methuen, 1992.

Arendt, Hannah. *On Violence.* New York: Harvest, 1970.

Armah, Ayi Kwei. *The Beautyful Ones Are Not Yet Born.* London: Heinemann, 1969.

Ashcroft, Bill. *Post-Colonial Transformation.* London: Routledge, 2001.

Ashcroft, Bill, Gareth Griffiths, and Helen Tiffin. *The Empire Writes Back: Theory and Practice in Post-Colonial Literatures.* London: Routledge, 1989.

– *Post-Colonial Studies: The Key Concepts.* London: Routledge, 2000.

Asmal, Kader, Louise Asmal, and Ronald Suresh Roberts. *Reconciliation through*

Truth: A Reckoning of Apartheid's Criminal Governance. 2nd ed. Cape Town: David Philip, 1997.

Attenborough, Richard, dir. *Gandhi*. 1982. DVD. Columbia Tristar, 2001.

Attwell, David, and Barbara Harlow. 'Introduction: South African Fiction after Apartheid.' *Modern Fiction Studies* 46:1 (Spring 2000): 1–9.

Bahri, Deepika. 'Disembodying the Corpus: Postcolonial Pathology in Tsitsi Dangarembga's "Nervous Conditions."' *Postmodern Culture* 5:1 (September 1994) <http://muse.jhu.edu/journals/postmodern_culture/v005/5.1bahri.html>.

Bartolovich, Crystal. 'The Eleventh of September of George Bush: Fortress US and the Global Politics of Consumption.' *Interventions* 5:2 (June 2003): 177–99.

Basu, Biman. 'Trapped and Troping: Allegories of the Transnational Intellectual in Tsitsi Dangarembga's *Nervous Conditions*.' *ARIEL* 28:3 (July 1997): 7–24.

Battle, Michael. *Reconciliation: The Ubuntu Theology of Desmond Tutu*. Cleveland: Pilgrim, 1997.

Bhabha, Homi K. 'In a Spirit of Calm Violence.' *After Colonialism: Imperial Histories and Postcolonial Displacements*. Ed. Gyan Prakash, 326–43. Princeton: Princeton University Press, 1995.

– *The Location of Culture*. London: Routledge, 1994.

– 'Translator Translated: Conversation with Homi Bhabha.' Interview with W.J.T. Mitchell. *Artforum* 33:7 (March 1995): 80–3, 110, 114, 118–19.

Bhargava, Rajeev. 'Restoring Decency to Barbaric Societies.' *Truth v. Justice: The Morality of Truth Commissions*. Ed. Robert I. Rotberg and Dennis Thompson, 45–67. Princeton: Princeton University Press, 2000.

Bharti, Brahm Datt. *Gandhi and Gandhism Unmasked (Was Gandhi Traitor?)*. New Delhi: Erabooks, 1992.

Biko, Steve. 'Black Consciousness and the Quest for a True Humanity.' *I Write What I Like: Selected Writings*, 87–98. Chicago: University of Chicago Press, 2002.

– 'Black Souls in White Skins?' 1978. *I Write What I Like: Selected Writings*, 19–26. Chicago: University of Chicago Press, 2002.

Bond, Patrick. 'South Africa's Resurgent Urban Social Movements: The Case of Johannesburg, 1984, 1994, 2004.' *Centre for Civil Society Research Report No. 22*. Durban, South Africa: Centre for Civil Society, October 2004.

Brydon, Diana, ed. *Postcolonialism: Critical Concepts in Literary and Cultural Studies*. London: Routledge, 2000.

Cabral, Amilcar. 'National Liberation and Culture.' *Colonial Discourse and Post-Colonial Theory: A Reader*. Ed. Patrick Williams and Laura Chrisman, 53–65. New York: Columbia University Press, 1994.

Césaire, Aimé. *Discourse on Colonialism*. 1955. Trans. Joan Pinkham. New York: Monthly Review Press, 1972.

Chadha, Gurinder, dir. *Bhaji on the Beach*. 1994. VHS. Columbia Tristar, 1996.

Chakrabarty, Dipesh. *Provincializing Europe: Postcolonial Thought and Historical Difference*. Princeton: Princeton University Press, 2000.

Chambers, Ross. *Room for Maneuver: Reading (the) Oppositional (in) Narrative*. Chicago: University of Chicago Press, 1991.

Chandramohan, Balasubramanyam. '"Hamlet with the Prince of Denmark left out?" The South African War, Empire and India.' *The South African War Reappraised*. Ed. Donald Lowry, 150–68. Manchester: Manchester University Press, 2000.

Chatterjee, Partha. 'Gandhi and the Critique of Civil Society.' *Subaltern Studies: Writings on South Asian History and Society*. Vol. 3. Ed. Ranajit Guha, 153–95. Delhi: Oxford University Press, 1984.

– *Nationalist Thought and the Colonial World: A Derivative Discourse?* London: Zed for the United Nations University, 1986.

Childs, Peter, and Patrick Williams. *An Introduction to Post-Colonial Theory*. London: Prentice Hall, 1997.

Chow, Rey. 'Where Have All the Natives Gone?' *Contemporary Postcolonial Studies: A Reader*. Ed. Padmini Mongia. London: Arnold, 1996.

Chrisman, Laura. 'Inventing Post-Colonial Theory: Polemical Observations.' *Pretexts* 5 (1995): 205–12.

Christie, Kenneth. *The South African Truth Commission*. New York: Palgrave, 2000.

Coetzee, J.M. *Waiting for the Barbarians*. New York: Penguin, 1980.

Cooper, Frederick. 'Conflict and Connection: Rethinking Colonial African History.' *American Historical Review* 99:5 (December 1994): 1516–45.

Dangarembga, Tsitsi. *Nervous Conditions*. 1988. Seattle: Seal, 1989.

'The Declaration of Independence.' 1776. United States Government. 2003. <http://www.archives.gov/exhibit_hall/charters_of_freedom/declaration/declaration_transcription.html> (accessed 24 January 2003).

Deegan, Heather. *The Politics of the New South Africa: Apartheid and After*. Harlow, UK: Pearson Education, 2001.

Dirlik, Arif. 'The Postcolonial Aura: Third World Criticism in the Age of Global Capitalism.' *Contemporary Postcolonial Theory: A Reader*. Ed. Padmini Mongia, 294–321. London: Arnold, 1997.

Dwyer, Susan. 'Reconciliation for Realists.' *Ethics and International Affairs* 13 (1999): 81–98.

Fanon, Frantz. *Black Skin, White Masks*. 1952. Trans. Charles Lam Markmann. New York: Grove, 1967.

- *Toward the African Revolution (Political Essays)*. 1964. Trans. Haakon Chevalier. New York: Monthly Review Press, 1967.
- *The Wretched of the Earth*. 1961. Trans. Constance Farrington. New York: Grove, 1963.

Flockemann, Miki. '"Not Quite Insiders and Not-Quite Outsiders": The "Process of Womanhood" in *Beka Lamb*, *Nervous Conditions*, and *Daughters of the Twilight*.' *Journal of Commonwealth Literature* 27:1 (1992): 37–47.

Foucault, Michel. *The History of Sexuality: An Introduction*. Vol. 1. 1976. Trans. Robert Hurley. New York: Vintage, 1990.

'The Freedom Charter.' 1955. <http://www.anc.org.za/ancdocs/history/charter.html> (accessed 3 April 2003).

Galtung, Johan. *Peace by Peaceful Means: Peace and Conflict, Development and Civilization*. London: Sage, 1996.

Gandhi, Leela. 'Concerning Violence: The Limits and Circulations of Gandhian *Ahimsa* or Passive Resistance.' *Cultural Critique* (Winter 1996–7): 105–47.
- *Postcolonial Theory: A Critical Introduction*. New York: Columbia University Press, 1998.

Gandhi, Mohandas K. *An Autobiography: Or, The Story of My Experiments with Truth*. 1927, 1929. Trans. Mahadev Desai. London: Penguin, 1982.
- *The Collected Works of Mahatma Gandhi*. 100 Volumes. Ahmedabad: Ministry of Information and Broadcasting, Government of India, 1962.
- *Hind Swaraj*. 1910. *Hind Swaraj and Other Writings*. Ed. Anthony J. Parel, 1–126. Cambridge: Cambridge University Press, 1997.
- *Sarvadoya (The Welfare of All)*. Ed. Bharatan Kumarappa. Ahmedabad: Navajivan, 1954.
- 'The Satyagraha Ashram.' *The Gandhi Reader: A Sourcebook of His Life and Writings*. Ed. Homer A. Jack, 136–44. New York: Grove, 1956.
- *Satyagraha in South Africa*. 1928. Trans. Valji Govindji Desai. Ahmedabad: Navajivan, 1950.
- *Village Swaraj*. Compiled by H.M. Vyas. Ahmedabad: Navajivan, 1962.

Gibson, James L. 'Truth, Justice, and Reconciliation: Judging the Fairness of Amnesty in South Africa.' *American Journal of Political Science* 46:3 (July 2002): 540–56.

Gikandi, Simon. *Maps of Englishness: Writing Identity in the Culture of Colonialism*. New York: Columbia University Press, 1996.
- 'Theory, Literature, and Moral Considerations.' *Research in African Literatures* 32:4 (Winter 2001): 1–18.

Gilroy, Paul. *Against Race: Imagining Political Culture beyond the Color Line*. Cambridge, MA: Belknap, 2000.

– *Postcolonial Melancholia*. New York: Columbia University Press, 2005.
Gordimer, Nadine. *July's People*. 1981. Middlesex: Penguin, 1982.
Gorle, Gillian. 'Fighting the Good Fight: What Tsitsi Dangarembga's *Nervous Conditions* Says about Language and Power.' *Yearbook of English Studies* 27 (1997): 179–92.
Guha, Ranajit. *Dominance without Hegemony: History and Power in Colonial India*. Cambridge, MA: Harvard University Press, 1997.
– 'The Small Voice of History.' *Subaltern Studies: Writings on South Asian History and Society*. Vol. 9. Ed. Shahid Amin and Dipesh Chakrabarty, 1–12. Delhi: Oxford University Press, 1996.
Gutmann, Ann, and Dennis Thompson. 'The Moral Foundations of Truth Commissions.' *Truth v. Justice: The Morality of Truth Commissions*. Ed. Robert I. Rotberg and Dennis Thompson, 22–44. Princeton: Princeton University Press, 2000.
Hallward, Peter. *Absolutely Postcolonial: Writing between the Singular and the Specific*. Manchester: Manchester University Press, 2001.
Hancock, W.K. *Smuts: The Sanguine Years, 1870–1919*. Cambridge: Cambridge University Press, 1962.
Hardiman, David. *Gandhi in His Time and Ours: The Global Legacy of His Ideas*. New York: Columbia University Press, 2003.
Hardt, Michael, and Antonio Negri. *Empire*. Cambridge, MA: Harvard University Press, 2000.
Harlow, Barbara. *Resistance Literature*. New York: Routledge, 1987.
Herman, Dominique. 'Fifty Per Cent of SA Citizens Live in Poverty.' *Pretoria News* (13 June 2006): 4.
Hill, Janice E. 'Purging a Plate Full of Colonial History: The *Nervous Conditions* of Silent Girls.' *College Literature* 22 (February 1995): 78–90.
Huttenback, Robert A. *Gandhi in South Africa: British Imperialism and the Indian Question, 1860–1914*. Ithaca: Cornell University Press, 1971.
Ignatieff, Michael. 'Articles of Faith.' *Index on Censorship* 5 (1996).
Ingham, Kenneth. *Jan Christian Smuts: The Conscience of a South African*. London: Weidenfeld and Nicolson, 1986.
James, C.L.R. *A History of Negro Revolt*. *Fact* 18 (September 1938).
JanMohamed, Abdul R. *Manichean Aesthetics: The Politics of Literature in Colonial Africa*. Amherst: University of Massachusetts Press, 1983.
Jefferess, David. 'Violence, Culture and Politics: A Reading of Chinua Achebe's *Things Fall Apart*.' *Peace Review* 13:2 (June 2001): 195–200.
Jolly, Rosemary. 'Desiring Good(s) in the Face of Marginalized Subjects: South Africa's Truth and Reconciliation Commission in a Global Context.' *South Atlantic Quarterly* 100:3 (Summer 2001): 693–716.

- 'Rehearsals of Liberation: Contemporary Postcolonial Discourse and the New South Africa.' *PMLA* 110:1 (January 1995): 17–29.
Krog, Antjie. *Country of My Skull: Guilt, Sorrow, and the Limits of Forgiveness in the New South Africa*. 1998. New York: Three Rivers, 2000.
Kureishi, Hanif. *The Buddha of Suburbia*. London: Penguin, 1990.
Lazarus, Neil. *Nationalism and Cultural Practice in the Postcolonial World*. New York: Cambridge University Press, 1999.
Little, David. 'A Different Kind of Justice: Dealing with Human Rights Violations in Transitional Societies.' *Ethics and International Affairs* 13 (1999): 65–80.
Macaulay, Thomas. 'Minute on Indian Education.' *The Post-Colonial Studies Reader*. Ed. Bill Ashcroft, Gareth Griffiths, and Helen Tiffin, 428–30. London: Routledge, 1995.
Magardie, Khadija. 'Blinded by Apartheid.' Interview with Neville Clarence. *Orbit* 78 (Autumn 2000): 8–9.
Magona, Sindiwe. *Mother to Mother*. Boston: Beacon, 1998.
Maluleke, Tinyiko Sam. 'Can Lions and Rabbits Reconcile? The South African TRC as an Instrument for Peace-Building.' *Ecumenical Review* 53 (2001): 190–201.
Mamdani, Mahmood. *Good Muslim, Bad Muslim: America, the Cold War, and the Roots of Terror*. New York: Three Leaves Press, 2004.
- 'Reconciliation without Justice.' *Southern African Review of Books* 46 (November/December 1996) <http://www.uniulm.de/~rturrell/antho3html/Mamdani.html>.
- 'When Does Reconciliation Turn into a Denial of Justice?' Pretoria: HSRC Publishers, 1998.
Mandela, Nelson. *Long Walk to Freedom: The Autobiography of Nelson Mandela*. Boston: Little, Brown, 1994.
Marks, Shula. *Reluctant Rebellion: The 1906–8 Disturbances in Natal*. Oxford: Clarendon, 1970.
McCabe, Colin. 'Foreword.' *In Other Worlds: Essays in Cultural Politics*. New York: Methuen, 1987: ix–xix.
McClintock, Anne. 'The Angel of Progress: Pitfalls of the Term "Post-Colonial."' *Colonial Discourse and Post-Colonial Theory: A Reader*. Ed. Patrick Williams and Laura Chrisman, 291–304. New York: Columbia University Press, 1994.
McWilliams, Sally. 'Tsitsi Dangarembga's *Nervous Conditions:* At the Crossroads of Feminism and Post-Colonialism.' *World Literature Written in English* 31:1 (1991): 103–12.
Meiring, Pieter. 'Truth and Reconciliation: The South African Experience.' *Race and Reconciliation in South Africa: A Multicultural Dialogue in Comparative Per-*

spective. Ed. William E. Van Vugt and G. Daan Cloete, 187–200. Lanham: Lexington, 2000.

Memmi, Albert. *The Colonizer and the Colonized*. Trans. Howard Greenfeld. Boston: Beacon Press, 1967.

Mishra, Vijay, and Bob Hodge. 'What Is Post(-)colonialism?' *Colonial Discourse and Post-Colonial Theory: A Reader*. Ed. Patrick Williams and Laura Chrisman, 276–90. New York: Columbia University Press, 1994.

Mondal, Anshuman. 'Gandhi, Utopianism and the Construction of Colonial Difference.' *Interventions* 3:3 (2001): 419–38.

Moore-Gilbert, Bart. *Postcolonial Theory: Contexts, Practices, Politics*. London: Verso, 1997.

Mukherjee, Arun P. 'Whose Post-Colonialism and Whose Postmodernism?' *World Literature Written in English* 30:2 (1990): 1–9.

Mukherjee, Subrata. *Gandhian Thought: Marxist Interpretation*. New Delhi: Deep and Deep, 1991.

Nagy, Rosemary. 'Reconciliation in Post-Commission South Africa: Thick and Thin Accounts of Solidarity.' *Canadian Journal of Political Science* 35:2 (June 2002): 323–46.

Nair, Supriya. 'Melancholic Women: The Intellectual Hysteric(s) in *Nervous Conditions*.' *Research in African Literatures* 26:2 (Summer 1995): 130–9.

Nanda, Bal Ram. *Gandhi and His Critics*. Delhi: Oxford University Press, 1985.

Nandy, Ashis. 'From Outside the Imperium: Gandhi's Cultural Critique of the "West."' *Alternatives* 7 (1981): 171–94.

– *The Intimate Enemy: Loss and Recovery of Self under Colonialism*. Delhi: Oxford University Press, 1983.

– 'Towards a Third World Utopia.' *Postcolonialism: Critical Concepts in Literary and Cultural Studies*. Vol. 4. Ed. Diana Brydon, 1749–75. London: Routledge, 2000.

Needham, Anuradha Dingwaney. *Using the Master's Tools: Resistance and the Literature of the African and South-Asian Diasporas*. New York: St Martin's, 2000.

Nehru, Jawaharlal. 'A Tryst with Destiny: A Speech Delivered at the Constituent Assembly, New Delhi, August 14, 1947.' *Postcolonialism: Critical Concepts in Literary and Cultural Studies*. Vol. 1. Ed. Diana Brydon, 340–1. London: Routledge, 2000.

Ngugi wa Thiong'o. *Barrel of a Pen: Resistance to Repression in Neo-Colonial Kenya*. Trenton: Africa World Press, 1983.

– *Decolonising the Mind: The Politics of Language in African Literature*. 1981. London: James Currey, 1986.

Norval, Aletta J. 'Reconstructing National Identity and Renegotiating Memory:

The Work of the TRC.' *States of Imagination: Ethnographic Explorations of the Postcolonial State*. Ed. Thomas Blom Hansen and Finn Stepputat. Durham: Duke University Press, 2001.

Noyes, John K. 'Nature, History, and the Failure of Language: The Problem of the Human in Post-Apartheid South Africa.' *Relocating Postcolonialism*. Ed. David Theo Goldberg and Ato Quayson, 270–81. Oxford: Blackwell, 2002.

Okri, Ben. *A Way of Being Free*. London: Phoenix, 1997.

Pagé, Lucie, prod. *South African Freedom Songs: Inspiration for Liberation*. Audio documentary. CD. Mayibuye Centre, 2000.

Pakenham, Thomas. *The Boer War*. London: Weidenfeld and Nicolson, 1979.

Pandey, Gyanendra. 'Peasant Revolt and Indian Nationalism: The Peasant Movement in Awadh, 1919–1922.' *Subaltern Studies: Writings on South Asian History and Society*. Vol. 1. Ed. Ranajit Guha, 143–97. Delhi: Oxford University Press, 1982.

Parel, Anthony J. 'Editor's Introduction.' *Hind Swaraj and Other Writings*. Ed. Anthony J. Parel. Cambridge: Cambridge University Press, 1997.

Parry, Benita. 'Liberation Movements: Memories of the Future.' *Interventions* 1:1 (1998): 45–51.

– 'Problems in Current Theories of Colonial Discourse.' *Postcolonialism: Critical Concepts in Literary and Cultural Studies*. Vol. 2. Ed. Diana Brydon, 714–47. London: Routledge, 2000.

– 'Reconciliation and Remembrance.' *Pretexts* 5:1–2 (1995): 84–96.

– 'Resistance Theory / Theorizing Resistance or Two Cheers for Nativism.' *Contemporary Postcolonial Theory: A Reader*. Ed. Padmini Mongia, 84–109. London: Arnold, 1997.

– 'Signs of Our Times: Discussion of Homi Bhabha's *The Location of Culture*.' *Third Text* 28/9 (Autumn/Winter 1994): 5–24.

Plasa, Carl. 'Reading "The Geography of Hunger" in Tsitsi Dangarembga's *Nervous Conditions*: From Frantz Fanon to Charlotte Brontë.' *Journal of Commonwealth Literature* 33:1 (1998): 35–45.

Pollard, Alton B., III. 'Rhythms of Resistance: The Role of the Freedom Song in South Africa.' *This Is How We Flow: Rhythm and Sensibility in Black Cultures*. Ed. Angela M.S. Nelson, 98–124. Columbia: South Carolina University Press, 1999.

Prakash, Gyan, and Douglas Haynes. 'Introduction: The Entanglement of Power and Resistance.' *Contesting Power: Resistance and Everyday Social Relations in South Asia*. Ed. Gyan Prakash and Douglas Haynes, 1–22. Berkeley: University of California Press, 1991.

Rao, Raja. *Kanthapura*. 1938. New York: New Directions, 1967.

Rose, Jacqueline. 'Apathy and Accountability: South Africa's Truth and Reconciliation Commission.' *Raritan* 21–4 (Spring 2002): 175–95.

Rotberg, Robert I. 'Truth Commissions and the Provision of Truth, Justice and Reconciliation.' *Truth v. Justice: The Morality of Truth Commissions.* Ed. Robert I. Rotberg and Dennis Thompson, 3–21. Princeton: Princeton University Press, 2000.

Roy, Arundhati. 'Ahimsa.' *War Talk*, 9–16. Cambridge, MA: South End, 2003.

– 'Confronting Empire.' *War Talk*, 103–12. Cambridge, MA: South End, 2003.

– 'How Deep Shall We Dig?' *An Ordinary Person's Guide to Empire*, 95–118. Cambridge, MA: South End, 2004.

– *Public Power in the Age of Empire.* New York: Seven Stories, 2004.

Sachs, Albie. 'Preparing Ourselves for Freedom.' *Writing South Africa: Literature, Apartheid, and Democracy, 1970–1995.* Ed. Derek Attridge and Rosemary Jolly, 239–48. Cambridge: Cambridge University Press, 1998.

Said, Edward W. *Culture and Imperialism.* 1993. New York: Vintage, 1994.

– 'Culture and Imperialism.' 1993. Interview with Joseph A. Buttigeg and Paul A. Bové. *Power, Politics, and Culture: Interviews with Edward W. Said.* Ed. Gauri Viswanathan, 183–207. New York: Vintage, 2002.

– *Humanism and Democratic Criticism.* New York: Columbia University Press, 2004.

– 'Language, History, and Knowledge.' 1996. Interview with Gauri Viswanathan. *Power, Politics, and Culture: Interviews with Edward W. Said.* Ed. Gauri Viswanathan, 262–79. New York: Vintage, 2002.

– 'My Right of Return.' 2000. Interview with Ari Shavit. *Power, Politics, and Culture: Interviews with Edward W. Said.* Ed. Gauri Viswanathan, 443–58. New York: Vintage, 2002.

– 'The Only Alternative.' *Al-Ahram Weekly On-Line* 523 (1–7 March 2001). 1 March 2005.

– *Orientalism.* 1978. New York: Vintage, 1979.

– 'Representing the Colonized: Anthropology's Interlocutors.' *Reflections on Exile and Other Essays*, 282–92. Cambridge, MA: Harvard University Press, 2003.

Saliba, Therese. 'On the Bodies of Third World Women: Cultural Impurity, Prostitution, and Other Nervous Conditions.' *College Literature* 22:1 (February 1995): 131–46.

Sanders, Mark. *Complicities: The Intellectual and Apartheid.* Durham: Duke University Press, 2002.

Sandoval, Chela. *Methodology of the Oppressed.* Minneapolis: University of Minnesota Press, 2000.

San Juan, E., Jr. *Beyond Postcolonial Theory.* New York: St Martin's Press, 1997.

Sarkar, Sumit. 'The Decline of the Subaltern in *Subaltern Studies.*' *Mapping Subaltern Studies and the Postcolonial.* Ed. Vinayak Chaturvedi, 300–23. London: Verso, 2000.

Schell, Jonathan. *The Unconquerable World: Power, Nonviolence, and the Will of the People.* New York: Metropolitan, 2003.

Scott, David. *Conscripts of Modernity: The Tragedy of Colonial Enlightenment.* Durham: Duke University Press, 2005.

Scott, James C. *Domination and the Arts of Resistance: Hidden Transcripts.* New Haven: Yale University Press, 1990.

Seekings, Jeremy. *The UDF: A History of the United Democratic Front in South Africa, 1983–1991.* Cape Town: David Hill, 2000.

Sekyi-Otu, Ato. *Fanon's Dialectic of Experience.* Cambridge: Harvard University Press, 1996.

Sen, Ashok. 'Subaltern Studies: Capital, Class and Community.' *Subaltern Studies: Writings on South Asian History and Society.* Vol. 5. Ed. Ranajit Guha, 203–35. Delhi: Oxford University Press, 1987.

Senghor, Léopold Sédar. 'Negritude: A Humanism of the Twentieth Century.' *Colonial Discourse and Post-Colonial Theory: A Reader.* Ed. Patrick Williams and Laura Chrisman, 27–35. New York: Columbia University Press, 1994.

– 'Negritude and African Socialism.' 1963. *Postcolonialism: Critical Concepts in Literary and Cultural Studies.* Vol. 3. Ed. Diana Brydon, 998–1010. London: Routledge, 2000.

Sepamla, Sydney Sipho. *A Ride on the Whirlwind.* 1981. London: Heinemann Educational, 1984.

Serote, Mongane. *To Every Birth Its Blood.* Johannesburg: Ravan, 1981.

Seth, Sanjay. 'A "Postcolonial World"?' *Contending Images of World Politics.* Ed. Greg Fry and Jacinta O'Hagen, 214–26. London: Macmillan, 2000.

Sharpe, Jenny. 'Figures of Colonial Resistance.' *Modern Fiction Studies* 35:1 (1989): 137–55.

Slemon, Stephen. 'Reading for Resistance in Post-Colonial Literature.' *A Shaping of Connections.* Ed. Hena Maes-Jelinek, Kristen Holst Petersen, and Anna Rutherford, 100–15. Aarhus, Denmark: Dangeroo Press, 1989.

Smith, Linda Tuhiwai. *Decolonizing Methodologies: Research and Indigenous Peoples.* London: Zed, 1999.

Smuts, Jan. *Selections from the Smuts Papers.* Vol. 3. *June 1910–November 1918.* Ed. W.K. Hancock and Jean Van Der Poel. Cambridge: Cambridge University Press, 1966.

– *Selections from the Smuts Papers*, Vol. 7. *August 1945–October 1950.* Ed. Jean Van Der Poel. Cambridge: Cambridge University Press, 1973.

Spivak, Gayatri C. *A Critique of Postcolonial Reason: Toward a History of the Vanishing Present.* Cambridge, MA: Harvard University Press, 1999.
- 'From Haverstock Hill Flat to U.S. Classroom: What's Left of Theory.' *What's Left of Theory.* Ed. Judith Butler, John Guillory, and Kendell Thomas, 1–39. New York: Routledge, 2000.
- 'Subaltern Studies: Deconstructing Historiography.' *In Other Worlds: Essays in Cultural Politics,* 197–221. New York: Methuen, 1987.

Stone-Mediatore, Shari. *Reading across Borders: Storytelling and Narratives of Resistance.* New York: Palgrave, 2003.

Switzer, Les. 'Gandhi in South Africa: The Ambiguities of Satyagraha.' *The Journal of Ethnic Studies* 14:1 (1986): 122–8.

Tendulkar, D.G. *Mahatma: Life of Mohandas Karmchand Gandhi.* Vol. 1. *1869–1920.* Delhi: Ministry of Education and Broadcasting, Government of India, 1960–3.

Thomas, Sue. 'Killing the Hysteric in the Colonized's House: Tsitsi Dangarembga's *Nervous Conditions.*' *Journal of Commonwealth Literature* 27:1 (1992): 26–36.

Tlali, Miriam. *Amandla.* Johannesburg: Ravan, 1980.

Truth and Reconciliation Commission of South Africa Report. Vols. 1–5. Cape Town: The Commission, 1998.

Tutu, Desmond. *No Future without Forgiveness.* New York: Image Doubleday, 1999.
- *The Rainbow People of God: The Making of a Peaceful Revolution.* Ed. John Allen. New York: Image Doubleday, 1994.

Uppal, J.N. *Gandhi: Ordained in South Africa.* New Delhi: Ministry of Information and Broadcasting, Government of India, 1995.

Uwakweh, Pauline Ada. 'Debunking Patriarchy: The Liberational Quality of Voicing in Tsitsi Dangarembga's *Nervous Conditions.*' *Research in African Literatures* 26:1 (1995): 75–84.

Villa-Vicencio, Charles. 'Restorative Justice in Social Context: The South African Truth and Reconciliation Commission.' *Burying the Past: Making Peace and Doing Justice after Civil Conflict.* Ed. Nigel Biggar, 207–22. Washington, DC: Georgetown University Press, 2001.

Viswanathan, Gauri. 'Introduction.' *Power, Politics, and Culture: Interviews with Edward W. Said.* Ed. Gauri Viswanathan, xi–xxi. New York: Vintage, 2002.

Watts, Jane. *Black Writers from South Africa: Towards a Discourse of Liberation* New York: St Martin's, 1989.

Williams, Raymond. 'Tragedy and Revolution.' 1966. *The Raymond Williams Reader.* Ed. John Higgins, 94–108. Oxford: Blackwell, 2001.

Wynter, Sylvia. 'Africa, the West and the Analogy of Culture.' *Symbolic Narratives/African Cinema: Audiences, Theory and the Moving Image*. Ed. June Givanni, 25–76. London: British Film Institute, 2000.

Young, Robert. *Postcolonialism: A Very Short Introduction*. London: Oxford University Press, 2003.

– *White Mythologies: Writing History and the West*. London: Routledge, 1990.

Yousaf, Nahem. 'Apartheid Narratives.' *Apartheid Narratives*. Ed. Nahem Yousaf, vii–xv. Amsterdam: Rodopi, 2001.

Index

Achebe, Chinua, 16, 195–6n42
African literature, 5–6, 8–9, 25, 156–7, 195–6n42. *See also July's People; Mother to Mother; Nervous Conditions; Waiting for the Barbarians*
African National Congress (ANC): ideology, 140–1, 145–6, 206n26; neo-liberal policies, 155–6, 185; and resistance, 146, 149, 150, 205n11; and 'rhetoric of denial,' 174, 176; and the 'Truth Commission,' 140, 143, 210n118
Against Race (Gilroy), 10, 188n18
agency: and anti-colonialism, 9, 61, 62, 64, 86, 87; and apartheid, 169, 170, 175; foreclosed, in Said's *Orientalism*, 28; in Gandhism, 122, 123–4, 125–6, 130, 132, 183; in *Nervous Conditions*, 64, 66; in postcolonial discourse, 30, 31, 40, 60, 131; and reconciliation, 169, 183; and resistance, 7, 26, 39; and Subaltern Studies, 7, 26–7, 28
ahimsa (nonviolence): and colonial power, 123, 184; ends and means, 120–2; as ethic of social conduct, 104, 113–14, 118–19, 122, 131; as ethic of struggle, 126, 132–3; in *Kanthapura*, 115, 116–18; and transformation, 17, 21, 96, 133, 134
Ahmad, Aijaz, 6, 34, 59, 82, 95, 103, 109
aid, foreign, 86
Algeria, 49, 66, 77, 119
alienation, 18, 69, 74, 104, 106, 183
alterity. *See* Manicheism; Other, the
Ambedkar, B.R., 111–12, 125, 201n48
ambiguity, 11; and apartheid discourse, 141, 157, 159, 162; as casualty of war (Werwoerd), 162; of colonial power, and conflict, 36; of Fanon's concept of liberation, 12, 57–8; in Gandhism, 101–2, 192n63; of Messeh and the 'English Book,' 42; in *Nervous Conditions*, 66, 67, 70, 71; in *Waiting for the Barbarians*, 24
ambivalence: of anti-apartheid resistance, 144; Bhabha's theory of, 7, 28, 31, 32–4, 38, 40, 43; of colonial authority, 34, 35, 37, 40, 140; in Gandhism, 105; in *Nervous Conditions*, 70, 71, 74; in *Waiting for the Barbarians*, 23
Anderson, Benedict, 33, 80–1

anorexia, 64, 65, 66, 67, 68, 70
antagonism: ANC ideology based on, 141; and the colonial relationship, 36–7; and Fanon, 12, 77; and Gandhism, 107, 126, 131, 132; and reconciliation, 145, 150, 157–8, 165, 167; and resistance, 17, 19, 20, 60–1, 63, 134; and Said, 133
anti-apartheid movement: and the African National Congress, 140, 205n11; as assertion of common humanity (Said), 94; and liberation, 145, 148; and literature, 136–9, 141, 157; and reconciliation, 141–2, 145, 146–9, 152; and resistance, 144, 147–8, 149–50, 152; and the 'Truth Commission,' 143; and violence, 140–1, 150, 151, 164
apartheid: and complicity, 138–9, 174, 175, 176, 210n124; end of, 22, 141, 144, 152; legislation, 149–50; in *Mother to Mother*, 162, 168–9; not a Manichean conflict, 146; power and resistance, 151–2, 154, 176, 204n1; and separation, 139, 149, 150, 167, 176; violence of, 136–7, 139, 142, 146, 147, 150–1, 153; women's experience of, 147, 150, 160–1
apartheid discourse: and ambiguity, 141, 157, 159, 162; and the apartheid system, 156, 172; distinct from colonial discourse, 204n1; and literature, 157–8; as oppositional, 176; and reconciliation, 141, 142–3, 145, 157, 165, 168, 205n20; and violence, 136–7, 151; and white 'security,' 138, 139, 147, 156, 173
apology/forgiveness: and 'colonizing of the mind' (Fanon), 77; and reconciliation, 153–4, 162–3; and the 'Truth Commission,' 169–71, 172–4, 176–7
Appiah, Anthony Kwame, 60, 61, 64
Arendt, Hannah, 18, 152
Armah, Ayi Kwei, 8
Ashcroft, Bill, 8, 15–16, 37–8, 61–2, 72, 82, 87
Asmal, Kader, 152
assimilation, 5, 13, 42, 43, 67, 81
Attwell, David, 205n20
Atwood, Margaret, 16
authenticity, 34, 35
Autobiography, An (Gandhi), 45, 47, 192n63
autonomy, 16, 27, 28, 43, 92. *See also* independence

Bahri, Deepika, 63, 64–5, 67, 69–70
Basu, Biman, 65, 73
Beautyful Ones Are Not Yet Born, The (Armah), 8
Benzien, Captain Jeffrey, 174
Beyond Postcolonial Theory (San Juan), 6
Bhabha, Homi K.: colonial authority, 28, 29–31, 36–7, 40, 42, 76; colonial subjects, 35–6; concept of mimicry, 28, 42–4; concept of resistance, 7, 8, 28–9, 31–7, 53 (*see also* 'spectacular resistance'); hybridity and ambivalence, 28, 29–31, 32–5, 39–42, 56; others' critiques of, 28, 31–2, 35, 40–1, 42, 43–4, 57, 60; 'sly civility,' 31, 37, 38, 43, 55
Bhaji on the Beach (Chadha), 34
Bhave, Vinoba, 203n104
Biehl, Amy, 157, 158–9, 173, 209n100
Biko, Steve Bantu, 148–9, 172–3, 175
Bisho massacre, 169

'Black Act,' 51, 52, 131
Black Consciousness movement, 136, 148–9, 152, 153
Black Jacobins, The (James), 49
Black Skin, White Masks (Fanon), 13, 35–6, 44–5, 49, 57, 75, 85–6, 87, 88, 181
blame. *See* 'politics/rhetoric of blame'
body, as site of resistance, 64–6, 67, 70–1, 72
Boer War, 46, 47, 50, 53, 176
Boesak, Allan, 147, 148
Bose, Nirmal, 118
Botha, General Louis, 55
Brydon, Diana, 194n1
Buddha of Suburbia, The (Kureishi), 34
bulimia, 64, 65, 66, 67, 68, 70
Burdwan Plan (1818), 41
Buthelezi, Mangosuthu, 143

Cabral, Amilcar: concept of liberation, 80, 82, 84, 120, 167; concept of resistance, 8, 59; critique of colonialism, 58; other theorists on, 62, 83–4, 92
capitalism: and colonial discourse theory, 57, 58; and concepts of resistance, 180; Gandhi's critique of, 99, 104, 105–6, 130; and humanism/identity, 10–11; and liberation/nationalism, 83, 85, 94, 97; in material analyses, 101, 103; racial, under apartheid, 153
Cavafy, C.P., 163
Césaire, Aimé, 8, 14, 20, 58, 84, 90, 99
Chakrabarty, Dipesh, 27, 33, 53
Chambers, Ross, 39
Chatterjee, Partha, 95, 96–7, 99, 100, 103, 109, 113

Chow, Rey, 35
Chrisman, Laura, 59
Christianity: and Indian peasants, 38, 40, 41, 42, 53; in *Nervous Conditions*, 74; and reconciliation in South Africa, 166, 169–70; and *ubuntu*, 209n91
Christie, Kenneth, 140–1, 151, 204n11
citizen rights: and duty/responsibilities, 55, 127; Gandhi's campaign for, 29, 45, 47, 50, 53–4, 88, 110, 192n63
civilization: and the Burdwan Plan, 41; discourses of, 5; European, and Smuts, 53; Gandhi's critique of, 101, 103, 104–6, 124
'civilizing mission,' the, 48, 62
Clarence, Major Neville, 164, 168
Coetzee, J.M., 14, 16, 23–5, 28, 136, 163, 176
colonial authority: agonistic *vs.* antagonistic, 36–7; as ambivalent, 34, 35, 37, 40, 140; and anti-colonialism, 31, 60; Bhabha's concept of, 28, 29–31, 36–7, 40, 42, 76; and concept of mimicry, 54–5; in Gandhism, 113, 114; and Indian resistance in South Africa, 55–6
colonial discourse: as complex and ambivalent, 35; as cultural violence, 19, 60, 61, 119, 132, 156; as object of reconciliation, 156; and resistance/liberation, 156; in *Waiting for the Barbarians*, 23–5
colonial discourse theory: and colonial power, 35; conceptual limits, 23, 27–8, 57, 58; and Fanon, 57, 59–60; and Subaltern Studies, 26–7
colonial education, 17, 42, 73–4, 196n45

colonial subject(s), 35–6, 77, 80, 123, 156
colonialism: and complicity, 70, 114, 175; as consciousness, 130; Fanon's critique of, 18, 32, 58, 59, 61, 75–6, 79, 85, 104, 106–7; inherent dualisms, 10; and modernity, 179; as negotiated concept, 74; and women, 18–19, 68, 69
colonizer and the colonized: and colonial discourse, 144; and decolonization (Fanon), 12, 77; and discourse theory, 16, 101; as oppositional paradigm, 15, 30; as single 'subject' (Bhabha), 35, 36; transformation of, 7. *See also* master/slave dialectic
complicity: and apartheid, 138–9, 174, 175, 176, 210n124; of colonial subjects, and colonialism, 70, 114
Congress Party (India), 84, 95, 96–7, 113–14, 116, 120
consciousness, 18; and colonial constructions of identity, 140; and decolonization (Fanon), 12, 77, 85–6, 88, 89; and education, in *Nervous Conditions*, 73–4; and historical discourse (Spivak), 26; Indian nationalist, 97, 101, 107; national, and Fanon/Said, 62, 89, 91, 171; and resistance, 39, 130, 185; and the 'Truth Commission,' 170, 175–6. *See also* Black Consciousness movement
Conscripts of Modernity (Scott), 9, 49
Contesting Power (Prakash & Haynes), 38, 39
Cooper, Frederick, 39
counter-discursive writing, 14, 16
Country of My Skull (Krog), 162

Critique of Postcolonial Reason, A (Spivak), 181, 182
cultural essentialism, 109
cultural production, 13, 156–7. *See also* literature
'cultural resistance,' 8, 14
'cultural violence,' 19, 60, 61, 119, 132, 156, 176
culture, 17, 80, 124. *See also* colonial discourse; literature
Culture and Imperialism (Said), 14, 28, 62, 63, 91, 92
cycle of violence: in Algeria, 66, 77, 119; and reconciliation in South Africa, 144, 165; and 'Soweto novels,' 137; and transformation, 82, 133 (Fanon). *See also* violence; violent resistance

Dangarembga, Tsitsi, 14, 18, 58, 63–75, 196n45
de Klerk, F.W., 141
decolonization: Fanon's concept of, 11–13, 18, 76–8, 83, 86–9, 132, 188n25; Ngugi on, 14, 17. *See also* liberation
'decolonization of the mind,' 14, 148
Decolonizing the Mind (Ngugi), 73
dehumanization, 71, 104, 156
democracy: and the anti-apartheid movement, 139, 145, 147, 148; and armed struggle (San Juan), 61; and Gandhi, 103, 109, 110, 132; and Said's language of freedom, 93
denial. *See* 'politics/rhetoric of denial'
Derrida, Jacques, 9, 182
development: and anti-colonial theories of liberation, 84, 86, 89; and the

Indian nation, 33, 84; as national project, 45, 79; separate, in apartheid (JanMohamed), 139; and term 'post-colonial' (McClintock), 92
dharma (duty), 127–8, 128–9, 130
Dirlik, Arif, 6, 7, 11, 57, 179
discourse. *See* apartheid discourse; colonial discourse; history; language; literature; memory; stories
discourse theory. *See* colonial discourse theory
'DissemiNation' (Bhabha), 33, 34
diversity, 10, 140
dominance. *See* colonial authority; hegemony; power
Dominance without Hegemony (Guha), 122–3, 127, 128, 129
Dubois, J.A., 42
Durban strikes (1973), 152, 153
duty, 127–8, 128–9, 130. *See also* loyalty; responsibility
Dwyer, Susan, 178

economy, colonial, 5. *See also* capitalism; colonialism
education, colonial, 17, 42, 73–4, 196n45
Empire: contemporary form of (Hardt & Negri), 151, 183; as contemporary problem (Roy), 184; in *Waiting for the Barbarians*, 23–4
Empire (Hardt & Negri), 8, 11, 99, 151, 183
enemy, 133, 134, 162–3, 183, 185
English language, 15, 69, 70, 196n45
'enlightened anarchy,' 97
entrapment, 71, 72
equality: and the 'Freedom Charter,' 145; Gandhi's belief in, 48, 49, 53–4, 55; in Gandhism, 109, 110, 130; in the 'new' South Africa, 177, 178; and sameness, 42, 44–5, 53, 54. *See also* citizen rights
Europe, 12, 86–7, 88–9
'everyday resistance,' 37–9
exploitation: and anti-colonial struggle, 75, 79, 83, 84; in Bhabha's concept of resistance, 29, 31, 32, 35, 41; and concepts of resistance, 6, 22, 180; and the 'discursive sphere,' 7, 13, 14, 19, 61, 62, 179; and Gandhian resistance, 104, 105, 108, 114, 118; liberation and *swaraj,* 125, 132; and nationalism (Fanon), 85, 120; reinforced by violent resistance, 119, 121; and the 'Truth Commission,' 153, 165, 172; understanding contemporary, 93–4, 183, 185

Fanon, Frantz: and colonial authority, 30, 31; and colonial discourse analysis, 57, 59–60; concept of colonization, 13, 77; concept of decolonization, 11–13, 18, 76–8, 83, 86–9, 132, 188n25; concept of liberation, 3, 4, 13–14, 57–8, 59, 62, 83, 85–7, 92, 144; concept of mimicry, 44–5, 54; critique of colonialism, 18, 32, 58, 75–6, 104, 106–7; on language and power, 93; and Manichean difference, 5, 31, 35, 59–60, 61, 76, 78, 89, 133; and national identity, 13, 58, 75, 78, 80, 171; on nationalism, 12–13, 78–80, 82–3, 172; and 'new humanism,' 13, 87–90, 93, 120, 133, 148, 167, 179, 181; and postcolonial theory, 4, 98–9; and resistance, 8, 20, 49, 59, 132; and Said, 62, 76, 89–94, 133, 171; and violent rebellion, 49, 66, 76–8, 79–80, 92–3, 98, 118,

230   Index

119, 146. *See also Black Skin, White Masks*; *Wretched of the Earth, The*
fear, 24, 123–4, 176
fearlessness, 124, 130, 134
femininity, 65, 67, 68, 71
feminism, 65, 67–8, 73, 92
Flockemann, Miki, 196n45
foreign aid, 86
Foucault, Michel, 8, 9, 11, 28, 30, 182
France, 44, 45
'Freedom Charter' (South Africa), 145–6, 147, 176
French language, 99
French Revolution, 48–9

Galtung, Johan, 18, 19
Gandhi (film), 116
Gandhi, Leela, 6, 10, 11; concept of liberation, 21; on Gandhi(sm), 118, 126, 132, 199n3; on Indian nationalist discourse, 107, 118; on postcolonialism, 5, 7, 99
Gandhi, Mohandas K.: and British ideals, 48, 126, 133; as 'conscript of modernity,' 45–6, 49, 100; as cultural/mythical symbol, 95, 96, 97–8; and duty to Empire, 46–7, 48, 49, 50; 'experiments with truth,' 48, 96, 108–9, 110–11; and General Smuts, 51–2, 53, 54, 55, 126; and Indian independence movement, 95–6, 97, 113–14, 120 (*see also* Gandhism); and Indian resistance in South Africa, 45–8, 49–56, 100, 118, 126, 127, 131, 192n63; as 'mimic-man,' 46, 48; as political figure, 97, 100, 101; and Subaltern Studies, 45, 46–8, 96–8; writings of, 22, 98, 106, 109, 110, 192n63
Gandhism, 4, 17, 21; and agency/power, 122, 123–4, 125–6, 130, 132, 183, 184; concept of liberation, 25, 101, 103, 104, 106–7, 109, 110, 113, 117, 119, 171; contemporary relevance, 184, 185; critique of colonialism, 103, 107; critique of modernity, 4, 96, 99, 100, 102–6, 107, 108, 115; and duty, 125, 127, 128–9; and 'fearlessness,' 124, 130, 134; and gender roles, 97, 100, 110, 111, 116, 117, 118; and Hindu idiom, 100, 115–16, 128; influences on, 99–100, 108; in *Kanthapura*, 97–8, 103, 115–16, 134; Marxist responses to, 105, 109, 112, 129; and master/slave dialectic, 46–7, 48, 126; others' critiques of, 46–8, 52, 96–7, 192n63, 201n48; and postcolonial theorists, 95, 96–7, 99, 199n3; rejection of violence, 121–2, 132, 133; and resistance as transformation, 20, 22, 96, 101, 105, 106, 108, 110, 113, 125, 130, 185; and suffering as resistance, 130–1; theory of trusteeship, 129–30, 184, 203n104; and untouchability, 110, 111–12. *See also ahimsa; sarvadoya; satyagraha*
Gates, Henry Louis, Jr, 30
gender: and apartheid, 150; and Gandhism, 97, 100, 110, 111, 116, 117, 118; in *Nervous Conditions*, 67–8, 72. *See also* feminism; women
Gikandi, Simon, 5–6, 10, 11, 99
Gilroy, Paul, 10–11, 19, 21, 30, 89, 181
Gordimer, Nadine, 136, 137–9, 167
Gorle, Gillian, 196n45
Gramsci, Antonio, 27
'great leap,' 83, 141, 172. *See also* 'leap forward'

Griffiths, Gareth, 15–16
Guha, Ranajit: on colonial authority, 18, 27, 53, 122–3; critique of Gandhi, 46–8, 52, 54, 96, 129, 192n63; on *dharma vs.* rights, 127–8; on the Indian nation, 82

Haitian Revolution, 9, 48–9
Hallward, Peter, 188n25
Hardiman, David, 98, 125
Hardt, Michael: concept of resistance, 8, 11, 151; critique of hybridity (Bhabha), 28, 35; and Empire as global power, 183; nation-state and modernity, 85, 99
Harlow, Barbara, 13, 205n20
Harris, Wilson, 16
hatred: in anti-apartheid discourse, 146, 148; colonial authority and resistance, 43, 55–6; and Gandhism, 50, 118, 134; in *Mother to Mother*, 158, 162, 173; and reconciliation in South Africa, 164. *See also* 'implacable enmity'
Haynes, Douglas, 38, 39
Hegel, Georg Wilhelm Friedrich, 48, 126
hegemony: and 'everyday resistance,' 39; requirements of, 124; *vs.* dominance (Guha/Gramsci), 18, 27, 53, 122, 123. *See also* colonial authority; power
Hill, Janice E., 65
Hind Swaraj (Gandhi), 101–4, 106, 108, 111, 120–1, 123, 124
Hinduism, 99–100, 108, 109, 115–16
history: and the anti-apartheid movement, 149; Indian, conceptualizations of, 120, 121; Kenyan, as history of opposition, 80; and the 'Truth Commission,' 154, 159–60; and *The Wretched of the Earth*, 76–7
History of Negro Revolt, A (James), 191n49
Hobsbawm, Eric J., 33
humanism: and anti-colonial theory, 9–10, 88–9, 99; and Biko, 148; as form of oppression, 87; and postcolonialism, 5, 6, 8, 81, 181, 187n2. *See also* 'new humanism'
humanity: and the anti-apartheid movement, 94; and colonialism, 10; impossibility and inferiority (Fanon), 45; loss of, in apartheid, 161; recognition of the Other's, 87, 133, 166–7, 179, 185; resistance as assertion of, 9, 49, 51, 55; and the 'Truth Commission,' 165, 166–7, 170, 207n54. *See also ubuntu*
hybridity, 3, 5; Bhabha's concept of, 7, 28, 29–35, 40, 56; and counter-discourse, 16; critiques of, 6, 28, 34–5, 68; in *Nervous Conditions*, 68, 71; and transformation of conflict, 156, 181

identity: collective/transnational, 10–11; colonial, 13, 14, 24; and counter-discourse, 16; cultural/national, 80–1, 83, 158; discourses of, 176, 183; and possibilities for liberation, 82; and reconciliation in South Africa, 176, 178; and resistance, 75–82, 167–8; and social relations (Gandhi), 104. *See also* national identity
Ignatieff, Michael, 155
immigration, 34
'implacable enmity,' 43, 60, 63, 89, 133. *See also* hatred

independence, 79, 107. *See also* Indian independence movement

India: anti-colonial politics, and 'duty' (Guha), 46; and colonial power, 122–3; and independence, 83, 84–5; nationhood and liberation, 41; peasants and the 'English Book,' 39–42; pedagogy *vs.* performance, 33; and Subaltern Studies, 25–7

Indian Ambulance Corps, 46, 50, 53, 54, 55, 56

Indian independence movement: and bourgeois nationalism, 96–7; ends and means, 120–2; and Gandhi(sm), 95–6, 97, 113–14, 120; nationalist ideology, 106; and the *swadeshi* movement, 124–5, 128. *See also* Gandhism

Indian literature, 18, 97–8, 103, 114–18, 132, 134

Indian middle/mimic-men, 40, 41, 42, 46, 48, 123

Indian Mutiny (1857), 19, 122–3

Indian National Congress (INC), 84, 95, 96–7, 113–14, 116, 120

Indian resistance in South Africa: about, 44–8, 49–56, 131; and colonial difference, 33, 52; as 'escape,' 72; as opposition, 29; and rights, 29, 45, 47, 53–4, 55, 88, 110, 127, 192n63; as subversion, 33, 53–4; as transformation, 55–6

inequality: and anti-colonial theory, 13, 87, 92, 98, 106–7; and apartheid discourse, 161, 162; and discourse, 74, 172, 179, 183; Gandhi's critique of, 100, 101, 106–7; and Gandhism, 128, 130, 135; and postcolonial theory, 5, 6–7, 16, 17, 19, 27, 32, 74; and reconciliation, 154, 156, 177

Ingham, Kenneth, 53

Inkatha Freedom Party, 143, 146, 166, 206n30

interdependence: and apartheid, 151, 160, 161, 167, 172; and Gandhi(sm), 107, 118, 128–9, 130; and liberation, 9, 19, 89, 183; and reconciliation, 142, 145; and San Juan's 'planetary' ethics, 6; and transformation of power structures, 17, 181

'intransitive resistance' (Moore-Gilbert), 31

Iqbal, Muhammad, 97, 200n8

Ismail, Abu Bakr, 164, 168

James, C.L.R., 4, 8, 9, 20, 48–9, 60, 191n49

JanMohamed, Abdul R.: apartheid as 'traditional' colonial power, 151; on apartheid literature, 137, 138, 139; critique of Bhabha, 35; on Manicheism, 59, 61

Jolly, Rosemary, 140, 166, 171, 176

July's People (Gordimer), 137–9, 142, 167

justice, and the 'Truth Commission,' 139–40, 144, 159, 162, 165–6, 171, 172

Kanthapura (Rao), 18, 97–8, 103, 114–18, 132, 134

Kasrils, Ronnie, 140

Kenya, 80

Krog, Antjie, 157, 162, 170, 174, 176, 210n124

Kureishi, Hanif, 34

La Guma, Alex, 139

language: English, 15, 69, 70, 196n45; French, 99; and history (Noyes), 160; hybridity and resistance

(Bhabha), 29; and power, 93, 196n45
Lazarus, Neil, 26
'leap forward,' 80, 82, 83, 120. *See also* 'great leap'
liberation: in anti-apartheid discourse, 145, 148; to anti-colonial theorists, 60, 80, 82, 83–5, 120, 167; conceptualizations of, 7, 8, 9, 180–1, 187n2; and 'decolonization of the mind' (Ngugi), 14; Fanon's concept of, 3, 4, 13–14, 57–8, 59, 62, 83, 85–7, 92, 144; Gandhi's concept of, 25, 99, 101, 103, 104, 106–7, 109, 110, 113, 117, 119, 171; national, and community, 75, 82–3; and 'new humanism,' 49, 167; as a process, 83, 90, 91, 92; reconciliation as, 144, 148, 149, 167; and resistance, 8, 9, 82, 182; Said's concept of, 5, 59, 62–3, 89–94, 171; in South Africa, 153, 155. *See also* independence; national identity
literature, 4, 13–17. *See also* African literature; Indian literature; stories
'literature of combat' (Fanon), 13
Location of Culture, The (Bhabha), 29, 44
L'Ouverture, Toussaint, 48, 49
love: Fanon on, 87; Gandhi on, 116, 133; in *Kanthapura*, 134; Mandela on, 146; as a praxis of resistance/liberation, 181–2, 184; and rebellion (Hardt & Negri), 183
loyalty, 46–7, 48, 49, 50. *See also* duty

Macaulay, Thomas, 39, 41, 42
Madlana, Margaret, 169
Magona, Sindiwe, 14, 18, 141, 142, 157–9, 161–2, 163, 168–9, 209n100
Maluleke, Tinyiko Sam, 207n54

Mamdani, Mahmood, 138, 151, 152, 153, 154, 167–8, 200n8, 204n1
Mandela, Nelson, 141, 145–6, 149, 151, 152, 163, 175, 206n26
Manicheism: and *ahimsa/sarvadoya*, 183; in anti-apartheid discourse, 138, 139, 157; and apartheid, 146; and colonial discourse theory, 59–61; and Fanon, 5, 31, 35, 59–60, 61, 76, 78, 89, 132, 133; as focus of postcolonial theory, 101, 140; in *Mother to Mother*, 161, 162; and reconciliation, 165, 183
Marxism: and conceptions of freedom, 92, 180; and critiques of colonialism, 83–4; critiques of Gandhi(sm), 105, 109, 112; and Subaltern Studies, 26–7
master/slave dialectic, 46–7, 48, 52, 118, 124, 126, 138
materialism, 6, 104, 105–6, 180. *See also* capitalism
Mau Mau uprising, 19, 80
Mbeki, Thabo, 141
McClintock, Anne, 92
Memmi, Albert, 14, 20, 75, 81, 82, 84, 167
memory, cultural/historical: and colonial constructions of identity, 140; and reconciliation, 139, 159, 160, 166, 167, 173; in South Africa, 138, 139, 158, 176, 178; and the 'Truth Commission,' 155, 159, 160, 167
Messeh, Anund (missionary), 40, 41, 42, 43
metropole, 15, 16, 29, 34, 53, 122–3
mimic/middle-men, 40, 41, 42, 46, 48, 123
mimicry, 3, 7; Bhabha's concept of, 21, 28, 42–4, 54, 56; and colonial

authority, 54–5; Fanon's concept of, 44–5, 55, 57; of Indians in South Africa, 46, 50, 52; in *Nervous Conditions*, 68; revolt as a form of (Memmi), 81; in *Waiting for the Barbarians*, 24

'Minute on Indian Education' (Macaulay), 39, 42

Mitchell, Captain Brian, 209n104

modernity, 5; and Gandhi(sm), 45–6, 49, 96, 99, 100, 102–6, 107, 108, 115; as goal of opposition, 81, 84; and the Haitian Revolution (Scott), 49; and human community (Williams/Fanon), 179; and hybridity, 29, 34, 35; and the nation-state, 33, 85, 99; in *Nervous Conditions*, 64, 67, 68, 69, 70, 71, 74. *See also* capitalism; neo-liberalism

Mondal, Anshuman, 102

Moore-Gilbert, Bart, 31–2, 35, 40–1, 44

Mortimer, General Deon, 175

Mother to Mother (Magona), 14, 18, 141, 142, 157–9, 160–2, 163, 168–9, 173, 209n100

Mukherjee, Arun, 16

Nair, Supriya, 67, 73

Nandy, Ashis: and Gandhi(sm), 96, 100, 106, 109, 122; on opposition to colonialism, 48; and oppression, 82, 133–4

national identity, 17; community and resistance, 80–1; Fanon on, 13, 58, 59, 75, 77–8, 80, 171, 172; focus on poverty *vs*. capitalism, 83; memory and *ubuntu* (Sanders), 167

National Party (South Africa), 143, 149, 152, 175–6

nationalism/nationalization. *See* independence; liberation

nation-state, 33, 82–3, 85

nativism, 81, 99, 109, 181

Ndebele, Njabulo, 157

Negri, Antonio: concept of resistance, 8, 11, 151; critique of hybridity (Bhabha), 28, 35; and Empire as global power, 183; nation-state and modernity, 85, 99

negritude (Senghor), 75, 80, 99, 109

Nehru, Jawaharlal, 83, 84, 95, 106, 120

neo-liberalism, 155–6, 183, 184, 185

Nervous Conditions (Dangarembga), 14, 18, 58, 63–75, 196n45

'new humanism': conceptual limits, 90, 91; and Fanon, 13, 49, 87–90, 93, 120, 133, 148, 167, 179, 181; planetary (Gilroy), 10–11, 181; and post-structuralism, 58; as resistance (*ahimsa*), 134; and Said (after Fanon), 9, 91, 93, 171

Ngewu, Cynthia, 165, 166

Ngugi wa Thiong'o, 7, 14, 17, 73, 80, 92, 118

nonviolence, 46, 118, 132. *See also ahimsa; satyagraha*

'novels of liberation,' 136

Noyes, John, 160

Okri, Ben, v, 3, 7, 20

opposition, 29, 48, 81, 82, 84, 187n2. *See also* resistance; resistance as opposition

oppositional paradigm: in Fanon, 12, 13, 88, 89; and impossibility of liberation, 94; in *Nervous Conditions*, 63–75; in Parry, 37; in postcolonial studies, 14, 15, 17, 59–62. *See also* Manicheism; Other, the

Orientalism (Said), 25, 26, 28, 30, 31, 32, 35, 91
Other, the: in apartheid discourse/ imagination, 176; in Bhabha's concept of resistance, 34, 48, 54; and Fanon's concept of liberation, 62, 87, 89; in Gandhism, 52–3, 104, 113, 133, 134, 185; in Gilroy's concept of humanism, 11; in Indian nationalist discourse, 107; in postcolonialism, 99; recognition as human, 87, 133, 166–7, 179, 185; and reconciliation in South Africa, 154, 185; in Said's concept of liberation, 90–1, 94; into the Same, as colonial project, 31; and the Self, transformation of relationship, 17. *See also* Manicheism

Pakistan, 97, 200n8
Palestinian struggle, 90, 91
Pan-Africanist Congress (PAC), 206n26
Pandey, Gyanendra, 96
Parry, Benita: on anti-capitalist resistance, 83–4; critique of Bhabha, 36–7, 44, 57, 60; and Fanon, 35, 57, 60, 61, 76; and postcolonial discourse theory, 6, 179; and South African history, 159
'passive resistance,' 118
patriarchy: and colonial violence, 19; in *Nervous Conditions*, 67, 69, 73, 74, 196n54; Saliba's characterization of, 68
peasants, 4, 26, 33, 39–42, 81, 134
pedagogy, 33, 61. *See also* colonial education
'planetary ethics' (San Juan), 6
'planetary humanism,' 10–11, 181

'politics/rhetoric of blame': and *ahimsa,* 114; and Fanon, 88; and 'politics/rhetoric of denial,' 142, 174, 176; Said's critique of, 63, 76, 88–90, 93, 133, 171; and Subaltern Studies, 134; and the 'Truth Commission,' 171–4, 178
'politics/rhetoric of denial,' 142, 173–7, 178
'post-colonial,' term, 92, 187n4
postcolonial literature, 4, 13–17. *See also* African literature; Indian literature; stories; *specific titles*
postcolonial studies: analysis and critiques, 4–7, 25, 57, 58, 83; critiques of colonial authority, 140; and cultures of 'contra-modernity' (Bhabha), 29; discursive *vs.* materialist analysis, 7, 11, 27, 58, 59, 101; and Gandhism, 95, 96–7, 99, 199n3; Leela Gandhi on, 5, 7, 99; and resistance, 3, 4, 7–9, 11, 17, 81, 180
'postcolonialism,' term, 187n4
poststructuralism: and Gandhism, 100; and humanism, 9, 58, 181; and postcolonial studies, 5, 6, 25, 57, 179; and resistance, 3, 8, 38; San Juan's critique of, 188n12
poverty: and apartheid policies, 153; and 'cultural violence' (Galtung), 18, 19; and education, 74, 196n45; and Fanon, 18, 32, 79, 85, 93, 98, 106, 172; and Gandhism, 46, 104, 105, 106, 129; and national identity, 83; in the 'new' South Africa, 156, 207n55
power: and anti-apartheid discourse, 146, 158; in apartheid South Africa, 151–2; and colonial discourse the-

ory, 35, 58; in colonial India, 122–3; complex relations of, 35, 39, 64, 71, 75, 76, 91, 144, 171, 180; contemporary forms of, 151, 182–3; diminished by state violence (Arendt), 152; Fanon's concept of, 58, 66, 80; Foucault's concept of, 28, 30; Gandhi's construction of, 123–4, 125–6, 132; in *Nervous Conditions*, 64, 68–9, 70, 71, 75, 91; and oppositional paradigm, 37, 59–62; and postcolonial studies, 11, 58; transformation of, 13, 17, 67, 122, 156, 179. *See also* agency; colonial authority; hegemony; master/slave dialectic

Prakash, Gyan, 38, 39

race, 18, 79

racial hierarchy, 147, 149, 192n63

racism: and agency, 170; and apartheid, 143, 153, 175; and apartheid discourse, 140; and the Black Consciousness movement, 148; and colonial violence, 19; Gandhi's experience of, 44–5

racist legislation, 50, 51, 52, 149–50, 175

Ramashala, Mapule F., 169

Rao, Raja, 18, 97–8, 103, 114–18, 132, 134

reconciliation, 82, 88, 94

reconciliation in South Africa: and agency/power, 153–4, 169, 171, 183, 184; and the anti-apartheid movement, 141–2, 145, 146–9, 152; and apartheid discourse, 141, 142–3, 156, 157, 165, 168, 205n20; and apology/forgiveness, 153–4, 162–3; contemporary relevance, 184–5; as ideal of liberation and praxis of resistance, 144, 148, 149, 167; ideals of, 164–5; and the 'new' South Africa, 177–8; and resistance as transformation, 4, 17, 20, 21, 22, 145, 156, 165, 167–8, 185, 204n1; and restoration of humanity, 166–7; as theory of praxis, 156, 165, 184, 185; and transformation of discourse, 144–5, 154, 157, 165, 168, 176, 177–8, 185; and the 'Truth Commission,' 143–4, 153, 156, 160. *See also* Truth and Reconciliation Commission (TRC)

religion, 128. *See also* Christianity; Hinduism

reparations, 86

resistance: absence of term, 8, 187n2; as antagonistic, 60 (*see also* antagonism); conceptual limits, 3, 4, 7–9, 11, 17, 58, 81, 180–1; and Empire (Hardt & Negri), 151; 'everyday resistance,' 37–9; Foucauldian concept, 8, 11; and liberation, 8, 82, 182; outmoded notions of, 182, 183; as reconciliation, 144, 149 (*see also under* reconciliation). *See also* 'cultural resistance'; 'intransitive resistance'; 'spectacular resistance'; violent resistance

resistance as negation (saying no), 21, 65, 71, 72, 82

resistance as opposition: and the anti-apartheid movement, 147, 149; and anti-colonial thought, 59–60; and colonial discourse theory, 58–9; conceptual limits of, 180; Fanon's conceptualization, 57–8, 59, 75–81; and Indian resistance in South Africa, 29; in *Nervous Conditions*, 58–9, 63–5, 66–7, 71, 74–5; in

postcolonialism, 3, 4, 17, 20; Said's conceptualization, 62–3
resistance as subversion, 3, 4, 20; and ambivalence in colonial discourse, 32–3; and the anti-apartheid movement, 149; Bhabha's conceptualization, 29, 31, 33, 48; conceptual limits, 32–3, 180; and Indian resistance in South Africa, 33, 53–4; in *Nervous Conditions*, 70, 72; *vs.* oppositional paradigm (Parry/San Juan), 37
resistance as transformation: and *ahimsa*, 17, 21, 133, 134; and anti-apartheid movement, 140, 148, 149; Gandhism and, 20, 22, 96, 101, 105, 106, 108, 110, 113, 125, 130, 185; and idea of love, 181–2; and Indian resistance in South Africa, 55–6; and *Nervous Conditions*, 71; and 'new humanism,' 49, 58; and reconciliation in South Africa, 4, 17, 20, 21, 22, 145, 156, 165, 167, 185, 204n1; and transformation of power, 20, 27
responsibility: and *ahimsa*, 104, 113, 114; and *dharma*, 128, 130; European, 41, 86; in Gandhism, 132, 171; of postcolonial theory, 159; and reconciliation in South Africa, 157; and the 'Truth Commission,' 162, 167, 169, 173, 177, 209n104. *See also* duty
revolution, 9, 179. *See also* violent resistance
Rhodesia, 64, 65. *See also* Zimbabwe
Rhys, Jean, 16
rights, 46, 91–2, 145, 192n63. *See also* citizen rights; equality
Rose, Jacqueline, 154

Roy, Arundhati, v, 10, 11, 21, 22, 183–4

Sachs, Albie, 144, 156–7, 207n54
Said, Edward: on the anti-apartheid movement, 94; on colonial literature, 14; concept of liberation, 5, 59, 62–3, 89–94, 171; and Fanon, 62, 76, 89–94, 133, 171; formulation of love, 181, 182; and Foucault's concept of power, 28; and 'new humanism,' 9, 93, 171; on the Palestinian struggle, 90, 91; and reconciliation in South Africa, 21
Saliba, Therese, 66, 68, 70
San Juan, E., Jr: concept of liberation, 21; concept of resistance, 8, 60–1, 62; critique of hybridity, 68; and discourse theory, 25, 188n12; and Fanon, 35, 57, 61; oppositional discourses of power, 37, 59; and postcolonialism, 6, 10, 11, 57, 188n12
Sanders, Mark, 166, 167
Sandoval, Chela, 182
Sarkar, Sumit, 26–7
sarvadoya ('the welfare of all'): about, 108–9, 110, 112–13, 184; as an alternative concept of resistance, 96, 101, 184; Congress's views of, 116; practices of, 111; and *swaraj*, 106; as transformation, 17, 21
sati, 118, 131
satyagraha ('truth-force'): about, 111, 114, 118–19; and absolute suffering, 131; acts of resistance, 51, 52, 125–6, 132–3; as an alternative concept of resistance, 96; and Indian independence, 120
Satyagraha in South Africa (Gandhi), 47, 50, 131

238   Index

Satyagraha Namak (1930), 111
Schobesberger, Colonel Horst, 169
Scott, David, 9, 49, 87, 100
Scott, James C., 38, 39
Sekyi-Otu, Ato, 12, 76–7, 93, 98
self-destruction, 65, 67, 68, 70, 195–6n42. *See also* suicide
Senghor, Léopold, 8, 58, 75, 80, 99, 109
Seth, Sanjay, 4
settlers, 13, 75–6
Sharpe, Jenny, 32, 42
Shona culture, 67, 68, 69, 70–1, 73
slave revolt, Haiti, 9, 48–9
slavery, 19, 49, 87, 104
Slemon, Stephen, 16–17
'sly civility' (Bhabha), 31, 37, 38, 43, 55
Smith, Linda Tuhiwai, 9
Smuts, General Jan, 51, 52, 53, 54, 55, 126
socialism, 26, 86, 108, 129, 147
songs of struggle, 141
South Africa: colonial, as space in transition, 53; and cultural memory, 139, 140, 176; liberation and, 153, 155–6; political will and transformation of power, 178; poverty and unemployment, 156, 207n55; security forces (*see* South African Defence Force); 'security state,' 150, 151, 173. *See also* anti-apartheid movement; apartheid; Indian resistance in South Africa; reconciliation in South Africa
South African Defence Force (SADF), 150, 161, 169, 174, 175
South Asia. *See* India; Pakistan
'Soweto novels,' 136, 139
Soweto uprising (1976), 137, 146, 152

'spectacular resistance' (Bhabha), 38; and colonial power/discourse, 8, 56, 130; compared to Gandhi(sm), 46; hybridization of the Bible as, 39, 43; as subversion, 29, 54, 55
Spivak, Gayatri Chakravorty: concept of liberation, 5, 180; critique of Subaltern Studies, 26, 179–80; and 'new humanism,' 10, 181, 182, 184; on *satyagraha,* 118; on suicide, 131
stereotypes, 35–6, 49, 50, 52, 53, 55
Stone-Mediatore, Shari, 18
stories: alternative, 178, 184; of apartheid abuse, 155, 159, 164, 170, 177; in *Black Skin, White Masks,* 35–6; colonial, function of (Said), 14; interpretation of term 'story,' 20; and transformation (Okri), v, 3–4, 7, 20; Xhosa, and cultural identity, 158. *See also* literature
Subaltern Studies collective: analysis and critiques, 7, 25–7, 179–80; and M.K. Gandhi, 45, 46–8, 96–8; and peasant insurgencies, 4, 81, 134
subjectivity: and Bhabha's concept of resistance, 33; deconstruction of, and Subaltern Studies, 25, 26, 28; and discourses of identity/power, 20; Fanon's conceptualization, 77, 87; and Gandhism, 105, 184; and Indian resistance in South Africa, 56, 72; and reconciliation in South Africa, 145, 167, 184; and retributive justice (Jolly), 166, 171. *See also* agency
subjects, colonial, 35–6, 77, 80. *See also* colonizer and the colonized
suicide, 102, 131, 195–6n42
swadeshi movement, 109, 124–5, 128
swaraj ('self-government'): about,

106–8, 132; as an alternative concept of resistance, 96, 101; and Indian nationalism, 97, 101–2, 112–13; in *Kanthapura*, 116, 117; as transformation, 103, 110, 119, 125, 126

tatvajnana, 131
Tendulkar, D.G., 50
Things Fall Apart (Achebe), 195–6n42
'Third Space' (Bhabha), 32, 38, 44
third world literatures, 4, 13–17. *See also* African literature; Indian literature
'Third World' (San Juan), 60
Thomas, Sue, 66
Tiffin, Helen, 15–16
transformation: of the colonizer and the colonized, 7; of discourse, 144–5, 154, 157, 165, 168, 176, 177–8, 185; of language, 29, 93; of power structures, 13, 17, 62, 67, 122, 172; of stories (Okri), v, 3–4, 7, 20; *swaraj* as, 103, 106–7, 110. *See also* resistance as transformation
Transvaal Asiatic Ordinance, 50, 51
Trust Feed massacre, 209n104
trusteeship, Gandhi's theory of, 129–30, 184, 203n104
truth, 154, 155–6, 159–60
Truth and Reconciliation Commission (final report), 177, 205n24, 209n104, 210n118
Truth and Reconciliation Commission (TRC): and the African National Congress, 140, 143, 210n118; and ambiguity, 157, 159, 162; and apartheid, 18, 142, 150, 151, 153, 173, 178; and apology/forgiveness, 169–71, 172–4, 176–7; criticisms of, 139–40, 143, 153, 165–6, 171–2, 207n54; and history/memory, 141–2, 143, 154–5, 159–60, 167; and humanity, 165, 166–7, 170, 207n54; and justice, 139–40, 144, 159, 162, 165–6, 171, 172; limits of, 18, 142, 163, 184–5; mandate, 143–4, 165, 171, 177; and 'moments' of reconciliation, 163–4, 170; and 'politics of denial,' 173–7, 178; and reconciliation, 143–4, 153, 156, 160, 168, 178, 205n24; and resistance as transformation, 21, 156; and responsibility, 162, 167, 173, 177, 209n104; and Truth, 154, 155–6, 159–60; and understanding, 172, 173; and white journalists, 210n124. *See also* reconciliation in South Africa
Tutu, Desmond: on apartheid discourse, 156, 162–3; on economic transformation, 153; on forgiveness, 165, 169–70; on freedom/reconciliation, 147, 147–8, 152, 165; on government lies, 175; and *ubuntu*, 166, 209n91; on whites under apartheid, 176

ubuntu, 21, 145, 161, 166, 167, 209n91
Umkhonto we Sizwe (MK), 140, 145, 164, 174
United Democratic Front (UDF), 146–7, 206n30
untouchability, 110, 111–12, 125–6
utopianism, 5, 107, 120, 181
Uwakwe, Pauline Ada, 70, 196n45

Victoria (queen of England), 48, 49
violence: of apartheid, 136–7, 139, 146, 147, 150–1, 160–1, and colonialism, 14, 123; Galtung's theory

of, 18, 19; as masculine, 67, 118;
in *Nervous Conditions*, 64, 65–7, 71;
in South African history, 139, 158,
176; by state diminishes power
(Arendt), 152; in *Things Fall Apart*,
195–6n42; and the 'Truth Commission,' 18, 142, 150, 153; in *Waiting for the Barbarians*, 24; in Zimbabwe,
65–6. *See also* 'cultural violence';
cycle of violence
violent resistance: Fanon's concept
of, 12, 49, 66, 76–8, 79–80, 82, 98,
119; Gandhi's critique of, 121–2,
132, 133; and humanity (Williams),
9; Mandela's view on, 141; as mimicry (Memmi), 81; and Said (after
Fanon), 92–3; San Juan on, 60–1; in
South Africa, 140–1, 150
Viswanathan, Gauri, 17

'Waiting for the Barbarians' (Cavafy),
163
Waiting for the Barbarians (Coetzee),
14, 23–5, 28, 163, 176

Walaza, Nomfundo, 176
Watts, Jane, 136
Werwoerd, Wilhelm, 162
'white man's burden,' 42, 48
Williams, Raymond, 9, 12
women: and apartheid, 147, 150, 160–1; and colonialism, 18–19; in *Kanthapura*, 117; in *Nervous Conditions*,
58–9, 63–75; and the 'Truth Commission,' 142, 150. *See also* gender
Wretched of the Earth, The (Fanon), 7,
11–12, 13, 57, 75–7, 78, 79, 86–7, 88,
89, 90, 133, 171, 179
writers and writing. *See* literature
Wynter, Sylvia, 91–2

Xhosa Cattle Killing, 158, 173

Young, Robert, 32, 91, 119, 199n3

Zimbabwe, 63, 65–6, 119
Zulu Rebellion, 46, 50, 53

CULTURAL SPACES

Cultural Spaces explores the rapidly changing temporal, spatial, and theoretical boundaries of contemporary cultural studies. Culture has long been understood as the force that defines and delimits societies in fixed spaces. The recent intensification of globalizing processes, however, has meant that it is no longer possible – if it ever was – to imagine the world as a collection of autonomous, monadic spaces, whether these are imagined as localities, nations, regions within nations, or cultures demarcated by region or nation. One of the major challenges of studying contemporary culture is to understand the new relationships of culture to space that are produced today. The aim of this series is to publish bold new analyses and theories of the spaces of culture, as well as investigations of the historical construction of those cultural spaces that have influenced the shape of the contemporary world.

Series Editors:
Richard Cavell, University of British Columbia
Imre Szeman, McMaster University

Editorial Advisory Board:
Lauren Berlant, University of Chicago
Homi K. Bhabha, Harvard University
Hazel V. Carby, Yale University
Richard Day, Queen's University
Christopher Gittings, University of Western Ontario
Lawrence Grossberg, University of North Carolina
Mark Kingwell, University of Toronto
Heather Murray, University of Toronto
Elspeth Probyn, University of Sydney
Rinaldo Walcott, OISE/University of Toronto

Books in the Series:
Peter Ives, *Gramsci's Politics of Language: Engaging the Bakhtin Circle and the Frankfurt School*
Sarah Brophy, *Witnessing AIDS: Writing, Testimony, and the Work of Mourning*
Shane Gunster, *Capitalizing on Culture: Critical Theory for Cultural Studies*
Jasmin Habib, *Israel, Diaspora, and the Routes of National Belonging*
Serra Tinic, *On Location: Canada's Television Industry in a Global Market*
Evelyn Ruppert, *The Moral Economy of Cities: Shaping Good Citizens*
Mark Coté, Richard J.F. Day, and Greig de Peuter, eds., *Utopian Pedagogy: Radical Experiments against Neoliberal Globalization*
Michael McKinnie, *City Stages: Theatre and Urban Space in a Global City*
Mary Gallagher, ed., *World Writing: Poetics, Ethics, and Globalization*
David Jefferess, *Postcolonial Resistance: Culture, Liberation, and Transformation*